Dear Graham
Thank you for
your help and hard work in my
new home in Penzance
with best wishes
Susan Soyinka

A SILENCE THAT SPEAKS

A FAMILY STORY THROUGH AND BEYOND THE HOLOCAUST

Susan Soyinka

Eliora  Books

SUSAN SOYINKA has worked as a teacher, lecturer and researcher, spending 10 years of her early career in West Africa. On her return to England, she retrained as an educational psychologist and, after discovering her Jewish roots, worked for nine years in the Jewish community in London. Retirement has given her the time and energy to develop a new career as a writer.

Her first book, *From East End to Land's End, The Evacuation of Jews' Free School, London, to Mousehole in Cornwall during World War Two,* was described by Aumie Shapiro, author of the Jewish East End photographic series, as an *"extraordinary, significant story of inter-faith and community harmony. A magnificent achievement."*

For further information about this book, please visit the author's blog:
http://susansoyinka.wordpress.com

First published in Great Britain in 2012 by The Derby Books Publishing Company Limited

This edition published in 2013 by Eliora Books

Produced by The Choir Press
Design by Simon Hartshorne

ISBN 978-0-9575614-0-3

A SILENCE THAT SPEAKS

A FAMILY STORY THROUGH AND BEYOND THE HOLOCAUST

Based on the original documents

A Journey in Time
The Story of My Search for My Mother's Family

The Family of Lucy Fowler Née Smetana
The History of the Smetana and Weinberger Families in Vienna Prior to World War Two

and

The Nazi Machine in Austria
As Made Evident in Nazi Files on Members of the Smetana and Weinberger Families in Vienna
1938--1945

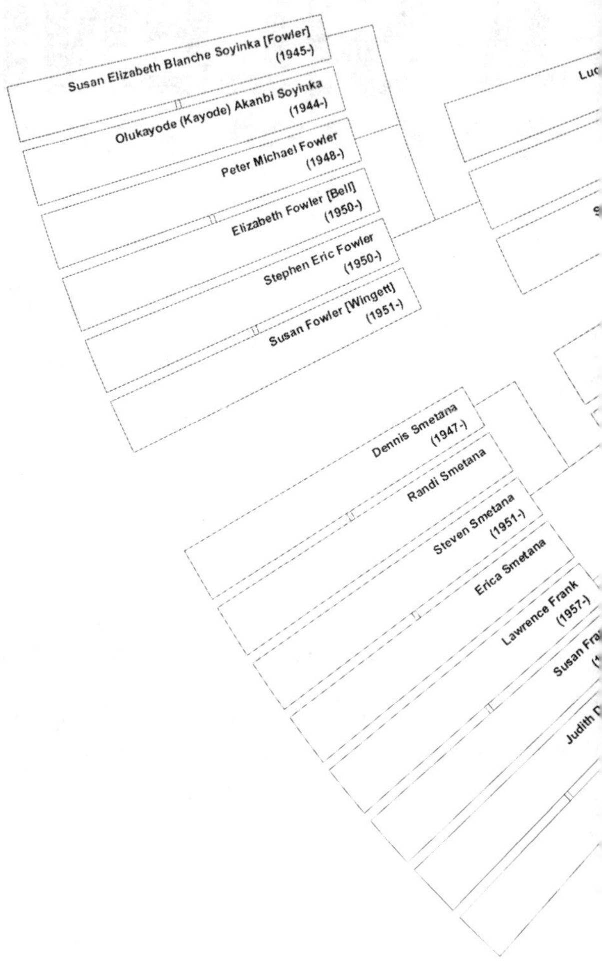

The Descendants of Josef and Cäcilie Smetana

Josef Smetana
(1858-1941)
Cacilie Smetana [Neumann]
(1863-1941)
Friedrich (Fritz) Smetana
(1889-1938)
Berta Smetana [Weinberger]
(1896-?)
Otto Smetana
(1891-1978)
Margaret (Grete) Smetana [Low]
(1901-1979)
Auguste (Gusti) Steininger [Smetana]
(1894-1989)
Jacques Steininger
(1892-1973)
Karl Smetana
(1899-1988)
Lilly Smetana [Bruchsteiner]
(1903-?)
owler [Smetana]
(1919-2003)
Francis Eric Fowler
(1925-1986)
te Renee Erika Smetana
(1927-?)
Peter Smetana
(1927-1991)
Gertrude (Trudy) Smetana [Jelinek]
(1926-2012)
Lori Frank [Smetana]
(1933-)
Robert Frank
(1932-)
Ully Redisch [Steininger]
(1919-2005)
Fred Redisch
(?-1983)
Helga Steininger
(1923-)
Stephen Angyal
(1914-2012)
Henry (Heinz) Stonnington
(1927-2009)
Constance Stonnington [Hamersley]
(1931-)
Gerda Weinreiter [Smetana]
(1929-)
Henry Weinreiter
(?-1997)
) Duff
(1953-)
Annette Schofield
(1944-)
Robert Angyal
(1949-)
Abby Angyal [Bloom]
(1951-)
Jane Hilary Leigh [Stonnington]
(1954-)
Anne Cecily Harber [Stonnington]
(1956-)
Sheldon Harber
(1957-)
Nicholas Henry Stonnington
(1957-)
Amanda Stonnington
(1969-)
Cynthia (Cindy) Margaret Weinstein [Stonnington]
(1960-)
James Weinstein
(1953-)
Sally Christine Chatelain [Stonnington]
(1963-)
John Chatelain
(1963-)
Michael James Stonnington
(1966-)
Katie Stonnington
(1964-)
Lynette Keil [Weinreiter]
(1956-)
Stephen Keil
Alan Wein
(1958-)
Caroline Wein [Sweet]
(1960-)
my HERITAGE
duced by Family Tree Builder, copyright © 2012 MyHeritage Ltd.

I wish to dedicate this book to:

The memory of my family who perished in the Holocaust: Fritz Smetana, Berta Smetana née Weinberger, Sonja Smetana, Josef Smetana, Cäcilie Smetana née Neumann, Cäcilie Weinberger née Klausner, Josef Weinberger, and Lydia Perlberger.

And to my mother, Lucy Fowler née Smetana, whose experiences have formed me, and whose courage has inspired me.

CONTENTS

FOREWORD

Every family has secrets. But few families have a past that is unknowable.

I have known Susan Soyinka since 1995 when she was an early and enthusiastic supporter of the Holocaust Centre in Nottinghamshire, England. From our early exchanges I was aware that she was on a quest to discover a family past that was deeply buried in the Nazi past. What I did not know was just how tenacious she would have to be to find the truth of what happened.

In this remarkable book, Susan has the patience and the desire to uncover one document at a time, one conversation at a time, one journey at a time, and create a detailed and moving picture of her family who had, until now, been a missing part of her life. Her quest to piece their lives back together was done in the face of considerable difficulty: missing fragments of information, resistance from those who could most help, uncertainty about whom she could turn to for reliable information, and from time to time a stroke of luck.

Genealogy is time consuming and tedious work, but when you have little information, it can only be a labour of love. That is what this book is – a true labour of love, to restore the lives of those who were lost and to find, in the traces of the past, dignity and true humanity. In her pursuit of truth she was able to fill the empty spaces of her family's past, turn a lonely suicide into a roll of honour, discover that her "bad" grandmother had in fact been a woman of tremendous courage in Auschwitz. She was able to give names to the nameless, faces to the faceless – and restore the wholeness of a family the Nazis had intended to destroy.

Her 18-year labour of love overcomes the void of memory, restores the dignity of loss and gives roots to future generations. Her courage, her honesty, her clarity and punctilious accuracy mean that her children and their children will always know who they are and where they came from. It restores life where there was death, presence where there was absence, roots where identity was lost, hope where there was despair. The Nazis had fully intended that Susan Soyinka's generation would never exist, but instead she has used the life she has, her sense of integrity and determination, to recover the legacy of the past. That is not only an act of commitment to the detail of history, but also an act of beautiful revenge.

Stephen D. Smith MBE

Executive Director, Shoah Foundation Institute, University of Southern California
Co-founder and former Director, Holocaust Centre, Nottinghamshire, UK (formerly Beth Shalom)
Co-founder Aegis Trust

Los Angeles 2012

PREFACE

"Most of us are dead. The few who remain are old. Our children must tell our story now. It is, after all, their story too." *Auschwitz survivor*

My mother was a Viennese Jew who came to England in 1938 to flee Nazi persecution. She lost many members of her immediate family, but did not speak of her experiences for decades. In 1995, I learned for the first time of other members of our extended family who had survived and were now scattered around the world. Thus began the search for my mother's family, and for the story of what had happened to them during that dreadful era.

In May 1996, I was asked to contribute to the National Life Story Collection, as part of the Living Memory of the Jewish Community Project. These collections are stored at the British Library National Sound Archive. In order to prepare myself for the interview, I wrote down what I knew of our family in a document entitled *A Journey in Time.* This was a narrative account of how my search began in October 1994 and the information I had managed to obtain since then. Over the next few years, the detective trail continued, and little by little, I pieced together the broader family history.

In September and October 2006, I went to Vienna for the first time with my daughter Bambo. We visited the *Israelitische Kultusgemeinde Wien,* the Jewish archives in Vienna, and also many of the former homes of my mother's family. The most moving occasion was our visit to the grave of my grandfather, Fritz Smetana. Much of what I learned during that visit was further supplemented by research carried out in the Czech Republic in 2011–12.

A Journey in Time now needed revision, and so by early 2012, I completed *The Family of Lucy Fowler née Smetana,* which draws upon, expands and considerably updates the original document, using much more factual information, though I still depended, to some degree, on the anecdotal accounts of relatives and others, as well as adding my own comments and reflections.

However, the task was still not finished. During 2011, I also received a huge number of Nazi documents from the Austrian State Archives detailing the Aryanisation of the properties and businesses of several family members. Since I did not want to include too much of this disturbing material in the family history, I wrote a supplementary document entitled *The Nazi Machine in Austria.*

These three documents, intended mainly for family members world-wide, were the culmination of almost two decades of research. Having now completed my task, as I thought, I was encouraged by family and friends to merge the three documents into one for wider publication.

Even during this process, new information continued to emerge. In July 2012, I attended a conference in Paris of the International Association of Jewish Genealogical Societies, where I obtained further details about the arrest of my grandmother and aunt in France, and their deportation to Auschwitz. Just days before the publication of this book, I received documentation from French archives which conveyed the horror of their final journey. Now, I could tell their full story.

Finally, I am able to make available to the wider public this remarkable story of my journey to meet my ancestors, a story of one family's struggle to deal with the impact and the legacy of the Holocaust. Just one of six million stories.

This work is a memorial to lost families and communities. I hope also to have given a voice to those who, through untimely death or trauma, were silenced.

Susan Soyinka, October 2012

ADDENDUM

This book was originally published by DB Publishing on 1 November 2012. Only two months later, this company went into liquidation, rendering my book out of print. Given the years I had devoted to bringing my family's story to light, this was a devastating blow. I could not allow the voice of my ancestors to be silenced yet again, and so took the decision to republish the book under my own publishing name of Eliora Books, with the assistance of the Choir Press.

Susan Soyinka, January 2013

Chapter One

A JOURNEY IN TIME: THE SEARCH BEGINS

1995 was for me an extraordinary year: a year when I travelled back more than 70 years in time to reach into the recesses of my family history. A year when I came face to face with myself.

My mother was an Austrian Jew. Throughout my life, I had known only the barest details about her background. Any attempt to find out more provoked hysteria. In about 1980, I persuaded her to watch with me the American TV miniseries *Holocaust*, the saga of a fictional Jewish family. The first few scenes consisted of archive footage of Nazi atrocities, and within seconds my mother ran out of the room screaming and hugely distressed.

I had thought that it would be helpful to her to confront her past. I was mistaken. She had carefully drawn a veil over her former life in order to suppress the pain. And so for many years, I let it lie, despite my curiosity.

Then, towards the end of 1994, I bought my husband, Kayode, a practising Christian, a leather-bound Bible for his 50th birthday. At the front was a chart in which to write the family tree. I did not even know the first names of my maternal grandparents. So, in order to fill in the chart, I once again started asking my mother questions, and this time got some hesitant answers.

At first, the information was very confused, and kept changing from one day, even one minute, to the next. *"I think I had two uncles, Karl and Otto. Uncle Karl went to Australia and Uncle Otto to New York. Or maybe it was the other way round, I can't remember."* My mother's age and failing memory, combined with the years of blocking out the pain, made recall difficult. Indeed, had I questioned her any later, it would have been too late.

After a few short minutes of such conversations, she would declare, *"I don't want to talk about it any more, it is all too painful."* So I would have to leave it for a while, and come back a few days later, to try once again to gently prise from her the information I was so desperate to discover.

I had always assumed that my mother's entire family had perished, other than one maternal aunt, Aunty Emmy, who also came to England, having lost her only daughter. She had died many years ago, leaving us with no one from that era. I was utterly astounded to hear that other members of the family had survived, including another aunt, an Aunt Gusti, as well as the two uncles. *"You mean we have relatives?"* I gasped. *"Why didn't you tell me?"*

"Oh, it was all too painful," came the sad reply. I was to hear this phrase many times.

Over the next few weeks, I contacted a number of people in various parts of the world with the family name Smetana, whose numbers I obtained through International Directory Enquiries. I had some fascinating conversations, but was unable to establish whether or not these were relatives. I obtained the number of a Dr Dennis Smetana in New York, but every time I rang, the number was on answerphone. I felt quite unable to leave a recorded message.

In early 1995, there was a lot of media coverage of the end of the war, and in particular, the commemoration of 50 years since the liberation of Auschwitz on 27 January 1945. It suddenly occurred to me that I was born nine months to the day after that, on 27 October 1945. Since I had reason to believe that my grandmother and aunt had died in Auschwitz, this struck me as extraordinarily symbolic. Not long after, I learned of another child of a survivor born on that same day.

I was moved by television reports on Friday 27 January to suggest to my mother that we should go the next day to the synagogue to honour her family. She agreed and next morning we went. It was the second time only in my entire life that I had entered a synagogue and the first time I had participated in a service.

Inevitably it was extremely moving and when we returned home, I was prompted once more to ring the New York number. This time, Dr Smetana answered and when I explained that I was looking for my mother's family and that she had an Uncle Otto who had gone to New York and set up a dry cleaning business, the astonishing response was: *"That was my grandfather. You have found us."*

Dennis put me in touch with his Aunt Lori, the daughter of Uncle Otto. Lori had left Vienna with her family at the age of five. Amazingly, when I first spoke to her, she had never known that she had had an Uncle Fritz and a cousin, Lucy (my grandfather and mother). Like my mother, her father, Otto, had remained silent about the past. But Lori did know of her cousins in Australia, and she it was who gave me their telephone numbers.

From that point on, it was only a matter of weeks before I traced the rest of the family: five living first cousins of my mother, three in Australia and two in America. The aunt and uncles had died only fairly recently. Phone calls, letters, photos and gifts followed. And then in April 1995, a visit from my mother's cousin Helga from Australia, followed in May by a visit from cousin Gerda, also from Australia. My mother had no recollection of any of her cousins other than Ully, Helga's older sister, so meticulously had she buried her past. But they remembered her and brought photos taken in the late twenties to prove it. One in particular portrays my mother playing happily with her cousin Helga.

Helga, Aunt Gusti's daughter, also brought with her an exquisite cut glass bowl. She gave this to my mother with the words *"Your father gave this to my mother many years ago. She gave it to me when I was married, and it has been sitting on my dressing table for 53 years. And now I am giving it back to you."*

Helga and Lucy playing happily together, c.1930

Lucy and Helga in England, April 1995. The small crystal bowl Helga gave to Lucy is in the left foreground

Another photo given to me by Helga shows my mother with her cousin Ully as bridesmaids at the wedding of Uncle Karl, Gerda's father. Once she saw this photograph, my mother remembered parading around the synagogue.

Ully and Lucy as bridesmaids at the wedding of Uncle Karl c.1927. Ully is wearing her "long blonde plaits"

Over the next few weeks and months, I was able to piece together the entire Smetana family tree: all the descendants of Josef Smetana, my mother's paternal grandfather. I was also able to reconstruct my mother's early life and relationships, though only to a limited degree due to her continued reticence. This was a painful process, as there were clearly, and quite normally, many family conflicts and tensions.

One of the tragedies of the Holocaust for survivors has been that there was never an opportunity to resolve such conflicts, so that the pain of that period remained. My mother remembered vividly her mother standing one day at the window saying that there was something important she would one day tell her. Of course, that story was never told.

In reconstructing my mother's story, I have come to realise what an enormous impact these events have had on my own life. This was brought home particularly strongly when, in June 1995, I attended a conference for the children of Holocaust survivors and refugees. Until then, I had thought of myself as a one-off, as being very different from anyone else I knew in my country of birth. Yet here I met so many people whose stories bore surprising similarities to my own.

At the conference, I participated in a workshop entitled *Loss of Jewish identity.* We sat in a circle and were asked to briefly describe our connection with the Holocaust. I began by saying, *"My mother came here from Vienna in 1938."* The next four people to my right uttered exactly the same words: *"My mother came here from Vienna in 1938." "My mother came here from Vienna in 1938." "My mother came here from Vienna in 1938." "My mother came here from Vienna in 1938."* All had been brought up with little or no knowledge of their Jewish background.

We then shared our stories. Stories, like mine, of travel around the world, of living in different continents, of marrying into different races and cultures. There was also a theme of trying out different religions, which for many of us had proved unsatisfactory.

So I was not as isolated or as unusual as I had thought. Could it be that our common experience of having been cut off from our roots had resulted in a lifetime of searching for those roots, of seeking an identity?

During 1995, I asked my mother if she had any photos from her childhood and she said yes, there was an old brown album somewhere in her house. I searched high and low for hours, but could not find it. Eventually I discovered the photos in a new red album. She had forgotten that she had transferred them. The album was lying on a small table just beside the chair in which she spent most of her time.

Among the photos were several of my grandmother, and I found myself looking into a mirror. This woman in the photos looked just like me, or rather, I looked just like her. When I suggested this to my mother, she became extremely agitated. *"You are nothing like my mother." "I may not be anything like her in personality, but I* ***look*** *like her,"* I replied.

Left: my grandmother, Berta Smetana, whose photo I saw for the first time in 1995. Right: myself in 2009. Mirror image?

My mother found this very hard to accept, as she had had a bad relationship with her mother. But the image of my grandmother continued to haunt me. What kind of person was this woman, whom I resembled so strongly? Could she really have been so bad? I desperately wanted to find something good about her and to know what happened to her. Strangely, I had a feeling I would find out ...

Here, then, is my mother's story and my own.

Chapter Two

A BRIEF INTRODUCTION

I hope you, the reader, will forgive the abundance of detail in Chapters Two and Three, but this is necessary to set the scene for the rest of the story. You may later find it helpful to refer back to these chapters.

I grew up with no relatives on my mother's side of the family, other than one rather eccentric great aunt from Vienna, who was an exotic reminder of distant places somehow associated with my mother. As a child, I was not consciously aware of this gap in my family, though the fact that I had no maternal grandparents, aunts, uncles and cousins must have registered at some subconscious level.

Looking back, I now know that the shadow of the Holocaust was hovering over me in some indescribable way. Not even knowing the names of my relatives made it difficult for me to imagine them as people, but as I grew older, I started thinking more about them, wanting to know who they were. At the age of 50, when I learned their names at last, this came as a great relief. It gave me a sense of connection and belonging, which I realised I had never quite had.

But to begin with, I only had the names, together with the handful of photos I had so recently discovered. My mother continued to be reluctant to talk, so it was to be many more years before I was able to gather enough information to recognise them as living breathing people, and to learn something of the lives they had lived and so tragically lost.

So here, to start my journey, and by way of introduction, are the barest details: names, dates, a few photos. Later, we will learn much more about who they really were and about how my own life was so intimately connected with theirs.

MY MOTHER'S IMMEDIATE FAMILY

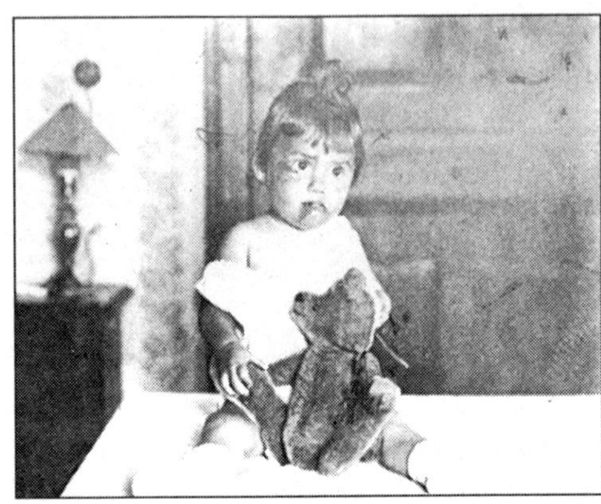

Lucy Smetana as a baby in Vienna, 1920

My mother, Lucie (later Lucy) Fowler, née Smetana, was born in Vienna, Austria, on 6 September 1919 to a Jewish family. Her father was Friedrich (known as Fritz) Smetana and her mother was Berta Smetana, née Weinberger.

Fritz was born in Vienna on 18 September 1889, son of Josef Smetana and Cäcilie Smetana, née Neumann.

Berta was born in Vienna on 9 January 1896, daughter of Heinrich Weinberger and Cäcilie Weinberger, née Klausner.

Fritz and Berta were married on 22 December 1918 in Vienna, but divorced on 26 April 1932.

Standing: Fritz Smetana and Ully Steininger. Seated: Cäcilie Smetana, Berta Smetana, Lucy Smetana and Jacques Steininger, Vienna late 1920s

My mother had a sister, Sonja (pronounced Sonya), born in Vienna on 1 December 1927. I was initially unable to trace Sonja's details because her birth-date was originally recorded at the *Israelitische Kultusgemeinde* as 30 December 1927, but was subsequently corrected. As a consequence, her name was missed out in the full entry but appeared in the index.

Sonja and Lucy Smetana, c.1930

My grandfather, Fritz, committed suicide on 31 May 1938, shortly after the *Anschluss*, when Hitler entered Austria. He was buried at the Jewish cemetery in Vienna.

My grandmother Berta and aunt Sonja, together with Berta's mother Cäcilie and brother, Josef, left Vienna in 1938–39 and escaped to France, where Cäcilie died. The others were eventually arrested and taken to Drancy, a transit camp on the outskirts of Paris, from where they were deported to Auschwitz in 1942.

My mother left Vienna on 27 August 1938, arriving in England in early September 1938.

THE SMETANA FAMILY

Josef Smetana, my great grandfather, was born on 5 July 1858, in what is now the Czech Republic. There is some reason to believe that he may have been the illegitimate son of the Czech composer Bedřich Smetana, which I will discuss in more detail later.

Cäcilie Smetana, née Neumann, my great grandmother, was born in Biala, Poland, on 2 October 1863. Her parents were Adalbert Neumann and Franziska Neumann, née Rippa, both of whom died in Bielsko, Poland, he in 1870 and she in 1890. Bielsko and Biala were two cities on opposite banks of the Biala River and were amalgamated in 1951 to form a single city Bielsko-Biala. Cäcilie was one of 12 children, of whom one was Alexander Neumann, born in 1856, who became a well-known architect in Vienna.

The Smetana family lived mostly in Hietzing, Vienna XIII, a wealthy suburb of Vienna where many Jews lived prior to the Second World War. The district is home to the renowned Schönbrunn, the summer palace of the Habsburgs.

Josef and Cäcilie had four children; Fritz, my grandfather, born in 1889, was the oldest. His younger siblings were Otto, born on 25 May 1891, Auguste (Gusti), born on 17 December 1894, and Karl born on 1 May 1899.

After working on the railways for 25 years, Josef became the proprietor of a dry cleaning factory, which eventually became a family business.

Josef and Cäcilie Smetana with all four children, in front of the family factory in 1900. Karl is seated on Cäcilie's knee, Gusti on her father's knee, while Fritz is lying on the ground to the left, and Otto to the right

A surprising development in my search was the discovery that the family name was originally SMETANY, but was changed by decree in 1902 to SMETANA. My mother's cousin, Helga, discovered this when looking at the birth certificate of her mother, Auguste Smetana, where she found the name change recorded. In a footnote dated 1899, the name was confirmed to be Smetany, but a footnote on the back of the certificate read:

Die K.K. Statthalterei hat mit Erlass vom 2 Juni 1902 den Kindeseltern und dessen Kinde die Änderung des Familiennamens Smetany zu Smetana bewilligt. (The Imperial Governor's Office has by decree on 2 June 1902 granted the parents and the child approval to change the surname from "Smetany" to "Smetana".)

It seems that all family members took the new name. This name change was later to prove significant in the unravelling of my family history.

Josef and Cäcilie Smetana committed suicide together on 2 December 1941, probably because they were about to be deported.

THE WEINBERGER FAMILY

Cäcilie Weinberger, my great grandmother, and her son, Josef Weinberger, Uncle Joshi

Heinrich Weinberger, my great grandfather, was born in Vienna on 7 October 1864, son of Josef Weinberger, from Holics in present-day Slovakia, and Fanny Weinberger, née Kuner. Heinrich was a book-keeper. He died on 20 February

1930 and was buried with his daughter Josefine, who had pre-deceased him.

Cäcilie Weinberger, née Klausner, my great grandmother, was born in Vienna on 1 September 1872. She was the daughter of Leopold (Leib) Klausner, born in 1830, a *Brandweiner* (spirit merchant) from Wiśnicz, Galicia, Poland, who died in Vienna on 30 November 1904, and Rebekka (Rifka) Klausner, née Gangel, born in 1840, and who died in Vienna on 24 February 1923.

Heinrich and Cäcilie were married on 19 February 1893, in a synagogue in the 2nd district of Vienna. They lived at Herminengasse 10, Vienna II. The Weinberger family lived mainly in central Vienna, in the 1st and 2nd districts.

Heinrich and Cäcilie had four children:

Berta, my grandmother, born in 1896, was the oldest. Her sister, Josefine, was born on 26 September 1897 but died young on 19 June 1918. The next sister, Emma (known as Emmy) was born on 26 April 1899. She married Ludwig Perlberger and had one daughter, Lydia, born on 11 July 1925. The youngest member of the family, Josef, known to my mother as Uncle Joshi, was born on 29 May 1902.

Cäcilie, Berta, Sonja, Josef and Lydia all perished in the Holocaust. Aunty Emmy, who came to England, was my mother's only surviving relative on the Weinberger side of the family.

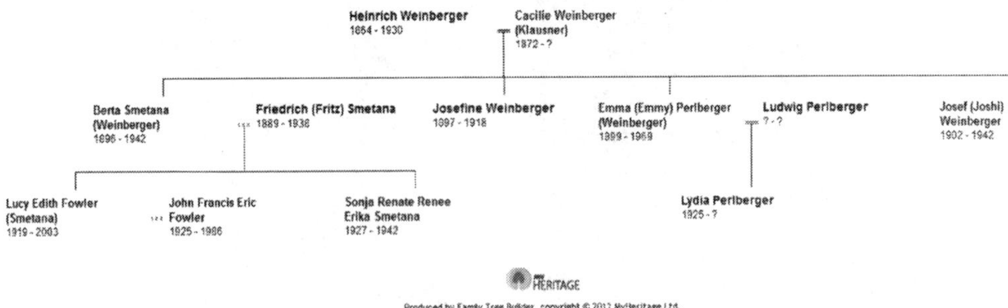

Note: House numbers in Austria follow the street name rather than precede it, as in England. The district numbers given throughout the book are those which were in use in the early part of the 20th century. These have now changed.

Chapter Three

AUNTS, UNCLES AND COUSINS A WORLD AWAY

During her childhood, my mother did, of course, have a full network of aunts, uncles and cousins and, as I later learnt, saw them on a regular basis until at least the age of 12. However, once they all fled to the far ends of the earth, she lost touch with them for almost 60 years. Since she never spoke of them, I was totally unaware of their existence.

When I first contacted my mother's cousin Helga in Australia in early 1995, she immediately passed my number to her older sister, Ully. Before I had the chance to ring her, Ully rang me. Her first words to me were, in a strong Viennese accent, *"Susie! Why have you not contacted us for all this time?"* She spoke as if she had known me all her life. I was amused and somewhat taken aback, but it was nevertheless pleasing to be recognised as a relative. Again, it gave me that feeling of belonging.

I went to Australia in 1997 to visit my new-found relatives. It was unsettling to meet people on the other side of the world who looked and spoke like my mother, and who shared her mannerisms. This made me acutely aware of the degree to which the Nazis had destroyed families whose traumatised survivors had been flung world-wide. This was emphasised yet again when, on my return from Australia, I received a visit from my mother's cousin, Lori, from America.

While my mother's immediate family still remained largely unknown to me for some time to come, here were flesh and blood relatives with whom I could communicate and share experiences. Hence, I came to know my mother's extended family before I was able to make the acquaintance of my own grandparents.

Here, in brief, are their stories.

THE FAMILY OF OTTO SMETANA

Left: Grete and Otto Smetana in 1964. Right: Trudy and Peter Smetana

Otto Smetana, my great uncle, married Grete Löw, a violinist. They had two children: Peter, born in 1927, and Loretta (Lori), born in 1933. Otto had a 30% share in the family dry cleaning business, which he owned jointly with his father, Josef, and brother, Fritz, my grandfather. Otto left Vienna with his family on 20 May 1939, having been given five days to leave, and only after being taken to court and signing over all his personal belongings and finances to the Nazis. The family eventually emigrated to the United States.

Otto's family first escaped to Paris together with the family of Grete's sister Olga, who was married to Fritz Kalmar, with whom they had lived at Einwanggasse 27, Vienna XIII, a huge house in Hietzing. The house had contained many flats, as well as a villa in the garden. They lived in hiding for two years on the outskirts of Paris, making and selling soap. Incredibly, I discovered that Fritz Kalmar was the great uncle of my colleague Joanna Grana, now Francis, who worked with me at Leicestershire Educational Psychology Service in the 1990s.

The two families eventually made their way to the United States, travelling over the mountains via Spain, carrying a rucksack and a Stradivarius violin. Otto again set up a dry cleaning business, joined for many years by his son Peter. Peter married Trudy Jelinek and had two sons: Dennis, born in 1947 and Steven, born in 1951. Lori married Robert Frank and they had a son Lawrence, born in 1957, and a daughter, Judith, born in 1960.

By another amazing coincidence, an Englishman, John Smetana, a distant relative who may also be related to the composer Smetana, met Peter, quite by chance, at a shop in New York. The two men and their wives dined together, but did not think that they were related. Peter died in 1991 and his wife, Trudy, also from Vienna, passed away in early 2012.

I was very pleased to meet my mother's cousin Lori when she visited England with her husband Robert in 1997. It was a memorable visit for them, because not only did they visit family they never knew they had, but they arrived in England on the same day that Princess Diana died. As they toured the country, people were gathering together in mourning in every church and historic building they visited. Lori told me that it had been fascinating to be in England at such a historically significant national moment.

Lori Frank, front left, my daughter Lara, back left, then me, my son Alex, Robert Frank and my mother on the right. Nottingham, 1996

THE STEININGER FAMILY

Auguste (Gusti) Smetana married Jacques Steininger. They had three children, Ully, born 1919, Helga, born 1923, and Heinz, born 1927. Prior to the Second World War, the Steininger family lived in Vienna in the same house as Josef Smetana, my great grandfather, but in a separate flat, at Kupelwiesergasse 13, Vienna XIII (Hietzing). I understand that my grandfather, Fritz Smetana, was very close to his sister, Gusti, and frequently visited her family, especially after his divorce in 1932. Gusti's three children all had fond memories of him.

Helga Steininger, Cäcilie Smetana, Heinz Steininger and Fritz Smetana, in the early 1930s

Jacques Steininger was a prominent lawyer in Vienna prior to the Second World War, one of his clients being the director and conductor of the Vienna opera. On 27 May 1938, he was arrested, together with about 2,000 others on that day, taken first to Dachau concentration camp, and then transferred to Buchenwald. It seems Gusti was instrumental in securing her husband's release, following a visit she made to an SS Officer in Weimar, Germany, to whom she was asked to pay 60,000 schillings (40,000 Reichsmark). The Reichsmark was the German currency of the period, which replaced the Austrian Schilling in 1938. (See Chapter Six for further information.)

She was told that they must leave the country within five days and tell no-one. Jacques was released on 1 February 1939, arriving home emaciated and with a shaven head. He had survived the camps by being vigilant, for example he noticed that men wearing spectacles were frequently beaten (an example of the often random and arbitrary nature of human violence), so removed his own spectacles. The couple left Vienna, as instructed, five days after his return.

Prior to that, Ully went to London in 1938, leaving behind her studies at art school, while Helga and Heinz travelled to England on the *Kindertransport* on 13 January 1939. In the meantime, their mother, Gusti, packed a large container and bought tickets to Shanghai, as she had managed to obtain a visa for there, though not for Australia. However, she and Jacques stopped off at Manila in the Philippines, where they had friends, and stayed there until they were able to get a permit to go to Melbourne. Jacques discovered that the Australian Governor General was a fellow Freemason, and he wrote to him and managed to obtain a visa on the basis of this connection.

They eventually arrived in Melbourne on 23 October 1939. The container was dropped off in Borneo, but was eventually found and sent on to Melbourne. In June 1940, the three children travelled from England to join their parents on the *SS Orcades*, a requisitioned troop ship. This was a dangerous voyage; the ship picked up survivors from a Greek boat which had been sunk near the Canary Islands. They arrived on 10 August 1940, just three weeks after the container had arrived. From then on, they were once again able to lead a relatively normal family life. Jacques taught at Wesley College, Melbourne, for 26 years from 1940 until 1966, when he and Gusti moved to Sydney to join some of their children and grandchildren.

Ully married Fred Redisch and remained in Melbourne. Helga married Stephen in Melbourne, and had two children, Annette, born 1944 and Robert, born 1949. They moved to Sydney in the late 1940s. (Helga's married name has been omitted for reasons of privacy.)

Heinz married Constance Hamersley, and they had six children, Jane, born in 1954, Anne, 1956, Nicholas, 1957, Cynthia, 1960, Sally, 1963, and Michael, in 1966, most of them born in Sydney.

Ully Redisch née Steininger, in Melbourne, still with her long blonde hair

I met Helga and Stephen when they visited England in April 1995, a very short time after I had first learned of their existence. A month later, we had a visit from their cousin, Gerda, Uncle Karl's daughter. In November 1996, Helga's daughter Annette visited me in England. Finally, I visited several of them in their various homes in Australia in August 1997. Luckily, I met Ully in Melbourne during that visit, as sadly she died in 2005.

Most of the family remained in Australia, but Heinz changed his name to Henry Stonnington and emigrated with his large family in 1969 to the United States, where he has many descendants. I was sorry not to meet him before he died in 2009, though we corresponded a great deal before that time.

THE FAMILY OF KARL SMETANA

Karl Smetana, my great uncle, married Lilly Bruchsteiner and they had one daughter, Gerda, born in 1929. They lived at Reithlegasse 16 (or possibly 14), Vienna XIX. Karl joined the paper manufacturing industry of his father-in-law, Richard Bruchsteiner, gaining a 30% share in the firm, together with Lilly's brother, Paul. Before the family's departure from Vienna, Lilly became ill and Gerda was looked after for a whole year by her maternal grandmother, who eventually died in Cuba.

Karl was interned for some time by the Nazis during 1938, and his grandson, Alan, recalls being told as a child that Lilly was required to hand over jewels and cash, before her departure, in order to get him released. Alan has a travel document dated 7 December 1938, giving the family permission to leave Vienna for Paris. However, Lilly, Gerda, and Lilly's best friend, Heller Schönbaumsfeld, travelled by train to Zurich, Switzerland, then on to Zug, where they remained for three months while trying to obtain a permit to emigrate to Australia. Heller, who was not Jewish, carried all Lilly's jewellery and money to get it safely over the border, an incredibly brave thing to do.

Karl was not with them at this stage, but on his release was granted a forged visa to leave Vienna, and eventually joined the rest of the family. They all arrived by boat in Melbourne on 20 June 1939. Karl set up a business selling cosmetic bags and changed his name to Charles Smeaton. By a strange coincidence, my childhood family home in Redhill, Nottingham, was bought from a family called Smeeton, with money my mother had inherited from the Smetana family.

Charles Smeaton (Karl Smetana) in Australia

Gerda married Henry Weinreiter but later divorced. She has two children: Lynette, born in 1956, and Alan, born in 1958. I met Gerda in May 1995 when she visited us in England and again in 1997 when I visited her at her home in Melbourne. I was struck by her remarkable resemblance to my mother.

Gerda with me and my mother, at my home in 1995

I had now discovered family living as far apart as England, Australia and the USA. But it seems that even before their flight from Vienna, this family had originated not in Vienna but in Poland and the present-day Czech Republic and Slovakia. Later I was to learn that the extended family had connections with at least 10 different countries in Europe prior to their departure. A family always on the move, like so many Jews throughout history.

Chapter Four

JOSEF SMETANA'S ANCESTRY: AN INNKEEPER'S SON OR SON OF A COMPOSER?

WAS JOSEF SMETANA RELATED TO THE COMPOSER?

The person I heard most about from my mother's relatives was Josef Smetana, our common ancestor. I wanted to find out more about this fascinating but ultimately tragic figure, and started to delve into his ancestry.

One of the few snippets of information I had learnt about the family, as a child, was that the Smetana family in Vienna was supposed, in some way, to be related to the Czech composer Bedřich Smetana, even though the composer was not himself Jewish. Intriguingly, I started to hear similar stories from my mother's cousins. My mother had never made an issue of the Smetana connection, though my father sometimes did. Not long before she died, I asked her again about this matter, and she confirmed that the family had claimed to be related to the composer, but she did not know what that relationship was.

I have now been conducting research into this issue for many years, but although I have uncovered many interesting facts, mystery continues to surround the parentage and birth of Josef Smetana, my great grandfather, almost as though someone has deliberately hidden the truth. Compounding the mystery is that evidence from different sources appears to be contradictory.

One source of information was my mother's cousin Ully, with whom I first spoke in 1995. Ully was a rather eccentric, albeit endearing, lady and I thought at first that she was possibly an unreliable witness. However, I later found that a number of the things she told me were indeed likely to be true.

Ully was convinced that Josef Smetana was related to the composer, and said that Josef was born in Litomyšl, the composer's birthplace, in Eastern Bohemia, 150 kilometres east of Prague in the current Czech Republic. (I have not yet had the opportunity to follow up this line of enquiry, so am unable to say whether or not there is any evidence to support this claim.) Ully also said that Josef was one of seven children, including a brother Julius, a dress designer who lived in Dresden, Germany. Apparently, Julius had a son Felix who was a set designer. There was also a story that Josef had a sister who married her uncle, and that he paid for her passage to Philadelphia, USA. According to Ully, Josef sent this sister his railway pension, a story also told by Ully's siblings, Helga and Heinz.

Some of Ully's story appeared to be confirmed when, quite accidentally, I came across a John Smetana, while I was working in the Jewish community in London between 1996 and 2005. John told me that his family believed themselves to be descended from the composer, and I said that his family and mine might therefore be related. When I asked how this relationship to the composer could be possible, since our families are Jewish and Bedřich Smetana was not, he said he could explain this.

Apparently, Bedřich Smetana spent a period of time in Göteborg, Sweden, between 1856 and 1861, with a further short visit in 1862. This period of the composer's life is well documented. During this time, Bedřich, who was himself married, had an affair with a married Jewish woman, Fröjda Benecke, by whom he allegedly had two illegitimate sons.

According to John's uncle, Erwin Smetana, who emigrated to Israel where he recently died, his father Adalbert or Albert Smetana (John's grandfather), born in 1873, was the grandson of the composer by this Swedish mistress. Erwin Smetana apparently also claimed that at some point after the composer died in 1884, Fröjda contacted the Emperor to request that her sons should be legitimised, and that this was granted by imperial decree.

John told me that he visited the Smetana museum in Prague many years ago, and that the museum was closed for half a day while he was shown documents not normally available to the public, including photos of Fröjda. He subsequently established contact with Dr Anders Carlsson, a doctor of music in Sweden who has carried out research into the composer, and whom I also later contacted.

There were two elements of John's story which struck a chord and made me believe that our two families could indeed be connected. One was that he spoke of a female relative living in Philadelphia, just as my mother's cousins had done. In fact John's father had visited a lady called June Smetana, and established that she was a relative, possibly his father Adalbert's niece. (June's married name has been omitted to protect her identity.)

The second and equally important point was that my great grandfather, Josef Smetana, had changed his name from Smetany to Smetana, by decree, on 2 June 1902. I later discovered that this was indeed an imperial decree. Since Josef was born on 5 July 1858 (that is, when the composer was in Sweden), this opened up the possibility that Josef was, in fact, one of the illegitimate sons.

When I contacted Dr Carlsson to discuss the possibility of Josef being one of Bedřich's sons, he took a great deal of interest in my story. Below is the e-mail he sent to me on 22 October 2006:

Dear Mrs Soyinka,

Thanks for your letter with a lot of interesting information and details ... I wrote my PhD dissertation about the musical life in Göteborg during the second half of the 19th century, unfortunately for you written in Swedish. A central part of this was the period when Bedřich Smetana stayed here. His contribution for the development of the musical life, repertoire, quality etc. was profound and essential. Smetana was also profitable to work with since he continuously wrote in his diary and also a lot of letters, mostly to his wife but also to colleagues for example Franz Liszt. It is obvious in Smetana's diary that he had an intimate relationship with Mrs Fröjda Benecke, born Gumpert and daughter to one of the most important booksellers in Göteborg at that time, Nathan Jacob Gumpert. (The Gumpert family - Jews - moved to Göteborg from Copenhagen where one of their friends was H.C. Andersen who also visited Göteborg and then stayed with the Gumpert family.) I could not in my dissertation pay any attention to the relationship between the two young people, and therefore I have not written anything about them there, more than just the fact that they had an intimate relationship.

However - privately - I have made some small research, and that started with Mr John Smetana, whom I came to know because he had visited the Smetana museum in Prague and talked to the museum director Mrs Doctor Olga Mojžíšová. Dr Mojžíšová and I have worked together a lot, and when she told me about John Smetana I called him. He told me immediately that he didn't know very much about his ancestors, and asked me instead to call his uncle Isaac Smetana (also called Erwin Smetana) who lives in Israel. I called this man and he told me that he as a young boy had been told that he and his family descended from Bedřich Smetana and a Swedish woman. This woman – Isaac Smetana had been told – got "*zwei Buben*" with Bedřich Smetana as father (Isaac Smetana only speaks German). These two boys were not twins but born separately. Fröjda went abroad, gave birth to the sons and in some way gave them a new home. After the death of Smetana in 1884, Fröjda wrote to Kaiser Franz Josef and asked for the permission for the two boys to take the name of Smetana. This Isaac Smetana told me, but he also made clear that there were no documents in his family since his father died before the Second World War; he himself flew before the Nazis came, and his mother was put in a concentration camp where she died and her home was burnt down ...

You tell me that your great-grandfather was born 5 July 1858. Well that makes it at least possible for Fröjda to be the mother, since she before that had given birth to a son 15 April 1857 (Wilhelm Nathan Benecke who died already 7 April 1859). I also found some interesting information in the log books for the passport police department in Göteborg from the time that is in focus for us. I was looking for some musicians when I found a note that Mr and Mrs Joseph Benecke (i.e. Joseph and Fröjda) had returned to Göteborg after a long stay abroad for several months. This could be one of these periods when Fröjda was pregnant and went abroad. And most certainly her husband was loyal to his wife and followed her abroad. I'm sorry to say that I at the moment cannot find my notes about this, so I don't know when they were abroad and when they returned to Göteborg. But it was in the years when Smetana stayed in Göteborg.

I don't know if this is anything of importance for you. But I am most certainly interested to know more about what you know and the photos you tell me about.

With kindest regards, Anders Carlsson

On 5 November 2006, Dr Carlsson wrote to me:

Smetana does not say explicitly in his diaries that he has an intimate relationship to Fröjda. However he writes in a manner that makes anything else than such a relation impossible. In the diary 5 January 1859 he writes: "*Urunglüllcklillicheser Tarag furür millich. F. garab millir eseillin Blaratt, woppe silliese millich deser Uruntreserouese beseschuruldilligt.*" And 7 January 1859 he wrote: "*F. barat milich uzum Vererzeseillhuzung, uzund weseillinesend stueillrztese Silliese iklin mereillinese Ararmese. Abend waren wir bei Pineus ...*"

This does not make much sense. What Smetana has done is to hide the real meaning by putting nonsense in-between. So if you take away letters that don't have any meaning you find for 5 January 1859 "*Unglücklicher Tag für mich. F. gab mir ein Blatt, wo sie mich der Untreue beschuldigt.*" (Unlucky day for me. F. gave me a sheet of paper, accusing me of infidelity.) And for 7 January 1859 "*F. bat mich um Verzeihung, und weinend stuerzte Sie in meine Arme* (F. asked me for forgiveness and crying, she fell into my arms). *Abend waren wir bei Pineus ...*"

Now why would a married woman accuse a married man, though not her husband, to be unfaithful? This is as far as I have seen the only part in Smetana's diaries where he tries to hide what he has written. And at the same time it is like a child's game. Everyone can in fact read what he has written. Please also note that it was only the part about Fröjda's accusation that was written in this manner. Immediately after that he shifted to the normal way of writing: "Abend waren wir bei Pineus ..."

There are some very important diaries of Smetana that are missing, those of the autumn of 1856, the second half of 1857 and all of 1858. There are some indications that the family still have these diaries in their private possession, but we don't know. The old director of the Smetana Museum in Prague, Dr Miloslav Malý, once told a Swede (Hans Abramson who in his turn told me) that he (Dr Malý) knew about these missing diaries and that they were kept by the Smetana family. But we cannot be so sure. And today Dr Malý is dead, and I don't think that Dr Olga Mojžíšová has an equally good contact/relation with the family as Dr Malý had. So Olga and I have discussed this over and over again: Has the family kept the diaries for themselves just because they want to hide something about Smetana's intimate relationship to Fröjda? Speculations.

Fröjda was married to Joseph Benecke who was a merchant but not with very good health. He died already in 1862 and after some years Fröjda remarried and got the name of Rubenson. So it must have been as Mrs Rubenson that she wrote to the emperor Franz Joseph, if this story is correct. She was once again a widow after her second husband and had a long life. But she didn't bequeath anything to some men that could be these two sons ... Please continue to inform me about what is happening in your investigations.

With kindest regards, Anders Carlsson

In 2007, I came across a book entitled *The Pain and the Glory: the Life of Smetana* by Liam Nolan and J. Bernard Hutton. Fröjda's name appears frequently in the book, which speaks of the life-long and passionate love between her and the composer, though appears to imply that they resisted a physical relationship, because of their respective marriages. Also, there is no mention of the fact that Fröjda was Jewish, so evidently, there was at least some editing of the truth.

Interestingly, the book states that Fröjda visited Smetana in Prague towards the end of his life, a detail not recorded elsewhere. If that is true, I wonder if she gained his agreement at that time to seek permission for the legitimisation of their sons after his death.

Since the book is written like a novel, it is very easy to read, and it gives some fascinating insights into the personality, life and relationships of the composer. I had never quite realised what a tragic life he led. Because of the way it is written, and because of the evident omissions, there is obviously a concern that some of it may be fanciful, and not based in reality. I therefore checked names, places, events and dates with the historical chronology provided in a book called *Smetana* by John Clapham, and they all correlated very closely. I think that all that is imagined is the dialogue, and even much of this may be based on diaries and letters seen by Hutton.

I have done some research on Hutton, who was the one with the knowledge of Smetana (Liam Nolan just wrote the book for him). Hutton was born in 1911, educated in Germany, but of Czech origin. He was a journalist, and I believe his original name was Hiesler. He had the advantage that he could read the original

Czech and German documents, and says he visited the Smetana museum many times in the 1930s, and again after the war, as well as visiting other archives and Smetana locations. It would seem therefore that he did his research thoroughly.

As far as I am aware, Hutton is the only author to write in such detail of the relationship between Fröjda Benecke and the composer, though there is some knowledge of the affair in academic circles. Even Wikipedia gives a tantalisingly brief reference to their relationship in an article about the composer:

"Back in Sweden (autumn 1857), Smetana found among his new pupils a young housewife, Fröjda Benecke, who briefly became his muse and his mistress. In her honour Smetana transcribed two songs from Schubert's Die schöne Müllerin *cycle, and transformed one of his own early piano pieces into a polka entitled* Vision at the Ball."

I asked Dr Carlsson about this relative lack of information about the full extent of the affair. He wrote back to me on 15 February 2007:

Dear Mrs Soyinka,

Yes, I have read the book you mention. There is also another one by Brian Large. And of course a lot of literature in Czech and also in German. Neither Clapham nor Large knows anything about the intimacies between Bedřich and Fröjda. Officially no one knows, and I have not seen it written anywhere. Even Mrs Mojžíšová, the director of the Smetana Museum in Prague, is not very happy to talk about it. Most people want to preserve the façade of "good bourgeois morality", whatever that is. A Czech professor and friend of mine, living in Sweden since 1968, told me many years ago to publish internationally what I knew about Bedřich and Fröjda. *"The Czechs will hate you for that but respect you,"* he said.

Yes, Fröjda and Bedřich were in contact with each other also after the Göteborg period. Bedřich wrote to Fröjda and told her about his deafness. There are some letters (in Prague) written in 1875, Bedřich got his ear problems the year before. He tried a lot to get cured but needed money to go abroad and visit some specialists in Würzburg, Frankfurt, Stuttgart, München and Wien. He asked Fröjda to arrange a benefit concert in Göteborg for him. Fröjda answered that it was not a very good idea since it was so late in the concert season - just before summer - and most

> of the ordinary concert visitors had already gone to their country houses. Instead she promised to raise a collection among the rich families where Bedřich had a lot of friends ... Fröjda kept her promise and sent Bedřich quite a large sum. Unfortunately nothing could help him, and after that, there are no more letters or other documents that tell us about a contact between the two.
>
> Kindest regards, Anders Carlsson

I subsequently carried out my own online research on Fröjda and her family using the FamilySearch website and discovered the following:

Fröjda was born Fröjda Gumpert in Göteborg on 19 March 1837, and died in 1923. Her parents were Nathan Jacob Gumpert, originally of Copenhagen, and Edla Nissen. She had five children from her two marriages to Joseph Benecke and Jacob Rubenson:

Nicolina Benecke, born in 1856, who married Carl Axel Stendahl in 1879;
Wilhelm Nathan Benecke, born on 15 April 1857 and died on 7 April 1859;
Agnes Rubenson, born 1867, died 1940, who married Jacob Philipson in 1888;
Axel Gumpert Rubenson, who was born in 1869 and died in 1908; and
Elsa Eufrosyne Rubenson, who was born in 1871 and died in 1925.

Fröjda's first husband, Joseph Benecke, was born in 1823 and died in 1862, while her second husband, Jacob Rubenson, was born in 1831 and died in 1898. Her marriage to Jacob Rubenson is recorded to have taken place on 10 June 1857, but this cannot be correct as she was at this time married to her first husband and had just given birth to her second child. According to Dr Carlsson, her second marriage in fact took place in 1866.

There was evidently a 10-year gap between the children of her two marriages, a gap probably filled by the birth of her two sons by Smetana. What is also clear is that she was very fertile, several of her children being born little more than a year apart. Had she had an affair in the intervening years when Smetana was in Sweden (1856–1862), this would have been likely to result in a child. Given that her second child by her husband was born in April 1857, the two sons she had by Smetana would have been born between April 1858 and 1863. My great grandfather, Josef, was born in July 1858, so that date fits.

I was puzzled by the 1873 date of birth of John Smetana's grandfather Adalbert, said to be the composer's grandson. If he was indeed descended from the composer, he would have been born later than 1873 if he were his grandson, but earlier if he were his son.

Bedřich had four daughters by his first wife, Katarina, of whom three died before he went to Sweden. He remained very close to his surviving daughter, Zofie. His first wife, whom he loved very much, died in 1859 and it appears to have been the custom at that time for a man with children to remarry quickly if his wife died. Indeed, the composer's father, František, had married three times for this very reason, and Bedřich was the son of his third wife, his first surviving son.

According to *The Pain and the Glory*, Bedřich begged Fröjda to marry him, but she was unable to do so as she was herself married. He therefore married his second wife, Bettina, in 1860, but this does not appear to have been a good marriage, though he subsequently had two further daughters. Ironically, Fröjda's own husband died in 1862, and had Bedřich not been so hasty, he could have married Fröjda, if this had been permissible, given that she was Jewish.

It seems highly likely that, having no sons within his marriages, Bedřich would have wanted to ensure that the two sons he had by the woman he loved passionately were properly cared for, and would also have wanted to give them his name. What better way of doing this than by placing them with a Jewish Smetana family to ensure that they had a Jewish upbringing, as I am sure would have been Fröjda's wish, and that they took the Smetana name?

THE SMETANY/SMETANA FAMILY IN UNGARISCH BROD (NOW UHERSKÝ BROD)

Note: While part of the Habsburg Empire, the towns and villages in this region were known officially by their German name, for example Ungarisch Brod ("Hungarian ford") and Hallenkau, now known by their Czech names, Uherský Brod and Halenkov. I have used the German names when referring to the 19th century, as that is what appears in the documentation, but the Czech names of the towns where the archives are now stored. (For further information, please see Appendix 15: A Note on Czech Jewish Genealogy.)

As I said earlier, evidence from different sources appears to be contradictory and confusing, and this has made it difficult to establish the facts. I was able to confirm that Josef was born to a Jewish family on 5 July 1858 and in two documents he

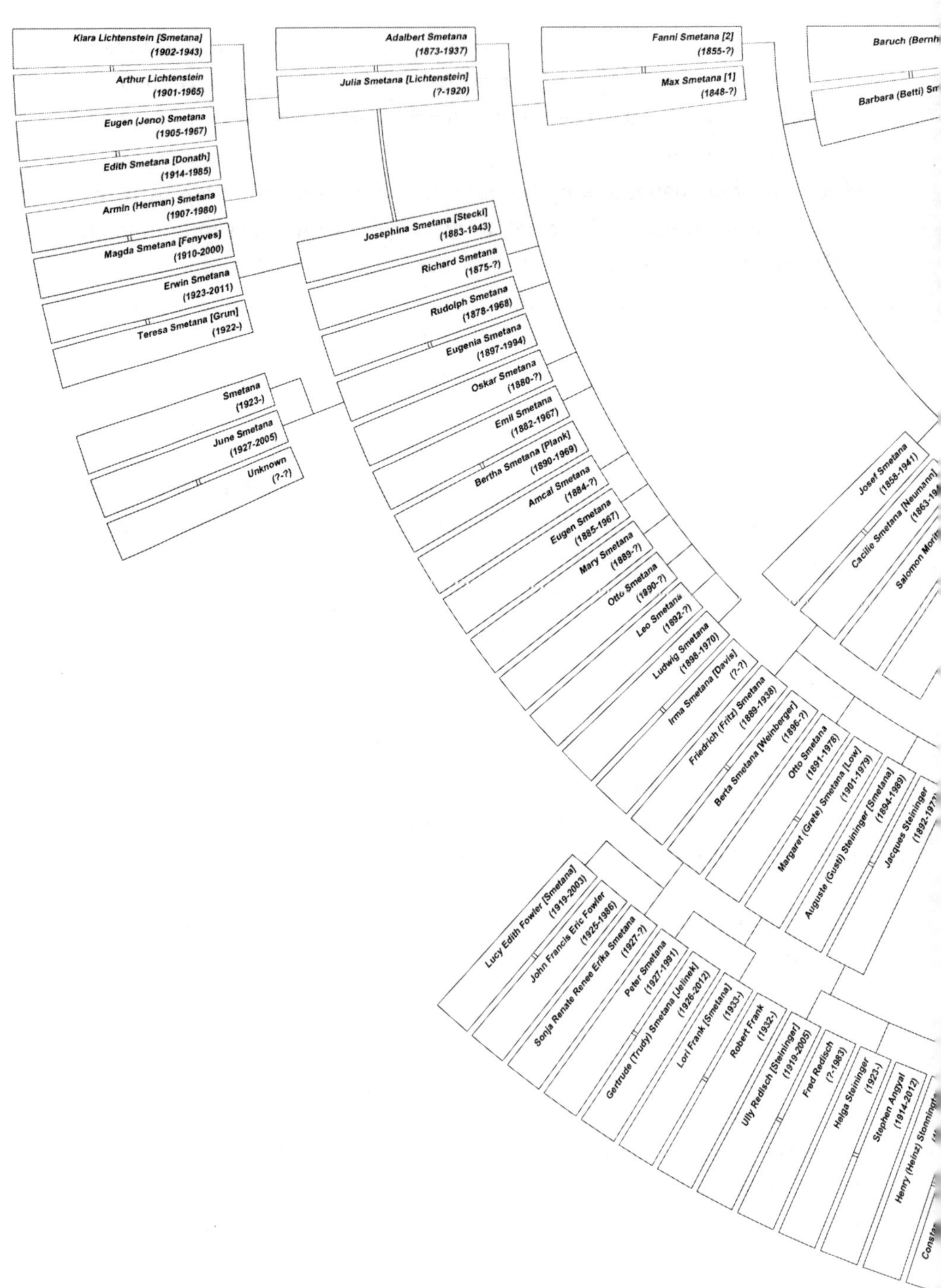

THE DESCENDANTS OF ABRAHAM HIRSCH SMETANY

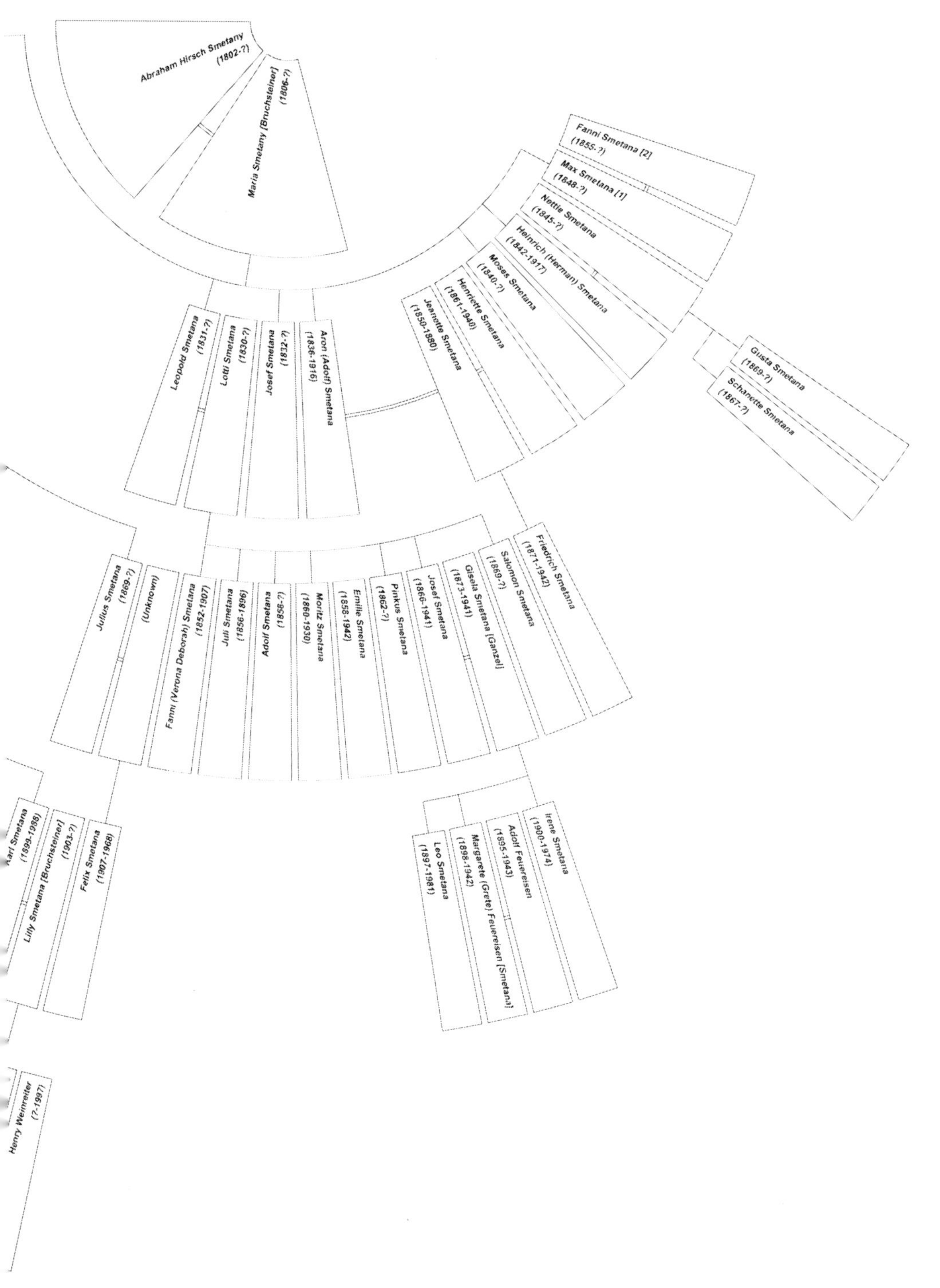

Abraham Hirsch Smetany (1802-?)
Maria Smetany [Bruchsteiner] (1806-?)
Fanni Smetana (1855-?) [2]
Max Smetana (1848-?) [1]
Nettie Smetana (1845-?)
Heinrich (Herman) Smetana (1842-1917)
Moses Smetana (1840-?)
Henriette Smetana (1861-1940)
Jeanette Smetana (1850-1880)
Gusta Smetana (1869-?)
Schanette Smetana (1867-?)
Leopold Smetana (1831-?)
Lotti Smetana (1830-?)
Josef Smetana (1832-?)
Aron (Adolf) Smetana (1836-1916)
Julius Smetana (1869-?)
(Unknown)
Fanni (Verona Deborah) Smetana (1852-1907)
Juli Smetana (1856-1896)
Adolf Smetana (1858-?)
Moritz Smetana (1860-1930)
Emilie Smetana (1858-1942)
Pinkus Smetana (1862-?)
Josef Smetana (1866-1941)
Gisela Smetana [Ganzel] (1873-1941)
Salomon Smetana (1869-?)
Friedrich Smetana (1871-1942)
Karl Smetana (1899-1988)
Lilly Smetana [Bruchsteiner] (1903-?)
Felix Smetana (1907-1968)
Leo Smetana (1897-1981)
Margarete (Grete) Feuereisen [Smetana] (1898-1942)
Adolf Feuereisen (1895-1943)
Irene Smetana (1900-1974)
Henry Weinreiter (?-1997)

stated that his birthplace was Hallenkau (now Halenkov), Moravia, in the east of the present Czech Republic, close to the border with Slovakia.

Other documents show that Josef's parents were Baruch Smetany, born in Ungarisch Brod in 1830, and Barbara Smetany, née Hirsch, born in Karlovitz (now Karlovice). Ungarisch Brod, a town to the south-east of Brno, not far from the border with Austria, had an important Jewish community, dating probably from the 13th century. It had had a troubled history, suffering several massacres, but was served by a number of noted rabbis.

Another record, dated 1941 (i.e. during the Nazi era, when people had to declare their ancestry), names Josef's parents as Bernhard Smetana, who was born in Wsetin (now Vsetín), near Hallenkau, and died in Philadelphia, and Betti Smetana, née Hirsch, who died in Wsetin. However, there is no record of Josef's birth in Hallenkau either in the Prague Archives or in the Vsetín District Archives.

Indeed, other than trade and police records placing Bernhard in Hallenkau between 1855 and 1872, there is no record of any Smetana family in either Wsetin or Hallenkau, though there were Hirsch families in Hallenkau. Neither is there any mention of Hallenkau at the *Israelitische Kultusgemeinde* (IKG), the Jewish archives in Vienna, and indeed here, once again, Josef is said to originate from Ungarisch Brod. There is no mention in the IKG records of Josef's parents.

Interestingly, census and other records show that there was an extensive Smetany family living in Ungarisch Brod throughout the 19th century, and it is clear that there was a degree of interconnection between the Smetany family of Ungarisch Brod and the Hirsch family of Hallenkau.

Abraham Hirsch Smetany, born on 7 July 1802, married Maria Bruchsteiner, aged 19, on 5 July 1826 in Ungarisch Brod. Their children included Baruch, born in 1830 at house number 69, Joseph, born in 1832 at house number 40, Aron (Adolf) born in 1836, Moses born in 1840, and Heinrich, born in 1842 at house number 40. The 1869 census for Ungarisch Brod shows that a Leopold, born in 1813, and Lotti Smetany, together with their seven children were living at Ungarisch Brod number 40.

Also living there in 1869 was a Mariana Smetany, born in 1805, almost certainly the widow of Abraham Hirsch Smetany. The same family appeared in the 1880 census, when "Mari" was said to be the house owner. It is likely that Leopold was one of Abraham's sons, since Mari is described as Leopold's mother in the 1880 census, in which case he must have been born later than 1813. It is possible that he could have been one of the other sons mentioned above (perhaps Josef born in 1832), but known by a different name.

A search of the US census records for Philadelphia showed a Fanni Smetana, born in Hallenkau in about 1855, married to a Max Smetana, born in Ungarisch Brod in 1848. They arrived in the USA in 1906–7 together with eight of their children: Rudolph, Emil, Amcal, Eugen, Mary, Otto, Leopold and Ludwig. Ship records show that Fanni had 12 children, of whom 11 survived.

The Fanni here is likely to have been the daughter of Baruch, since, like Josef, she was born in Hallenkau, and it was said to be his sister whose passage to the USA he paid, and to whom he sent his railway pension. Other records show that Fanni was born Smetana, and since she still had that name, this indicates that she married a relative, confirming Ully's story that Josef's sister married her uncle.

Furthermore, I discovered that John Smetana's relative, June Smetana of Philadelphia, was the daughter of Rudolph Smetana, son of Max and Fanni, born in 1878. This means that John Smetana's family and my family are almost certainly related.

But that is not all. When Max arrived in New York in 1906, he was required to give the name of a relative with whom he would be staying. The name he gave was Bernhard Milk of Bohemia, born about 1835, who arrived in the USA in 1884 (1870 according to one record) and who Max described as his step-brother. I think it is likely that Bernhard Milk was in fact Baruch/Bernhard Smetana, Josef's father, who according to records in Vienna died in Philadelphia, but of whom there is no record in the USA. He must have changed his name to Bernhard Milk when he emigrated, perhaps because he wanted a less foreign-sounding name. He may have chosen the name Milk because Smetana means cream.

It is also possible that he was trying to cover his tracks. There is some evidence that he had a police record in Hallenkau, having been arrested several times, once for illegally transporting wood and on another occasion for illegally serving brandy together with a number of other young men, in 1857, for which they all received a severe reprimand. He was also given notice of non-payment of taxes.

Indeed, he seems to have been something of a jack-of-all-trades, as he clearly tried his hand not only as an innkeeper and timber merchant, but also as a grocer and restaurateur. In Philadelphia, as Bernhard Milk, he became a ball stitcher. He appears to have abandoned his family, since his wife Betti was still alive in 1890. A record in Ungarisch Brod shows her to have been living at that time in Hallenkau with her son, Julius.

Yet, Baruch remarried in the USA in 1891 (if indeed he was Bernhard Milk) and had another child, Bertha. According to my mother's cousin, Heinz, he died at the age of 104. Baruch appears to have been an altogether different character

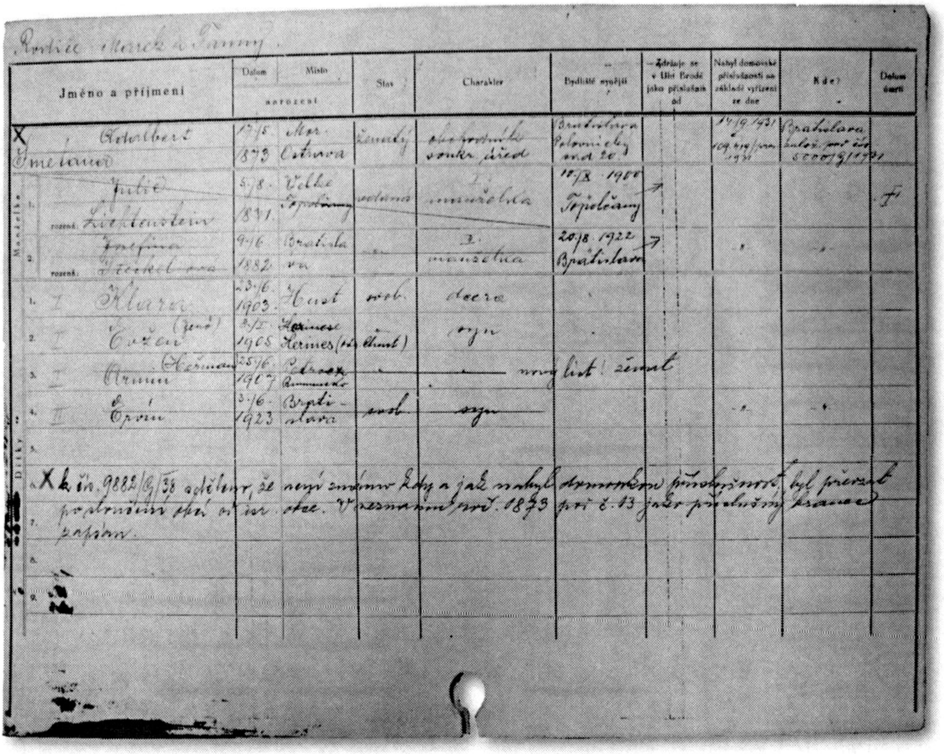

Document showing that Adalbert Smetana's parents were Marek (Max) and Fanni. Armin (Herman) Smetana listed here is John Smetana's father

from his son, Josef, who was in every respect a hard-working, upstanding citizen and dedicated family man.

Further searches in the records of the Jewish community in Ungarisch Brod resulted in some startling findings. It seems that Adalbert Smetana (John Smetana's grandfather) was born in Ostrau (now Ostrava), in the north-east of the current Czech Republic, on 17 May 1873, and was one of the three children of Max and Fanni who remained in Europe, the other two being Richard, born in 1875, and Oskar, born in 1880. They were recorded in the Ungarisch Brod records because Max was born there.

These documents also revealed that Max's original name was Marek or Markus. Unless he was not the real son of Max and Fanni, and was born 10 years earlier, or 10 years later, this means that Adalbert could not have been the composer's son/grandson. If he was not, how is it that his descendants have carried the story of the composer's illegitimate sons, and in such precise detail? There must have been some element of truth in the story.

Intriguingly, the census records for 1900 show that there was another Marek/Markus Smetana, born in 1855, living in Ungarisch Brod at that time, who also had a son Albert, born in 1888. This Markus, and his other son Leo, or Lev, were innkeepers and restaurateurs, like Baruch. Could this Markus have been Baruch's son, and therefore Josef's brother? This family did not appear in the Ungarisch Brod census records for 1869 and 1880, so may well have been living in Hallenkau at those times.

And why do all the trails lead back to Ungarisch Brod? What is of particular significance about the Smetany family living in Ungarisch Brod is the fact, already mentioned, of a change of name for the whole family from Smetany to Smetana in 1902. Permission for this name change was issued from the *Kaiserlich Königliches Innenministerium* (Imperial Royal Ministry of the Interior) in Vienna and was instigated by my great grandfather, Josef Smetana, proving conclusively that he was related to the family in Ungarisch Brod, even though there is no record of him ever having lived there. It seems that because his father, Baruch, had been born there, he had an inherited right of domicile.

Copies of the name change were sent to the *Statthalterei* (governorship) in nearby Brno and also to Lwów (Lemberg), now in Ukraine, indicating that some member of the family had moved east. Could this have been Max and Fanni, who were living by this time in Poland, or Adalbert, who moved still further east and later died in Serbia?

Furthermore, the involvement of the *Kaiserlich Königliches Innenministerium* confirms that the decree declaring the change of name was issued from the Imperial Office, which chimes with the story provided by John Smetana's family regarding the birth of two illegitimate sons to the composer and his mistress, and their legitimisation by imperial decree after the composer's death in 1884.

Details of the family name change are contained in a 51-page document, copies of which I have managed to obtain from the Brno Archives. The male members of the family, in addition to Josef, were listed as Abraham Hirsch (1802), Baruch (1830), his uncles Josef (1832), Aron or Adolf (1836), Moses (1840), Heinrich (1842), and also Salomon Moritz (1862), Eduard (1863) and Julius (1869). Leopold and Max were not on the list, but were almost certainly Abraham's sons. The second Markus was not on this list either.

The only female members of the family listed were the wives of Abraham and Baruch, as it was judged that women born Smetana would take the name of their husbands. The name of Augusta was mentioned, possibly Josef's sister or aunt, who had apparently died, and to whom therefore the name change did not apply.

Correspondence in the documents spans a period of time from 29 November 1899 to 8 July 1902. Throughout most of that time, there was an insistence, on the part of the imperial authorities, that the correct family name was Smetany. As late as 2 May 1902, the Imperial District Commissioner declared that:

> In accordance with the execution of the order dated 27th March 1902, no. 12906, it is submitted, with the report, that all relevant members of the Smetany family are notified of the decision by the Imperial Ministry of the Interior of 11th March 1902, no. 7896, and the appeals submitted by Adolf Smetana and Julius Smetana for change of name of the same are simultaneously turned down.

Then suddenly, and without any explanation, it was confirmed on 2 June 1902 that the *"Lower Austrian Governor's Office notifies the approval of the change of name to Smetana granted to Josef Smetany in Vienna, his wife and his children."*

What brought about this sudden and inexplicable change of mind?

The document includes an extract from the IKG registry of births in Ungarisch Brod, confirming that Josef Smetany, son of Baruch and Barbara, was born on 5 July 1858 in Hallenkau and was circumcised on 12 July 1858. This would appear to indicate that Josef was not, after all, the son of the composer.

However, some aspects of this record remain puzzling. The extract shown above was issued in 1899, with notes added in 1902, and Josef shares the entry with his uncle Aron, born in Ungarisch Brod in 1836. Bizarrely, Josef's entry appears before that of his uncle. Why would a birth in Hallenkau be registered in Ungarisch Brod, when there is no record of Josef's birth, or indeed of his existence, in the Hallenkau records?

Another interesting piece of information to emerge from Josef's birth record is the confirmation that the occupation of Baruch Smetany was that of *Schänker*, a term meaning innkeeper, surprisingly a fairly common occupation for a Jewish person of that period. Is it a coincidence that the occupation of František Smetana, father of the composer, was that of brewer? Were the two families in some way connected, at an earlier period, through their occupations? It is known that František Smetana travelled widely throughout the country, working in numerous locations, while building up his brewery business. This is speculation, of course, but an intriguing thought, nevertheless.

It seems Josef also had to provide a birth certificate, which was returned to him and was not therefore amongst the papers. However, a reference to it states that his birth certificate was issued on 7 June 1888, 30 years after his birth, and four years after the death of the composer.

The Brno document appears to imply that Salomon Moritz, Eduard and Julius (born in 1862, 1863 and 1869 respectively) were the sons of Abraham and Maria, but this could not have been the case, as they would have been too old by this time. It is more likely that they were the children of Baruch, and therefore Josef's brothers. Indeed the document shows that Julius went to Dresden, thus confirming Ully's story that Josef had a brother Julius who went to Dresden.

However, although Salomon Moritz, Eduard and Julius would appear from this document to have been born in Ungarisch Brod, they do not appear, as does not

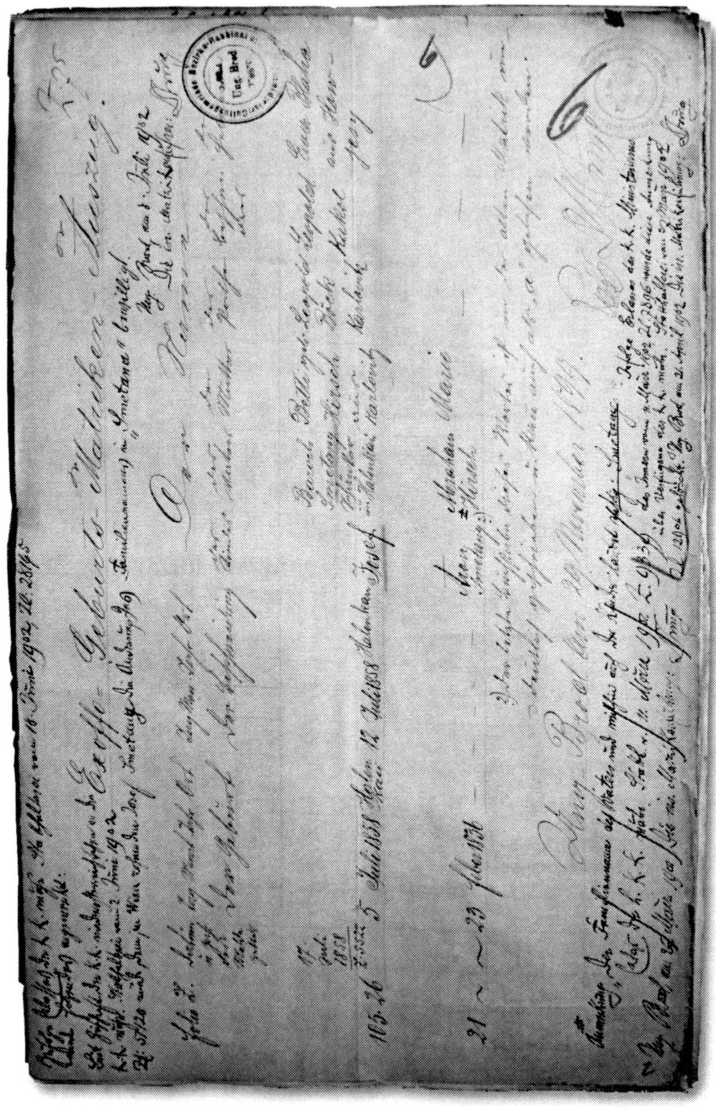

Extract from the Jewish registry of births in Ungarisch Brod, showing details of Josef Smetana's birth in 1858 (translation Appendix 1)

Josef, in either the 1869 or 1880 census for that town. In fact, even though he was said to be born in Hallenkau, I still have not found any census or other records showing the whereabouts of Josef and his immediate family between the time of his birth in 1858 and 1874 when he went to work for the railways.

Why has evidence of Josef's early childhood proved so elusive? It is true that the 1869 census records for Hallenkau are missing, but the family does not appear in any of the other census records for that town either. Sadly, for the time being, many questions remain unanswered.

When John Smetana, whom I met by chance, first sent me his own family tree several years ago, it appeared to bear no relation whatsoever to my own. What we did share was the family name of Smetana, and an oral family history claiming a relationship with the Czech composer, Bedřich Smetana. No doubt, many families bearing that name make a similar claim. What makes this story a little different is that the families making this claim were Jewish when the composer was not, and that a Jewish link to the composer has been established.

Obviously, it would be difficult to prove conclusively whether or not my great grandfather, Josef Smetana, was indeed the illegitimate son of the composer. Some of the information I have unearthed points in that direction, while other evidence would suggest otherwise.

At the very least, this has been a fascinating piece of research which has not only enabled me to establish that my family is related to the family of John Smetana (indeed it would seem that our grandfathers were cousins); it has also unearthed our shared family histories, which unfolded during a significant period of European Jewish history.

There is a final footnote to this story: I received two photographs of Fröjda Benecke from Dr Carlsson, and discovered that I bear a most uncanny resemblance to her.

REFLECTIONS ON ANCESTRAL BONDS

I have found in the course of my family research that, even though one has many ancestors, certain ancestors seem to stand out more than others. One can feel a much greater connection or affinity with some, whereas others hardly register at all. It is as though one has received more genes, more history, from certain ancestors than from others.

Of my two possible great great grandparents, it is Fröjda rather than the composer to whom I feel drawn, and with whom I feel a connection. When I first looked into her eyes, I got the same tingling sensation that I had when first I looked at the photograph of my grandmother, Berta, even though the two of them were not blood-related. A nerve-tingling sense of recognition, as if I were looking into a mirror. It was almost as if I knew her.

When I first received the photos from Anders Carlsson, I asked my husband, Kayode, to take a look at them, to see if he thought I could be related to her. He stared at the photo on the computer screen in silence for a full 15 minutes, until I finally prompted him by asking, "*Well, do you think I could be descended from her*?" He replied very slowly, "*Ye...es, I should think so.*"

Above left and bottom left: Fröjda Benecke. Top right and bottom right: two passport photos of myself, taken in my youth

As I started to learn more about her life, I realised that, just as with my grandmother, she had taken actions or perhaps made mistakes very likely to be frowned upon by society. "Mistakes" that I also had made, long before I had ever known anything about either of them. In particular, all three of us had, as married women, had a child by another man.

One thing that has troubled me about Fröjda's history is the loss of her two-year-old son, Wilhelm, in 1859, and of her husband, Joseph, in 1862, both during the period of her affair with the composer. One has to question whether these untimely deaths were in any way related to her affair, to the possible neglect of her duties, to the fact that her attention was elsewhere. I imagine she must have carried an enormous burden of guilt throughout her life. Guilt is another prevalent theme in my own family history.

But what if, in the final analysis, it could be proven that Josef was not the son of Bedřich and Fröjda, and that I could not therefore be descended from them? Would this matter to me? There would be a certain sense of disappointment, even surprise, that I was not descended from this woman with whom I have identified so strongly. However, the thought of not being a blood relative of the Smetana family of Ungarisch Brod, in which Josef was raised, also leaves me feeling somewhat deprived. Having taken so much time and trouble to track them down, I would feel a certain sense of relief that I was in fact descended from this remarkable family whose history I have found so fascinating.

Whatever the truth, unearthing this story has caused me to give a great deal of thought to the nature of inheritance. We all know that looks are inherited, but it is generally assumed that a large part of human behaviour is learned. Could it be that the actions we take, or at least our character and personality, are also derived, in part, from some inherited pattern?

On a separate, but similar vein, I believe it may be possible that trauma, too, could be inherited, or in some measure and in some unknown way, passed on from parent to child. In the course of my search, I have come across the phrase "intergenerational transmission of trauma", which resonates with me. I am not suggesting that behaviour is predetermined, or that human beings should not be responsible for their own actions, but rather that there are many complex and interacting factors which shape human behaviour, and that inherited trauma could be one of those factors in some instances.

One thing of which I am certain is that the impact of individual actions, and more importantly of historical events, can cascade down the generations. These are some of my thoughts whenever I witness the reporting of some major catastrophic event in one part of the world or another. As well as the dreadful impact on human beings right now, how will these events affect the generations to come?

Chapter Five

THE JEWISH COMMUNITIES OF BOHEMIA AND MORAVIA

The historical information in this chapter is based mainly on articles written by Czech Jewish genealogist, Dr Julius Müller, published on his website www.toledot.org, with his kind permission.

It would be helpful at this point to pause briefly from the family history, and to examine the context in which the family of Josef Smetana lived. During the medieval period, some horrific atrocities were committed against Jews, for example in Prague in 1389, the Catholic Church being the major source of anti-Semitism at that period.

Between 1526 and 1918, the Czech lands of Bohemia to the west and Moravia to the east were part of the Habsburg Empire, ruled from Vienna. While all subjects were victim to some oppression over the centuries, Jews in this region, in particular, were subjected to severe restrictions, though this kind of persecution did not usually take the form of pogroms.

In fact, Jewish communities in southern Moravia increased in size as they absorbed waves of refugees expelled from Moravian royal towns in the 15th and 16th centuries, then Jews fleeing terror from Poland, Latvia and Belarus in the 17th century, and in 1670, those expelled from Vienna and Lower Austria.

However, as a consequence of this swell in numbers, numerous attempts were then made to decrease the Jewish population. In 1724, the first census of Jews in Czech lands was carried out. The data collected was intended to serve as a basis for the reduction of the number of Jewish families to what it had been in the year 1618 and to identify those who were supposed to leave the country. At that time, approximately 30,000 Jews inhabited 168 towns and 672 villages in Bohemia, and about 20,000 lived in Moravia in 52 communities, mostly in towns.

In 1726, a decree issued by Emperor Karl VI limited the number of Jewish families to 8,541 in Bohemia, and 5,106 in Moravia. This was later increased to 8,600 and 5,400 respectively. According to this *Familianten Ordnung* (Family Decree or Family Law), only the first-born son of each Jewish family was allowed to marry and have children. To ensure enforcement of this law, lists of *Familien* were compiled into *Books of Jewish Families.*

The Family Decree was introduced in Bohemia and Moravia but not in other lands of the Empire. As a consequence, between 1730 and 1790, 30,000 Jewish families migrated from Bohemia and Moravia, mainly to Upper Hungary (now Slovakia), though the decree did ensure that some Jews were allowed to remain in the country, and ultimately it was never fully enforced. Nevertheless, the population restrictions of the 1726 decree dramatically changed the social life of Jewish families for the next 120 years. This law was not rescinded until 1849, and even then was partly re-introduced and not fully annulled until 1867.

The existence of the Family Law also affected the legitimacy of children. Since only first-born sons were allowed to marry, the children of other couples were considered illegitimate and bore the mother's surname. I have noticed during my research that a number of Jewish women of that period married a relative bearing the same name, and wonder if this may have been a way of counteracting this discriminatory law. After 1849 when the decree was lifted, many couples sought to legitimise their children.

Although Abraham Hirsch Smetany, born in 1802, had many sons, only one, Leopold, remained in Ungarisch Brod by the mid-19th century. Baruch went first to Hallenkau, then to the USA, while Aron went to Vienna and Heinrich to Ostrava (German, Ostrau), in the north-east of the present Czech Republic.

Max and Fanni were particularly mobile and, before the family finally emigrated to the USA, lived in numerous locations, where their 12 children were born: Ostrava, then nearby Český Těšín, Belgrade in the former Yugoslavia (now Serbia), Orsova in Romania, and Wygoda in Poland. Their eldest son, Adalbert, born in Ostrava, moved east to Bratislava, then to Petrőc, now Bački Petrovac in Serbia, where he died.

Many of Abraham's grandchildren also moved further afield, including of course Josef to Vienna and his brother Julius to Dresden in Germany. It is likely that the widespread dispersal of the Smetana family was due at least in part to these repressive laws.

Interestingly, I came across another extensive Jewish Smetana family, very probably related, living only 30 miles away in Trenčín, just over the border in the present-day Slovakia (then Hungary). It is very possible that they migrated there in the18[th] century in order to avoid the Family Decree, restricting marriage to the first-born son. Their patriarch, Simon Smetana, was born in 1800. The members of this family, unaffected by the laws, were far more likely to remain in their home town, as borne out by the fact that many descendants have been able to trace their ancestors and construct family trees. As far as I am aware, I am the only person to have built the family tree of the Smetanas from Ungarisch Brod. Of course, many members of both these Smetana families were victims of the Nazis, and became widely dispersed, or perished in concentration camps.

A further decree which was to impact considerably on Jewish life was issued in 1787 by Joseph II, who ordered that all Jews should have officially recognised German first names and surnames. A Jewish census carried out in 1793 was the first to list the newly adopted surnames of Jewish families. Prior to this, Jewish surnames had usually been patronyms or place names, but the new names were often related to professions or to roles in the community. It would seem likely, therefore, that the Smetany/Smetana family name came into existence at this point. It is interesting to surmise whether the Smetana name change in 1902 was in some way related to this decree or indeed to the Family Decree.

The Jewish populations were also subject to occupational restrictions. From medieval times till 1841, 1861 in some areas, Jews were forbidden to own land, and they were not allowed to manufacture goods until the end of the 18th century. The few crafts they were permitted to practise were mostly those within the community, for example, baker, shoemaker and tailor, so as not to provide competition with the non-Jewish population. Their primary sources of income were peddling and trading in agricultural products. They were also allowed to rent potash houses and distilleries.

Though he may well have been a rogue, Baruch Smetany's brushes with the police may have been due to these restrictions on Jewish trade, and he seems to have been spirited enough to challenge them.

Migration and the search for work were facilitated from the mid-19th century onwards with the building of the railways, on which Josef himself worked for 25 years. The railways also provided employment for other members of the Smetana family in Ungarisch Brod, including Josef's namesake, Josef, son of Leopold, born in 1866, who moved to Bohumín (German name Oderberg), a railway hub near Ostrava.

Many Jews also migrated in order to escape from the harsh conditions of the densely populated Moravian Jewish quarters. In 1726 the Austrian government tried to isolate Jewish communities from their non-Jewish neighbours. Although Jews in Bohemia often lived scattered among their fellow countrymen, Jewish families in Moravia usually lived in a designated Jewish street close to the church, so that they could be supervised, and near the overlord's manor, so that they could be "protected". The small houses were often subdivided into a number of sections to provide housing for several families, and were interconnected by corridors, passages and bridge-paths.

Many Jews from this region migrated to Vienna, including several members of the Smetana family. In general, the phenomenon of migration and resettlement reflected the troubled history of the Jewish people of Central Europe. The mutual support and solidarity of Jewish communities was often the only mechanism for survival, later facilitated by the emancipation and civic liberation of the 1850s and 1860s, which brought new opportunities.

For a tragically brief period, these new opportunities, together with family bonds and the tradition of trading, enabled Jewish entrepreneurs, such as my great grandfather, Josef Smetana, to flourish and to contribute to the larger society, economically, politically, socially and culturally. The catastrophe which then ensued was to engulf the Smetana family along with the rest of European Jewry.

Map of Europe, 1871, courtesy of the University of Texas Libraries

The synagogue in Ungarisch Brod was destroyed by the Nazis in 1941 and the communists demolished the town's Jewish quarters in 1950. Remarkably, three Torah scrolls from the synagogue survived and have found homes in congregations in the USA. (For further information on the rescue of hundreds of Czech scrolls, see Appendix 15: A Note on Czech Jewish Genealogy.)

In January 1943, Ungarisch Brod became an assembly point for Jews from the surrounding region, and 2,637 Jews were deported from the town, in three transports, first to Theriesenstadt and later to Auschwitz. Only 81 survived. All that remains of a once thriving Jewish community is the cemetery containing 1,085 tombs, among them those of Markus Smetana, 1855–1922, and Julie Smetana, daughter of Leopold, 1858–1896.

Map of Central Europe, 1996, courtesy of the University of Texas Libraries

Chapter Six

THE NAZI MACHINE IN AUSTRIA

AS MADE EVIDENT IN NAZI FILES ON MEMBERS OF THE SMETANA AND WEINBERGER FAMILIES IN VIENNA 1938–1945

"Monsters exist, but they are too few in numbers to be truly dangerous. More dangerous are ... the functionaries ready to believe and act without asking questions." *Primo Levi, author and Auschwitz survivor*

INTRODUCTION

During the late 1990s, when I first embarked on my journey of discovery, I obtained a number of Nazi documents from the Austrian State Archives. These consisted largely of forms which all Jews had had to complete, acknowledging that they were Jewish and declaring their assets, together with a small amount of associated correspondence.

In early 2011, I started to compile the family history, based on these early documents and also on a number of other sources, mainly the *Israelitische Kultusgemeinde Wien* (IKG), the Jewish Archives in Vienna, and oral family history.

Having almost completed my project, I wanted to check out a few facts before going to print, and thus contacted once again the Austrian State Archives. In particular, I wanted to know whether they could confirm that my great grandfather, Josef Smetana, had been the Commissioner for Railways in Vienna, as this was information given to me by one of my mother's cousins in Australia. This eventually proved not to be the case, though he did hold a fairly senior position in the railways. Helga had thought his title was *Kommissariat*, whereas in fact it was *Kommerzialrat*.

This was a fortuitous mistake, as it led to my discovery of new evidence on a different and more important matter. For, to my astonishment, while I was not given an answer to my question regarding Josef's title, I received instead, in June 2011, a thick file several hundred pages in length. This set out in grim detail how Josef's dry cleaning and dyeing business (jointly owned with my grandfather, Fritz, and his brother, Otto) was Aryanised.

I asked why I was being sent this file now, rather than with the earlier collection, and was told that it had only come to light in 2000–02. I asked, therefore, whether there were recently discovered files on other members of my family. At the end of July 2011, after several weeks of silence and with little explanation, I received a box containing about 2,500 further pages of documents concerning several family members, as well as other people of whom I had no knowledge.

The largest files were on my great uncle, Otto Smetana, my maternal great grandmother, Cäcilie Weinberger, and on a firm I had never heard of called *Isothermol*, owned by Oskar Freund. Again, these files related largely to the Aryanisation of the property of these family members and others, some in the most astounding detail. In addition, there was a long list of people, including my great uncle Otto, falsely accused of being *Schuldner*, debtors. There was also a lengthy file on my grandfather, Fritz, who had committed suicide on 31 May 1938, and had consequently not completed the form declaring his assets. The original information on him had therefore been sparse. This new file outlined in detail his bank accounts and estate, and the attempts of the Nazis to track down my grandmother, mother and aunt in order to deprive them of their inheritance.

It was chilling to read that my mother's name had been sent to the *Geheime Staatspolizei Staatspolizeileitstelle* (secret state police headquarters, i.e. the Gestapo) in Vienna, and then on to *Der Chef der Sicherheitspolizei* (the head of the security police) in Berlin.

NAZI GERMANY AND THE ANSCHLUSS

In order to place this account in its historical context, I have provided here a very brief summary of the Nazi era. Nazi Germany, known also as the Third Reich, was a totalitarian state which dominated Europe from 1933 until 1945, when it was defeated at the end of the Second World War.

Adolf Hitler came to power in Germany in 1933 when he became Chancellor, having previously established himself as leader of the *National Sozialistische Deutsche Arbeiter Partei* (NSDAP), the Nazi Party. Germany had suffered considerably during the Great Depression which followed the First World War, and Hitler gained enormous popularity by restoring the country to prosperity.

(Durchschrift)

Geheime Staatspolizei
Staatspolizeileitstelle Wien
Tgb. Nr. 3243 IV B 4 a

Wien, den 18. September 1942.

6

An das

Reichssicherheitshauptamt
— Referat IV B 4 b-4 —

in Berlin

Betrifft: Vermögensverfall bei Juden auf Grund der 11. Verordnung zum Reichsbürgergesetz vom 25. November 1941 (RGBl. I S. 722 ff.)

Bezug: Ohne.

Anlagen: 1 Durchschrift.

Ich bitte, die Feststellung zu treffen, daß das Vermögen des (der) nachstehend aufgeführten Juden (Jüdin), der (die) zuletzt die deutsche Staatsangehörigkeit besessen hat, auf Grund der 11. Verordnung zum Reichsbürgergesetz vom 25. November 1941 (RGBl. I, S. 722 ff.) dem Reiche verfallen ist.

Kartei

1. Name: (bei Frauen auch Geburtsname) Smetana — Vornamen: (Rufnamen unterstreichen) Lucie Sara
2. Geburtstag: 6.9.1919
3. Geburtsort und Kreis: Wien
4. Letzter inländischer Wohnsitz: (genaue Anschrift) Wien 1., Schubertring 12
5. Zeitpunkt der Abwanderung: 27.8.1938 nach England abgemeldet
6. Inländische Vermögenswerte:
   a) Art und Wert des Vermögens: Sie ist Miterbin nach der Verlassenschaft Friedrich Smetana. Die Verlassenschaftsabhandlung wird vom Amtsgericht Hietzing Zahl: 7 A 843/38-36, geführt. Bei der Creditanstalt Bankverein, Zweigstelle Hietzing, besteht das Anderkonto hi 203/8.
   b) Sicherstellung erfolgt? Nein
7. Angaben, ob Renten, Versorgungsgebühren usw. bezogen wurden und Einstellung der Zahlung veranlaßt ist: Nein

Im Auftrage:

Geheime Staatspolizei Staatspolizeileitstelle Wien

Verbr. 33 abgef. 16.10.44

Details about my mother, Lucy, here also called "Sara" by the Nazis, which were sent to the Gestapo in Berlin (translation Appendix 2)

However, he maintained absolute and unquestioned power and authority over his country by ruthlessly and brutally crushing all opposition, and establishing himself as the *Führer* (leader) who was above the law.

The main agents of oppression were the *Gestapo*, the secret state police, and the *Schutzstaffel* (protection squadron or defence corps), known as the SS. Concentration camps were established from as early as 1933, initially to deal with political opposition, but increasingly to exterminate Jews and others perceived as "inferior" human beings, such as homosexuals, gypsies and the mentally and physically ill.

Hitler considered himself to be leader of the "superior" Aryan or Master Race, a theory he expounded in his book, *Mein Kampf*, "my struggle", written in 1925. He blamed Jews for all the troubles which had befallen the nation, and set about aggressively implementing anti-Semitic laws aimed at depriving Jews of their citizenship and driving them out of the Reich. This ultimately led to the Final Solution: the plan to exterminate all Jews.

It was Hitler's intention to "unite" all German-speaking peoples, at that time living in several European countries, into one German nation, and he thus began an aggressive territorial expansion. On 12 March 1938, German troops marched into Austria, where they were enthusiastically received, and the next day Austria was incorporated, by law, into Germany. This annexation of Austria is known as the *Anschluss*.

A few days later, Hitler proclaimed to the crowds gathered in the *Heldenplatz* (Heroes' Square) in central Vienna that Austria and Germany had now been united. The Nazi regime and anti-Semitic legislation were implemented with astonishing rapidity, preparing the way for the brutality and violence already underway in Germany, and of which the coming pages bear witness.

Great Britain entered the war in September 1939, when Germany invaded Poland.

THE PROCESS OF ARYANISATION IN AUSTRIA

Of course, the German obsession with record-keeping is common knowledge, and there has never been any doubt about the depths to which the Nazis stooped in order to achieve their aim of exterminating the Jews and plundering their assets. However, to read in such detail how they went about this process, and in particular how they attempted to justify what they were doing, was for me a complete revelation.

What became abundantly clear when reading the documents was the attempt, by the Nazis, to make the seizure of Jewish assets appear to be a legitimate and legal process. This perhaps goes part way to explaining the abundance of correspondence.

Immediately following the *Anschluss*, the Nazis and their many collaborators in Austria wasted no time in setting up departments and producing a proliferation of forms, all with weird and wonderful titles which would be laughable if they were not so sinister.

Already established government departments were also drawn into the process. The sheer number of departments and officials involved testifies to the degree of complicity within the Austrian government and the broader Austrian society. A law was enacted on 27 April 1938 legitimising the seizure of Jewish assets, and over the next few weeks and months, Jews were required to declare all aspects of their financial situation.

For those who were immediately arrested and detained, including Josef Smetana and his son-in-law, Jacques Steininger, it was impossible to comply with this requirement, and it was often the wives, left alone and terrorised, who were obliged to supply the information demanded of them.

There then followed a systematic process of humiliation and degradation. Jews were referred to in correspondence as "the Jew" or the "Jewess", while all males had to use the name "Israel" and all females the name "Sara". Hence, *der Jude Fritz Israel Smetana und seine Kinder Lucie Sara Smetana und Sonja Sara Smetana* or *die Jüdin Berta Sara Smetana.*

This labelling was accompanied by a process of vilification and criminalisation, in which a narrative was created where Jews were presented as villains whose suspect and anti-social behaviour constituted a danger to the Austrian economy and to the safety, security and well-being of Austrian citizens. Citizenship to which Jews were naturally not entitled and were obliged to renounce. The ever-tightening and vicious grip of the Nazis led inexorably, as we know, to the isolation, ostracism, expulsion and ultimately extermination of millions of Jews.

The impact of this process on one elderly Jewish couple, my great grandparents Josef and Cäcilie Smetana, will be conveyed in Chapter Seven (having been included here in the original document). Below is a brief description of what happened to the estate of my grandfather, Fritz Smetana. His story is followed by several lists of forms, departments, officials, and terms, all used extensively in the documents I received from Vienna. These lists demonstrate better than any complex analysis the nature of the Nazi machine as it manifested itself in Austria.

THE ESTATE OF FRITZ SMETANA

The suicide of my grandfather, Fritz, on 31 May 1938, meant that he did not complete the form declaring his assets. This appeared to place the Nazis in a dilemma, as in order for them to seize Jewish assets "legally" according to the law enacted on 27 April 1938, it was necessary for Jews to sign over their assets.

The legal heirs of my grandfather were my grandmother, Berta (even though my grandparents were divorced), my mother Lucy, and my aunt Sonja. The Nazis went to great lengths to track them down. They were aware that my mother had left for England on 27 August 1938, and that my grandmother and aunt had left on 8 October 1938 for an unknown destination abroad. In fact, Berta and Sonja went to France and were ultimately deported from Drancy to Auschwitz on 2 September 1942.

It would seem that in order to deal with cases such as this, an 11th decree relating to the law concerning citizenship of the Reich was enacted on 25 November 1941. A great deal of correspondence on Fritz's file between 1942 and 1944 was devoted to determining whether this decree was applicable to Fritz's estate.

It was first established that the Josef Smetana company was so heavily indebted that Fritz's 30% share in it was worthless, and was not therefore included in the estate. In July 1943, it was declared that, on the basis of the 11th decree, Berta Smetana owed taxes of over 18,000 Reichsmark.

Finally, and after various downward adjustments of the value of the estate, it was declared, in February 1944, that Berta's assets (and therefore those of my mother) inherited from Fritz had become the sole property of the Reich.

FORMS AND STANDARD LETTERS USED DURING ARYANISATION

Ansuchen um eine Verkaufsbewilligung
Application for Permission to Sell

Josef Smetana appears to have written and signed a letter with this subject heading on his own headed note paper, though there is some doubt as to whether the signature could have been his, as it is accompanied by someone else's signature, and his first name is missing.

Certainly, it was not Josef who composed this letter. The date was 28 April 1938, only one day after the enactment of the new law and three months before Josef was able to complete his declaration of assets, as he was in custody throughout June and July. In it, he purportedly says that he is willing to sell his company for the protection of the Austrian economy and in the interests of his workers.

It would seem, therefore, that the plans to seize Jewish assets must have been well advanced, even prior to the *Anschluss*. There were clearly people in place ready and willing to take the necessary actions to implement the new law as soon as it was enacted, using pre-prepared bureaucratic machinery.

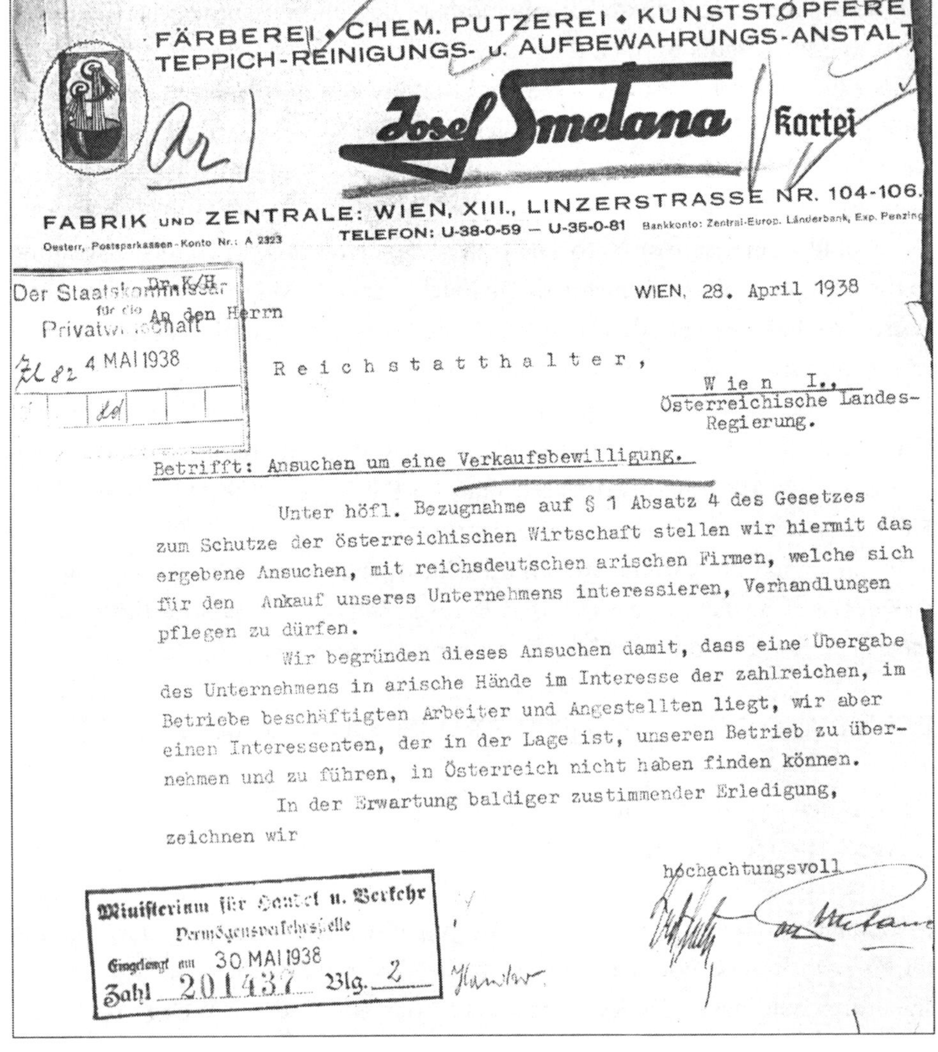

FÄRBEREI • CHEM. PUTZEREI • KUNSTSTOPFEREI
TEPPICH-REINIGUNGS- u. AUFBEWAHRUNGS-ANSTALT

Josef Smetana

Kartei

FABRIK UND ZENTRALE: WIEN, XIII., LINZERSTRASSE NR. 104-106.
TELEFON: U-38-0-59 — U-35-0-81
Oesterr. Postsparkassen-Konto Nr.: A 2323
Bankkonto: Zentral-Europ. Länderbank, Exp. Penzing

Der Staatskommissar für die Privatwirtschaft
4 MAI 1938

Dr.K/H.

WIEN, 28. April 1938

An den Herrn
Reichstatthalter,
Wien I.,
Österreichische Landes-Regierung.

Betrifft: Ansuchen um eine Verkaufsbewilligung.

Unter höfl. Bezugnahme auf § 1 Absatz 4 des Gesetzes zum Schutze der österreichischen Wirtschaft stellen wir hiermit das ergebene Ansuchen, mit reichsdeutschen arischen Firmen, welche sich für den Ankauf unseres Unternehmens interessieren, Verhandlungen pflegen zu dürfen.

Wir begründen dieses Ansuchen damit, dass eine Übergabe des Unternehmens in arische Hände im Interesse der zahlreichen, im Betriebe beschäftigten Arbeiter und Angestellten liegt, wir aber einen Interessenten, der in der Lage ist, unseren Betrieb zu übernehmen und zu führen, in Österreich nicht haben finden können.

In der Erwartung baldiger zustimmender Erledigung, zeichnen wir

hochachtungsvoll

Ministerium für Handel u. Verkehr
Vermögensverkehrsstelle
Eingelangt am 30 MAI 1938
Zahl 201437 Blg. 2

Letter in which Josef Smetana purportedly requested the sale of his company (translation Appendix 3)

Ansuchen um Genehmigung der Veräusserung
Request for Approval of Sale

This form, filled in by Jews, made it appear that the Jewish owner of a property was engaging willingly in the sale. The applicant was required to declare his Jewish status and the term *Jude*, Jew, was pre-printed on the form. Josef completed this form on 3 August 1938 **after** agreement had been reached with the purchaser, Franz Hotschewar.

Ansuchen um Genehmigung der Erwerbung
Request for Approval of Acquisition

This was a form completed by prospective purchasers of Jewish properties. Applicants declared their Aryan status with great flourish.

Fristgesuch zur Einbringung des Vermögensverzeichnisses nach dem Stande vom 27 April 1938
Application for the extension of the deadline for the submission of asset inventory in accordance with the law of 27 April 1938

Jews who were unable to complete the form declaring their assets within the required time frame (for example those who had been arrested and detained) had to apply for an extension of the deadline. This clearly instilled fear and placed applicants in a position where they had to beg to their persecutors.

Sicherheitsbescheid
Security notice

This was a document issued to Jews who had applied to leave the country, setting out the amount they would have to pay, and the conditions of their departure. It was issued by the *Finanzamt Innere Stadt-Ost Reichsfluchtsteuerstelle*, the Office for Tax on Flight from the Country. The document noted that there was a right of appeal but that there would be no delay in implementation.

Verzeichnis über das Vermögen von Juden nach dem Stand vom 27 April 1938
List of assets of Jews in accordance with the law of 27 April 1938

This was the form all Jews had to complete by 30 June 1938, which marked the beginning of the stripping of their assets. From the Nazi perspective, it was probably the most important document in each individual's file. Incredibly, even though completion of the form was compulsory, Jews had to pay 50 pfennig in order to obtain it!

Vor Ausfüllung des Vermögensverzeichnisses ist die beigefügte Anleitung genau durchzulesen!

Zur Beachtung!

1. **Wer hat das Vermögensverzeichnis einzureichen?** Jeder Anmeldepflichtige, also auch jeder Ehegatte und jedes Kind für sich. Für jedes minderjährige Kind ist das Vermögensverzeichnis vom Inhaber der elterlichen Gewalt oder von dem Vormund einzureichen.
2. **Bis wann ist das Vermögensverzeichnis einzureichen? Bis zum 30. Juni 1938.** Wer anmelde- und bewertungspflichtig ist, aber die Anmelde- und Bewertungspflicht nicht oder nicht rechtzeitig oder nicht vollständig erfüllt, **setzt sich schwerer Strafe (Geldstrafe, Gefängnis, Zuchthaus, Einziehung des Vermögens) aus.**
3. **Wie ist das Vermögensverzeichnis auszufüllen?** Es müssen sämtliche Fragen beantwortet werden. Nichtzutreffendes ist zu durchstreichen. Reicht der in dem Vermögensverzeichnis für die Ausfüllung vorgesehene Raum nicht aus, so sind die geforderten Angaben auf einer Anlage zu machen.
4. Wenn Zweifel bestehen, ob diese oder jene Werte in dem Vermögensverzeichnis aufgeführt werden müssen, sind die Werte aufzuführen.

07027

Verzeichnis über das Vermögen von Juden

nach dem Stand vom 27. April 1938

~~des~~ der Berta Smetana (Zu- und Vorname), Privat (Beruf oder Gewerbe)

in Wien I. Schubertring (Wohnsitz oder gewöhnlicher Aufenthalt) Straße, Platz Nr. 12

Angaben zur Person

Ich bin geboren am 9/I 1896

Ich bin Jude (§ 5 der Ersten Verordnung zum Reichsbürgergesetz vom 14. November 1935, Reichsgesetzbl. I S. 1333) und — deutscher¹) — .... — Staatsangehörigkeit¹) — ~~staatenlos¹)~~ —.

Da ich — Jude deutscher Staatsangehörigkeit¹) — ~~staatenloser Jude~~ ¹) — bin, habe ich in dem nachstehenden Vermögensverzeichnis **mein gesamtes** inländisches und ausländisches Vermögen angegeben und bewertet¹).

~~Da ich Jude fremder Staatsangehörigkeit bin, habe ich in dem nachstehenden Vermögensverzeichnis mein inländisches Vermögen angegeben und bewertet¹).~~

Ich bin ~~verheiratet mit~~ gerichtlich getrennt geb. Weinberger (Mädchenname der Ehefrau)

Mein Ehegatte ~~ist~~ war der Rasse nach — jüdisch¹) — ~~nichtjüdisch¹)~~ — und gehört ist gestorben der jüdischen Religionsgemeinschaft an.

Angaben über das Vermögen

I. Land- und forstwirtschaftliches Vermögen (vgl. Anleitung Ziff. 9):

Wenn Sie am 27. April 1938 land- und forstwirtschaftliches Vermögen besaßen (gepachtete Ländereien u. dgl. sind nur aufzuführen, wenn das der Bewirtschaftung dienende Inventar Ihnen gehörte):

Lage des eigenen oder gepachteten Betriebs und seine Größe in Hektar? (Gemeinde — Gutsbezirk — und Hofnummer, auch grundbuch- und katastermäßige Bezeichnung)	Art des eigenen oder gepachteten Betriebs? (z. B. landwirtschaftlicher, forstwirtschaftlicher, gärtnerischer Betrieb, Weinbaubetrieb, Fischereibetrieb)	Handelte es sich um einen eigenen Betrieb oder um eine Pachtung	Wert des Betriebs RM	Bei eigenen Betrieben: Wenn der Betrieb noch Anderen gehörte: Wie hoch war Ihr Anteil? (z. B. 1/4)
1	2	3	4	5
—	—	—	—	—

II. Grundvermögen (Grund und Boden, Gebäude) (vgl. Anleitung Ziff. 10):

Wenn Sie am 27. April 1938 Grundvermögen besaßen (Grundstücke, die nicht zu dem vorstehend unter I und nachstehend unter III bezeichneten Vermögen gehörten):

Lage des Grundstücks? (Gemeinde, Straße und Hausnummer, bei Bauland auch grundbuch- und katastermäßige Bezeichnung)	Art des Grundstücks? (z. B. Einfamilienhaus, Mietwohngrundstück, Bauland)	Wert des Grundstücks RM	Wenn das Grundstück noch Anderen gehörte: Wie hoch war Ihr Anteil? (z. B. 1/4)
1	2	3	4
—	—	—	—

¹) Nichtzutreffendes ist zu durchstreichen.

Vermögensverzeichnis (VO v. 26. 4. 38).

First page of form completed by my grandmother, Berta Smetana, declaring her assets. The heading, written in Gothic script, looks extremely intimidating (translation Appendix 4)

OFFICES, DEPARTMENTS AND ORGANISATIONS INVOLVED IN OR DEALING WITH JEWISH MATTERS

Abteilung Auflagenberechnung
Office for the Calculation of Surcharges

This was the office charged with the task of working out the fee for the "dejewification" process. Although Jewish properties were bought at knock-down prices, the purchaser had to pay a fee to the government.

Abteilung "Betriebsentjudung"
Office for the "Dejewification" of Companies

The name of this department appears in a letter from the Industry Department, dated 29 August 1940, requesting a review of Franz Hotschewar's purchase of the Smetana company.

Abteilung Vermögensanmeldung
Department for the Registration of Assets

Abteilung Wirtschaftsprüfer
Department of Auditors

Abwicklungsstelle der Vermögensverkehrsstelle
Processing Office for the Transfer of Assets

Sub-section of the *Vermögensverkehrsstelle,* Office for the Transfer of Assets. Forced sales of properties were processed through this office, for example the sale on 14 May 1940 of Josef Smetana's property at Mariahilfestrasse 66, Vienna IX.

Amt für Betreuung
Office for Support

The name of this department appears in a letter from the Office for the Transfer of Assets, dated 8 December 1938, in which Franz Hotschewar is pursued for non-payment of the "dejewification" fee.

Die Deutsche Arbeitsfront
The German Labour Front

Devisenstelle Wien
Foreign Exchange Office, Vienna

The involvement of this office, and several other offices and departments listed below, is a clear indication of the way in which ordinary bureaucrats became involved in the Nazi agenda.

Fachrechnungsabteilung
Specialist Accounting Department

Finanzamt Innere Stadt-Ost Reichsfluchtsteuerstelle für das Land Österreich
City-East Office for Tax on Flight from the Country of Austria

Jews had to apply to this department if they wished to leave the country. Successful applicants were required to give up their abode and pay a hefty fee. (See *Sicherheitsbescheid* above.)

Finanzlandesdirektion für Wien
Head Tax Office for Vienna

Geheime Staatspolizei Wien
Secret State Police (i.e. Gestapo) in Vienna

Geheime Staatspolizei Staatspolizeileitstelle Wien
Secret State Police Headquarters in Vienna

Landesgericht für Strafsachen
Provincial Court for Criminal Matters

Many Jews were taken to court, falsely accused of criminality in relation to the declaration of their assets, to intimidate them into giving up their property.

Leitung der Auslands-Organisation
Management of Overseas Organisation

Ministerium für Handel und Verkehr
Ministry for Trade and Commerce

Nationalsozialistische Deutsche Arbeiterpartei
The National Socialist Labour Party (i.e. Nazi Party)

Nationalsozialistischer Dozentenbund
The Nazi Lecturers' Association

Nationalsozialistischer Rechtswahrerbund
The Nazi Legal Workers' Association

It is clear that highly educated professionals such as lecturers and lawyers were signed up to the Nazi agenda.

Oberfinanzkasse
Chief Cashier's Office (of the Tax Office)

Österreichische Landes-Regierung
Austrian Regional Government

Reichskuratorium für Wirtschaftslichkeit
Curator's Office in the Reich for the Economic Sustainability of Firms

Reichssicherheitshauptamt in Berlin
Reich Security Head Office in Berlin

Staatliche Verwaltung des Reichsgaues Wien
State Administration for Vienna District

Überwachungsstelle für kommissarische Verwaltung
Provisional Administration Monitoring Office

Vermögensverkehrsstelle im Ministerium für Wirtschaft und Arbeit
Office for the Transfer of Assets in the Ministry of Commerce and Labour

This department was responsible for the seizure of Jewish assets, and is the one that appears most frequently in the documents. It had several sub-sections.

Vermögensverwertung Aussenstelle
Branch Office for the Recovery/Utilisation of Assets

This office was involved in trying to track down my grandmother, mother and aunt, so that their inheritance could be seized from them.

Wirtschaftsamt der Nationalsozialistische Deutsche Arbeiterpartei
The Trade and Industry Office of the Nazi Party

OFFICIALS INVOLVED

Buchsachverständiger/Notar
Accountant/Notary

Accountants and notaries were involved in valuing Jewish properties. One of the accountants involved, Josef Anton Herz, was clearly a member of the Nazi Party, and of the *NS Rechtswahrerbund,* the Nazi Legal Workers' Association. Correspondence from a number of banks and bankers was also contained within the documentation, so one must also suspect their complicity.

Chef der Sicherheitspolizei Berlin
Chief of Security Police, Berlin

Gerichtskommissär
Court Commissioner

The courts were involved in proceedings against Jews accused of criminality. Again, as with the accountants and notaries mentioned above, we see here examples of the way in which hitherto ordinary citizens became involved in the Nazi agenda.

Gestapo Wien
The Gestapo in Vienna

Kurator der gesetzlichen Erben
Curator of Legal Heirs

A person was appointed to oversee the legal inheritance of my grandmother, mother and aunt, but far from representing their interests, found ways to deprive them of their legal inheritance.

Leiter der Geschäftsabteilung
Head of Business Department

Oberbürgermeister der Hauptstadt Innsbruck
Mayor of the City of Innsbruck

The person occupying this position, Dr Denz, wrote on 5 July 1938 to the leader of the local Nazi Party asking him to put in a good word for the buyer of the Smetana family dry cleaning business, Franz Hotschewar, whose outstanding behaviour in support of the Nazi Party he praised.

Oberfinanzpräsident Berlin-Brandenburg
President of Tax Office in Berlin-Brandenburg

Oberfinanzpräsident Wien-Niederdonau
President of Tax Office in Vienna-Lower Danube

Reichsbeauftragter für Österreich
Reich Representative for Austria

Reichstatthalter
Reich Governor

Staatskommissär für die Privatwirtschaft
State Commissioner for Private Industry

SS. Obersturmbannführer
Stabsführer beim Staatskommissär für die Privatwirtschaft
SS Senior Assault Unit Leader
Staff leader to the State Commissioner for Private Industry

The person occupying this position, Dr Hans Georg Bilgeri, was clearly a Nazi Party member, and must have been placed in this department to ensure that Aryanisation proceeded in accordance with Nazi plans. He was probably instrumental in securing Franz Hotschewar's purchase of the Smetana company. He was addressed as *du* (i.e. in familiar terms) by Dr Amann, leader of the Innsbruck Nazi Party, who wrote to him asking him to support Hotschewar's application.

Wirtschaftsberater
Economic Adviser

Wirtschaftsprüfer der Wiener Magistrat
Auditor for the Vienna City Council

OTHER TERMS AND PHRASES ASSOCIATED WITH THE NAZI ERA AND WITH ARYANISATION

Abstammungsnachweis
Certificate of racial origins/ancestral proof

The Nazis were obsessed with race and ancestry, and from 1933 onwards, numerous laws were enacted establishing legal rights on the basis of "racial" status. By the end of the war, almost every citizen of Nazi Germany was required to provide evidence of their Aryan ancestry, including applicants for Jewish property.

There were two types of ancestral proof: one was a short version, shown below, the *Kleiner Abstammungsnachweis.* The reverse of this certificate gives details of the applicant's parents and grandparents, which had to be supported by birth and marriage certificates. A more detailed document, the *Grosser Abstammungsnachweis,* traced the person's ancestry back to 1800.

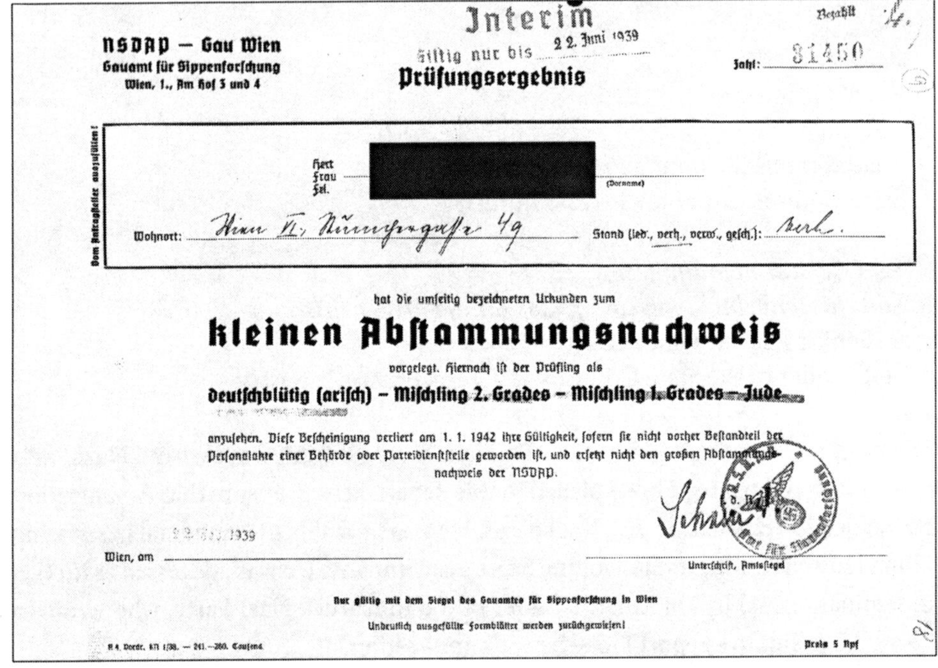

Interim

NSDAP — Gau Wien
Gauamt für Sippenforschung
Wien, 1., Am Hof 3 und 4

Gültig nur bis 22. Juni 1939

Prüfungsergebnis

Bezahlt 4.

Zahl: 31450

Vom Antragsteller auszufüllen!

Herr
Frau
Frl. (Vorname)

Wohnort: Wien VI, ... 49

Stand (led., verh., verw., gesch.): verh.

hat die umseitig bezeichneten Urkunden zum

kleinen Abstammungsnachweis

vorgelegt. Hiernach ist der Prüfling als

deutschblütig (arisch) – ~~Mischling 2. Grades – Mischling 1. Grades – Jude~~

anzusehen. Diese Bescheinigung verliert am 1. 1. 1942 ihre Gültigkeit, sofern sie nicht vorher Bestandteil der Personalakte einer Behörde oder Parteidienststelle geworden ist, und ersetzt nicht den großen Abstammungsnachweis der NSDAP.

Wien, am 22. ... 1939

Unterschrift, Amtssiegel

Nur gültig mit dem Siegel des Gauamtes für Sippenforschung in Wien

Undeutlich ausgefüllte Formblätter werden zurückgewiesen!

R4. Vordr. 6/1 1/38. — 241.–280. Tausend.

Preis 5 Rpf

Certificate of racial origins completed by woman seeking to buy a property for which Cäcilie Weinberger had provided a mortgage (translation Appendix 5)

Aktion Gildemeester

Aktion Gildemeester was set up in Vienna in the spring of 1938 and enabled wealthy Jews to emigrate, provided that they agreed to hand over their entire fortune. The action was open mainly to *nichtgläubige Juden,* that is, non-believing Jews. Several members of the Smetana and Weinberger families were involved in this process.

Altreichdeutsch
Nationality of old German Reich

This term was specific to the period and in use for 10 years only. It was used by

Wolfgang Richter, one of the applicants wishing to purchase Josef Smetana's company.

Beschlagnahmt
Seized

This term appeared, without explanation, next to some of the items, often cars, listed in the forms in which family members declared their assets.

Bilanzkonto
Balance sheet

The value of Jewish properties was worked out in detail by accountants, often as part of a larger exercise of valuation. (See *Schätzung*, meaning valuation, below.)

Entjudung
Dejewification

Entjudungsauflage
Dejewification fee/order/surcharge

Purchasers of Jewish properties had to pay a fee, usually then deducted from the amount the Jewish "vendor" received.

Gesetz zum Schutze der österreichischen Wirtschaft
Law for the Protection of the Austrian Economy

Heil Hitler!
Nazi salutation

This was the greeting used at the end of most of the official correspondence.

Judenvermögen
Jewish assets

This term was used to describe the property found on Josef and Cäcilie Smetana following their suicide.

Krida
Fraudulent bankruptcy/falsely declaring bankruptcy

This was a specifically Austrian term of that period, used as a device to take Jews to court.

Kriegszuschlag
War surcharge

There were many instances of concocted charges designed to justify taking funds out of Jewish accounts. This charge was made to my great grandmother, Cäcilie Weinberger. Other charges levied against her, at various times, were *Judenvermögensabgabe* (tax on Jewish assets), *Pfändungsgebuhr* (seizure fee) and *Säumniszuschlag* (lateness fee).

Lieber Parteigenosse
Dear Party Comrade

Used in correspondence from one party member to another.

Meldung über den Betriebsführer und Arisierer
Notice concerning the Company Director and Person Responsible for Aryanisation

Name des Juden
Name of the Jew

A derogatory expression used on many forms and letters.

Rassezugehörigkeit
Racial identity

This term was used on forms to establish people's racial identity. On forms to be completed by Jews, the term *Jude* was pre-printed, so that it would be difficult for them to avoid answering the question.

Reichsmark (RM)
German mark

German currency of the period, which replaced the Austrian Schilling in 1938. The Austrian National Bank calculated that 1RM in 1938 was equivalent to 4.17 Euros or US$4.91 in May 2003. According to Götz Aly, writing in 2006, 1RM in 1940 was equivalent to 10 Euros.

Rückstandsausweis
Record of outstanding amount owed

Many Jews were accused of owing large amounts of money.

Schätzung
Estimate/valuation

Detailed reports and inventories of Jewish properties were provided by architects or surveyors in order to establish their value.

Schuldner(in)
Debtor

Many Jews were accused falsely of debts they did not have, or were forced into situations where they inevitably built up debt, and were then accused of criminality because of this. Among the documents was a long list of "debtors", which included my great uncle, Otto Smetana.

It would appear that some Jewish people were given loans to enable them to leave the country, but this amount, together with charges, was then held against the value of their property which was seized by the Reich prior to their departure and sold off. The loans were made by a government-appointed audit company, said to be trustees and administrators of Jewish assets, who supposedly were taking care of their clients' interests.

Steuerrückstände
Tax arrears

There are many instances in the files where tax arrears appear to have been concocted in order to justify taking further funds out of Jewish accounts. (See *Kriegszuschlag,* war surcharge, above.)

Für die Überführung in nichtjüdischen Besitz vorgemerkt
Earmarked for transfer to non-Jewish ownership

Memo dated 29 June 1938 regarding Josef Smetana's company. An attached handwritten note from the company administrator, Eduard Mahel, talks of the transfer of assets to a "party comrade".

Der Verbotszeit
The period of prohibition

The Nazi party was banned in Austria between 1932 and 1934, but revived and made part of the German Nazi party after the annexation of Austria in 1938.

Verfallenes Vermögen
Forfeited assets

This term was used in relation to the estate of my grandfather, Fritz Smetana.

EXTRACTS OF NAZI CORRESPONDENCE

Ein altes bewährtes Parteimitglied interessiert sich für die nichtarische Firma Josef Smetana in Wien
An old and trusted party member is interested in the non-Aryan company of Josef Smetana in Vienna

Ausgesprochen jüdische Geschäftsusancen
Decidedly Jewish business activities

This phrase, clearly intended as derogatory, was used in an angry letter written on 8 August 1938 by a representative of the Dry Cleaners' Association to the Office for the Transfer of Assets. He regarded the Josef Smetana company as a rival, and wanted it liquidated rather than Aryanised, to remove the competition. He strongly disputed a claim in a government report that the Smetana firm was well-run and its workers were happier than his own.

Die Firma Smetana ist 100%ig in der Deutschen Arbeitsfront
The Smetana firm is 100% in the German Labour Front

Declaration issued on 18 July 1938, just four months after the *Anschluss*!

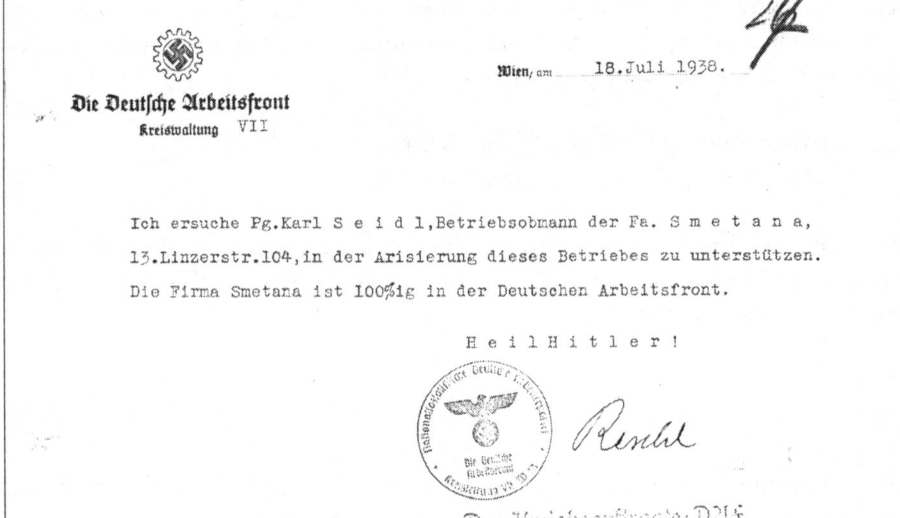

Die Deutsche Arbeitsfront
Kreiswaltung VII

Wien, am 18.Juli 1938.

Ich ersuche Pg.Karl S e i d l,Betriebsobmann der Fa. S m e t a n a, 13.Linzerstr.104,in der Arisierung dieses Betriebes zu unterstützen.
Die Firma Smetana ist 100%ig in der Deutschen Arbeitsfront.

H e i l H i t l e r !

Der Kreisbeauftragte DAF.

Document declaring that the Smetana firm is 100% in the German Labour Front! (translation Appendix 6)

> *Schaginger möchte noch das Geschäft ... um seiner alten Mutter zum Muttertag eine Freude zu machen*
> Schaginger would like to buy the business ... to give pleasure to his elderly mother on Mother's Day

Correspondence relating to the sale of Josef Smetana's company, dated 12 May 1940. Clearly the same consideration was not given to elderly Jewish people!

> *Eine Übergabe des Unternehmens in arische Hände (liegt) im Interesse der zahlreichen, im Betriebe beschaftigten Arbeiter und Angestellten*
> A handover of the company into Aryan hands is in the interests of the numerous workers and employees employed in the business

This comment was made in a letter dated 28 April 1938 on Josef Smetana-headed notepaper, and supposedly written by him. It was a frequently stated Nazi view, as the example below shows.

> *Eine jüdische Firma (geht) in arische Hände über und die Existenz der Belegschaft (ist) damit sichergestellt*
> A Jewish company passing into Aryan hands ensures the livelihood of the workforce

This sentiment was expressed by the Trade and Industry Department of the Nazi Party in Vienna in letters dated 3 October and 11 November 1938.

> *Die Veräusserung und Übertragung der Firma Josef Smetana ... des Gesetzes vom 27. IV. 1938, Gesetzblatt des Lands Österreich Nr. 103/38 genehmigt*
> The sale and transfer of the Josef Smetana company (and other properties listed) is approved (in accordance with) the law of 27 April 1938, Austrian Law Gazette no. 103/38

This was the wording of a contract between Franz Hotschewar and Josef Smetana dated 26 November 1938, following their appearance in court chambers the previous day. Josef and Cäcilie (also present in court) were to be left in no doubt that this was an entirely legal process, even though they emerged from it with not a single penny from the sale.

> *Bitte um Genehmigung der Arisierung der Firma Josef Smetana*
> Request for approval of the Aryanisation of the Josef Smetana company

This phrase appeared on the front sheet of the application of one of the applicants, Rudolf Vierthaler, a university lecturer.

Bezüglich meiner arischen Abstammung verweise ich auf meine Parteizugehörigkeit, anderseits lege ich die nachstenden Standesdokumente ...

With respect to my Aryan descent, I refer to my Party affiliation (and) offer you the following documents ...

Part of Rudolf Vierthaler's personal statement in his application, followed by a long list of his Aryan ancestors.

Wolfgang Richter ist langjähriges Mitglied der N.S.D.A.P. und sowohl in politischer wie charakterlicher Hinsicht einwandfrei

Wolfgang Richter is a long-standing member of the Nazi Party and is therefore of unblemished political record and character

Wolfgang Richter was another applicant wishing to buy the Josef Smetana company.

Anfang 1933 der NSDAP beigetreten ... Waffen und Munitionslager in der Wohnung. Hietzinger Mitlgiederkartei im Hause

Joined Nazi Party in 1933 ... Kept weapons and armament store in flat. Hietzing membership records (i.e. of Nazi Party members) kept in house

Part of Wolfgang Richter's personal statement when applying for purchase of Josef Smetana's company. Hietzing is a suburb of Vienna where many wealthy Jews lived at the time, including the Smetana family. This statement shows that plots against the Jews in the area well preceded the *Anschluss* and were taking place even during the period when the Nazi Party was banned in Austria.

Ein altes bewährtes Parteimitglied, Franz Hotschewar ... interessiert sich für die nichtarische Firma Josef Smetana ...

An old and trusted party member, Franz Hotschewar ... is interested in the non-Aryan firm of Josef Smetana ...

This was part of a letter written on 19 July 1938 by Dr Amann, a lawyer in Innsbruck, and leader of the local Nazi Party, to a Nazi colleague in the Industry Department, *SS. Obersturmbannführer* Dr Hans Georg Bilgeri, asking him to do what he could to help Franz Hotschewar in his acquisition of the Smetana company.

Wie aus dem Akt ersichtlich, scheint Hotschewar, abgesehen von Machenschaften, die seiner persönlichen Bereicherung dienen, auch den Angestellten gegenüber ein asoziales Verhalten an den Tag zu legen. ... Hotschewar (hat sich) einen Mercedes Personenkraftwagen um RM 18.000 gekauft. Diesem Volksschädling gegenüber ist m.E. kein wie immer geartetes Entgegenkommen am Platz

As can be seen from the file, quite apart from machinations that serve his personal enrichment, Hotschewar demonstrates antisocial behaviour towards his employees ... Hotschewar has bought a Mercedes car for 18,000 RM. In my opinion, it is inappropriate to show this vermin any consideration

Part of an extraordinary letter dated 29 August 1939, sent by the Tax Department to the correction section of the Office for the Transfer of Assets, following Hotschewar's refusal to pay the "dejewification" fee of 5,000 RM for his purchase of Josef Smetana's company. As far as I can ascertain, he never did pay this fee, in spite of threats to take him to court. His escape from censure was no doubt due to his connections in the Nazi Party.

There is some evidence that there may have been criminal proceedings against him after the war. There are many other examples in the documents of this kind of nastiness, not just towards Jews, but of one official or Nazi Party member towards another.

Es ist mir nicht bekannt, ob es sich diesbezüglich um einen Arier oder Juden handelt

I don't know whether this person is an Aryan or a Jew

Odd comment made by a dentist, in a letter dated 21 December 1944, in relation to an outstanding dental bill of Fritz Smetana, following his death. Possibly the dentist was attempting neutrality, or pleading ignorance, for fear of censure for treating a Jew.

Da es uns als Vollariern natürlich nicht angenehm sein kann, Miteigentümer einer polnischen Jüdin zu sein

Since as full Aryans, it cannot be pleasant to be co-owners with a Polish Jewess

Comment made by a woman purchasing the part of a house she co-owned with a Jewish woman, Rosa Hermann. Rosa had been given a mortgage to purchase her part of the property by my great grandmother, Cäcilie Weinberger.

> *Anzeige gemäss § 7 der 11. Verordnung zum Reichsbürgergesetz von 25 November 1941*
> Notice pursuant to section 7 of the 11th decree relating to the Reich Citizenship Law, 25 November 1941

Law used to deprive my grandmother, mother and aunt of their legal inheritance.

> *Es ist gemäss § 8, Ziffer 1 vorbezeichneter Verordnung festgestellt, dass das Vermögen obgenannter Person dem Reich verfallen ist*
> Pursuant to section 8, clause 1 of the above-mentioned decree, it is established that the assets of the aforementioned person have been forfeited to the Reich

Declaration made on 7 February 1944 in relation to the right of my grandmother, Berta Smetana, to inherit from her former husband, Fritz. This act was said to be done *im Namen des Grossdeutschen Reiches,* in the name of the Greater German Reich.

> *Der Grossdeutsche Reich (Reichsfinanzverwaltung), dessen an Stelle der Testamentserbinnen Berta Sara Smetana, Luzie Sara Smetana und mj. Sonja Sara Smetana auf Grund des Gesetzes und der Elften Verordnung zum Reichsbürgergesetz zum ganzen Nachlass abgegebene bedingte Erbserklärung vom 30 März 1944 zu Gericht angenommen wurde, als Alleinerben eingeantwortet und das Abhandlungsverfahren damit für beendet erklärt*
> The Greater German Reich (the tax administration of the Reich), whose conditional declaration of 30 March 1944 of acceptance of inheritance in place of the heirs Berta, Lucie and the minor Sonja Smetana, on the basis of the law and the 11th decree relating to the Reich Citizenship Law, has been accepted by the court, has transferred the assets as the sole heir, and the probate proceedings have now been declared concluded

Here, my family's legal inheritance is handed to the Reich, now considered sole heir. This impenetrable statement, written on 23 December 1944, demonstrates the tortuous lengths to which the Nazis went in order to make their theft of Jewish assets appear legal.

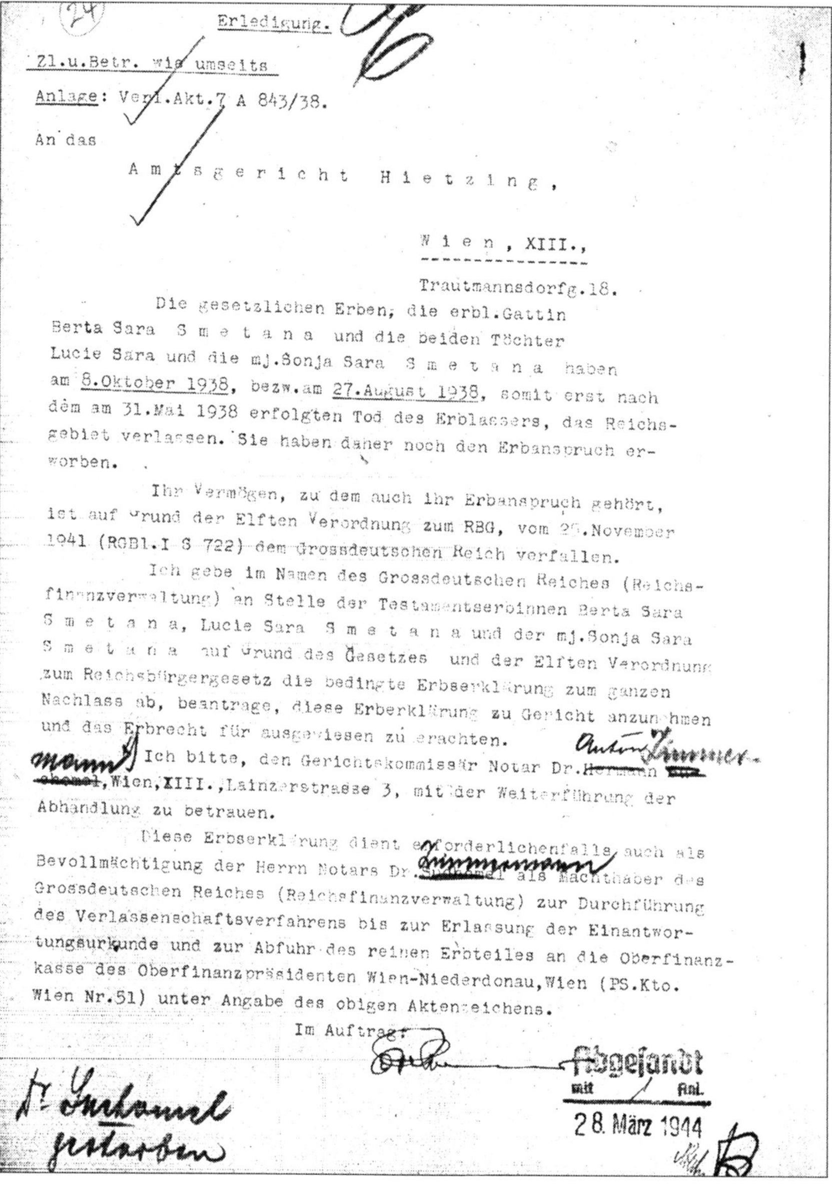

Erledigung.

Zl.u.Betr. wie umseits

Anlage: Verl.Akt.7 A 843/38.

An das

Amtsgericht Hietzing,

Wien, XIII.,

Trautmannsdorfg.18.

Die gesetzlichen Erben, die erbl.Gattin Berta Sara Smetana und die beiden Töchter Lucie Sara und die mj.Sonja Sara Smetana haben am 8.Oktober 1938, bezw.am 27.August 1938, somit erst nach dem am 31.Mai 1938 erfolgten Tod des Erblassers, das Reichsgebiet verlassen. Sie haben daher noch den Erbanspruch erworben.

Ihr Vermögen, zu dem auch ihr Erbanspruch gehört, ist auf Grund der Elften Verordnung zum RBG, vom 25.November 1941 (RGBl.I S 722) dem Grossdeutschen Reich verfallen.

Ich gebe im Namen des Grossdeutschen Reiches (Reichsfinanzverwaltung) an Stelle der Testamentserbinnen Berta Sara Smetana, Lucie Sara Smetana und der mj.Sonja Sara Smetana auf Grund des Gesetzes und der Elften Verordnung zum Reichsbürgergesetz die bedingte Erbserklärung zum ganzen Nachlass ab, beantrage, diese Erberklärung zu Gericht anzunehmen und das Erbrecht für ausgewiesen zu erachten.

Ich bitte, den Gerichtskommissär Notar Dr. ~~Hermann Schamel~~ Anton Zimmermann, Wien, XIII., Lainzerstrasse 3, mit der Weiterführung der Abhandlung zu betrauen.

Diese Erbserklärung dient erforderlichenfalls auch als Bevollmächtigung der Herrn Notars Dr. ~~Schamel~~ Zimmermann als Machthaber des Grossdeutschen Reiches (Reichsfinanzverwaltung) zur Durchführung des Verlassenschaftsverfahrens bis zur Erlassung der Einantwortungsurkunde und zur Abfuhr des reinen Erbteiles an die Oberfinanzkasse des Oberfinanzpräsidenten Wien-Niederdonau, Wien (PS.Kto. Wien Nr.51) unter Angabe des obigen Aktenzeichens.

Im Auftrag:

Abgesandt mit / Anl.
28. März 1944

Dr. Schamel gestorben

Declaration that Fritz's estate has been forfeited by his heirs and has become the sole property of the German Reich (translation Appendix 7)

Note: According to Dr Kristen Rundle (see page 205) the 11th decree relating to the Reich Citizenship Law pronounces that "a Jew who resides abroad permanently cannot be a German subject" *(para 1), and* "if the Jew loses his status as a German subject on these grounds, he/she also forfeits his property to the Reich" *(para 3, section 1). Para 3, section 2 then adds:* "The forfeited assets are intended for the promotion of measures that contribute to the solution of the Jewish problem." *(Dr Rundle is quoting here from Karl Schleunes.)*

I came across one comment in the files which stood out from the rest:

> *Josef Smetana hingegen, ist anderslautenden Mitteilungen praktisch schuldenfrei ... Bei Besichtung der Betriebe durch das RKW konnte bei Smetana wesentlich grösserer Arbeitseifer in der Belegschaft festgestellt werden, als bei der Konkurrenzfirma*
>
> Josef Smetana, however, contrary to reports otherwise, is virtually debt-free ... RKW noted that workers in the Smetana factory show considerably more enthusiasm for work than in rival firms.

This positive report of the Smetana company, written by Herr Kreindl on behalf of the *Reichskuratorium für Wirtschaftlichkeit* (Curator's Office in the Reich for the Economic Sustainability of Firms) is perhaps the only chink of light, a small act of honesty and humanity, in the otherwise dark and chilling saga which emerges from the 3,000 pages of these extraordinary files.

I am indebted to Margret Vince, who spent several days with me translating some sections of the files, and who edited the original document.

Chapter Seven

THE LIFE AND FATE OF JOSEF AND CÄCILIE SMETANA

Left: Cäcilie and Josef Smetana with two of their children, Karl and Gusti, in 1900

Below: Cäcilie and Josef Smetana in their later years

BUILDING A NEW LIFE: FAMILY AND BUSINESS

All my new-found relatives were on the Smetana side of the family. The person who loomed large in their stories was Josef Smetana, the patriarch, and my great grandfather.

Prior to the Second World War, Josef and Cäcilie lived at Kupelwiesergasse 13, Vienna XIII (Hietzing), in the top flat which they reached via a lift, while Ignaz, the chauffeur, lived on the ground floor. The Steininger family occupied the mezzanine of the same house, and consequently my mother's cousins, Ully, Helga and Heinz (later Henry) knew their grandfather, Josef, well, and spoke a good deal of him. I was therefore intrigued and keen to find out more about this dominant figure in the family history.

Initial enquiries bore little fruit. Neither his birth, nor his marriage was recorded at the *Israelitische Kultusgemeinde Wien,* the Jewish Archives in Vienna, meaning apparently that these events took place outside Vienna. I was told that Josef originated from a town called Ungarisch Brod, but, rather puzzlingly, that this did not necessarily mean that he was born there. Eventually, and after a good deal of digging, I uncovered the story of his origins that I have already told.

In the course of my enquiries, I obtained Josef's railway service record which indicated that he married Cäcilie Neumann on 20 August 1888, and another document dated 23 April 1941, during the Nazi era, which shows that they were married in Biala, Poland, where Cäcilie was born and her mother still lived.

Josef's railway service record also shows that he worked for the Moravian border railways and then the Imperial Ministerial Commission from 1 June 1874 to 1 July 1898. He worked in various locations, including Hannsdorf and Schönberg, both in the present day Czech Republic, and Steyr and Villach, in Austria. (The Czech name for Hannsdorf is Hanušovice, and for Schönberg is Šumperk.) His final posting was at the central office in Vienna, where he worked as a civil servant. He must have held a senior position as he received an annual salary, and a large supplement for accommodation.

He had worked briefly in Vienna in 1878 and again in 1884, moving permanently to the city in 1889, shortly after his marriage, so this is clearly when the young married couple settled down and had their four children: Fritz, my grandfather, Otto, Auguste (Gusti), and Karl. After his marriage, Josef continued to work for the railways for 10 more years.

Around the time he left the railways at the end of the 1890s, Josef set up a dry cleaning business which became very successful. There was a large factory at Linzerstrasse 104–106, Vienna XIII, and eventually over 50 branches in Vienna, with

K. k. Ministerial-Commission für die Verwaltung der k. k. Dniester- und Tarnów-Leluchower Staatsbahn, der Erzherzog Albrechtbahn und der Mährischen Grenzbahn.

Dienst-Tabelle.

Zuname: Smetana		Vorname: Josef
Geburts- / Zuständigkeits-	Tag	5 Juli 1857
	Ort	Hattenbau · Bezirk — · Land Mähren
Bildung	Studien	Real & Handelsschule
	Sprachkenntnisse (spricht / schreibt)	deutsch & böhmisch
	Sonstige Kenntnisse	—
Praktische Verwendung vor dem Eintritte in den Dienst der k. k. Ministerial-Commission		Beamter der mährischen Grenzbahn durch achtzehn Jahre und zwar durch fünf Jahre beim ... als Cassa & Verkehrsbeamter und die folgende Zeit in der Einnahmen Controlle
Wehrpflicht	Linie	Assent-Tag / Truppenkörper / beurlaubt seit / Charge: —
	Reserve	eingetheilt seit / Ergänzungsbezirk Nr. / beurlaubt seit / Charge —
	Landwehr	eingetheilt seit / Evidenzhaltung Nr. zu / Charge —
	Verabschiedet mit (ohne) Certificat für Civil-Anstellung Nr. vom 18	—
	Patental- (Vorbehalts-) Invalide	
	Vom Militärdienste gänzlich befreit	befreit

Familien-Stand.

Datum der Bewilligung und Trauung	Frau: Vor- und Familienname	Frau: geboren am	Kinder: Name	Kinder: geboren am
7/8 1888, T.R. 20/8 1888	Cäcilie Neumann	2/10 1863	Friedrich	18/9 889
			Otto	7/5 1891
			~~[illegible]~~	7/12 1894

Unterschrift des Vorgesetzten: [illegible]

Eigenhändige Unterschrift (Handzeichen) des Angestellten: J. Smetana

Josef Smetana's railway service record (first of three sheets) dating from 1874 to 1898. Josef's birth year is given as 1857, whereas all other documents show it to be 1858 (translation Appendix 8)

about 300 employees. I understand that Cäcilie was the driving force and the one with the shrewd business sense, so it was likely to have been she who encouraged her husband to go into business.

My grandfather Fritz and great uncle Otto each had a 30% share in the company, while Josef, as proprietor, retained a 40% share and the trading name of the firm was *Josef Smetana.*

FÄRBEREI • CHEM. PUTZEREI • KUNSTSTOPFEREI
TEPPICH-REINIGUNGS- u. AUFBEWAHRUNGS-ANSTALT

Josef Smetana

FABRIK UND ZENTRALE: WIEN, XIII., LINZERSTRASSE NR. 104-106.
Oesterr. Postsparkassen-Konto Nr.: A 2323 R/I TELEFON: U-38-0-59 – U-35-0-81 Bankkonto: Zentral-Europ. Länderbank, Exp. Penzing

Letter heading of the Josef Smetana company

Josef, Fritz and Otto at the factory on the occasion of Josef's 70th birthday in July 1928. Fritz is with his father, top left, and Otto is with his father top right

Josef and Cäcilie also owned other properties in Hietzing and in central Vienna, including a house on Mariahilfestrasse, Vienna VII. Their home at Kupelwiesergasse 13 was designed by Alexander Neumann, Josef's brother-in-law, who, I understand, designed several major buildings in Vienna.

According to my mother's cousin, Helga, Josef was treated with great respect wherever he went, and earned the title *Kommerzialrat*, an honorary title sometimes given to highly regarded businessmen at that period.

The Smetana family in Vienna was very privileged and cultured. There were cooks and maids, and the children had nannies. There were many trips to the opera and to concerts, as well as to skiing and lakeside resorts in Yugoslavia and Italy. There was a family car driven by the chauffeur, Ignaz. My mother remembered a blue Daimler. She spoke also of two well-known brother pianists who played at Josef Smetana's house. I was told too that Josef was quite religious and regularly attended synagogue. He made a major contribution to the synagogue which was built in Hietzing in 1928, but which was destroyed by the Nazis in 1938.

Speaking of his grandfather, Heinz wrote to me: "*I was very close to him. Each Sunday we would walk up to a Heuriger* (a wine tavern), *have a Frankfurter and a glass of wine. My grandmother and my mother would come later, driven there by the chauffeur. They would drive back and the two of us would walk home.*"

These few words conjure up an image of a lost world.

THE FATE OF JOSEF AND CÄCILIE UNDER THE NAZIS

This world was to be shattered by Hitler's annexation of Austria on 13 March 1938. Immediately following the *Anschluss*, Josef and Cäcilie returned from their annual holiday in Merano, Italy. Subsequently, Josef's son-in-law, Jacques Steininger, was arrested on 27 May 1938 and interned for eight months in Dachau and Buchenwald concentration camps.

Four days later, on 31 May 1938, Josef's son Fritz, my grandfather, committed suicide. Josef himself was arrested on 3 June 1938, but released in July 1938, shortly after his 80th birthday. Josef's other children and grandchildren fled to various parts of the world in 1938–39. During the period leading up to and following the departure of their family, Josef and Cäcilie were systematically persecuted by the Nazis.

I had originally learned something of Josef and Cäcilie's fate at the hands of the Nazis in a small number of documents which I received in the late 1990s. In the course of my continued investigations, I was the incredulous recipient, in 2011, of some 3,000 pages of Nazi documents on various family members, the details of which have been outlined in Chapter Six. The documents contained a large file on the Aryanisaton of Josef's dry-cleaning firm, and the way in which this elderly couple, whose entire family had by then fled, were treated. There is no doubt that thousands of others in Vienna were dealt with in a similar manner, but this one story, revealed in all its gory detail, demonstrates in chilling terms the individual human suffering involved.

As I read the documents (with the helpful assistance of translator Margret Vince), what soon became apparent to me was that the political circumstances of the period meant that for some time the family business had not been able to trade properly, resulting in an accumulation of debts.

Josef, together with Cäcilie and also their son Otto before his departure, were taken to court accused of "falsely declaring bankruptcy" or *Krida* (a specifically Austrian term of that period). One of the Nazi strategies was to criminalise Jews in order to make the seizure of their assets appear legal. The case was dropped in February 1939, once Otto had agreed to pay a large sum of money in order to be allowed to leave the country.

Josef's car, a Renault, at the time valued at 3,500 Reichsmark, was seized, and the elderly couple were obliged to "sell" their beautiful home at Kupelwiesergasse 13, supposedly to pay off the health insurance of the workers at the factory. This did not in fact get paid, so the money must have been misappropriated. All their other properties and assets were also "sold", including the house at Mariahilfestrasse 66, sold for 128,000 RM to August Kovats. This gentleman had to pay a fee of 27,000 RM for the purchase and this amount was deducted from the amount at which the house was valued, making it even more difficult for Josef to pay off his supposed debts.

On 28 April 1938, and before Josef had even completed his declaration of assets, a letter was written on Smetana headed paper, in which Josef purportedly requested the sale of his company in the interests of the Austrian economy and of his workforce. The signature appears to be forged or at least written under duress.

On 12 July 1938, while he was still in custody, he wrote a pitiful statement in which he explained that he was in no position to declare his assets. Once released, he was obliged to sign a form declaring that he was willing to sell the factory at Linzerstrasse, and what ensued was an unseemly struggle between several Nazi party members to acquire the business.

The successful applicant was Franz Hostchewar of Innsbruck, an unsavoury character by all accounts, who bullied the workforce. This is ironic in view of the fact that one of the justifications given for the sale of the business was the protection of its 230 largely non-Jewish workers and employees.

The factory was sold for 70,000 RM, well below its market value. Josef did not receive any money from the proceeds of the sale, since, supposedly, this was used to pay off debts. Franz Hostchewar sold off the many branches and instead focused on taking bulk orders for the cleaning of army and Nazi party uniforms. It would be difficult to imagine a more distasteful use of a Jewish business of that era.

Several detailed inventories were made to ascertain the value of the company, and during the process of inspection, photographs were taken, showing the machinery, and the workforce in the ironing department (*Büglerei*) looking quite evidently afraid, even though they were not Jewish and their own position was not, therefore, threatened. The inspection was clearly intimidating.

Left: Photo of chemical plant at the Smetana factory, taken during a Nazi inspection to ascertain its value

Below: Photo of the workforce at the Smetana factory taken during Nazi inspection

Ich bin seit 3.Juni 1938 verhaftet. Durch diesen Umstand bin ich ausserstande, die Unterlagen für das Vermögensverzeichnis rechtzeitig zu beschaffen. Ich bin auch nicht in der Lage, aus meiner Erinnerung das Verzeichnis zu verfassen, da ich 81 Jahre alt und krank bin. Im Wesentlichen besteht mein Vermögen aus meinem Anteil als Firmengesellschafter der Firma Josef Smetana, Wien, 13., Linzerstrasse 104, ferner aus dem Hause Wien, 7.,Mariahilferstrasse 66 und aus der Liegenschaftshälfte Wien, 13.,Trazerberggasse 4. Eine genaue Bewertung dieses Vermögens anzugeben, bin ich gegenwärtig ausser-stande. Ich schätze das Haus in der Mariahilferstrasse auf mindestens RM 100.000.-- und die Fabriksrealität mindestens mit demselben Betrage.

Ich bitte, mir zur Einbringung des vermögensverzeichnisses eine Frist bis 14 Tage nach meiner Haftentlassung, jedenfalls aber bis 31.August.1938 zu gewähren.

Wien, am 12.Juli 1938.

Josef Smetana

Statement made by Josef on 12 July 1938, while still in custody. There were a number of statements in this format, written not only by Jews, but also by people applying to buy Jewish properties, presumably to make this look like a fair and equal process

Josef's statement reads:

I have been under arrest since 3 June 1938. Due to this circumstance I am not in a position to acquire the documents for the list of assets on time. Nor am I able to compile the list from memory, since I am 81 years old, and sick. Essentially, my assets consist of my share as a shareholder in the firm Josef Smetana, Linzerstrasse 104, Vienna 13; also the house at Mariahilferstrasse 66, Vienna 7; and half of the real estate at Trazerberggasse 4, Vienna 13. I am at present unable to state the value of these assets. I estimate the value of the house in Mariahilferstrasse to be at least 100,000 Reichsmark, and the factory real estate at least the same amount.

I request that to allow me to submit the list of assets, I be granted a period of 14 days following my release from custody, but at any rate until 31 August 1938.

Vienna, 12 July 1938. Josef Smetana

Ich bin 75 Jahre alt und schwer herzkrank. Mein Mann, Herr Josef Smetana, der meine geschäftlichen Angelegenheiten führt, ist seit drei Wochen in Haft. Ich bin ausser Stande selbst die Unterlagen für das Vermögensverzeichnis rechtzeitig zu beschaffen. Mein Mann ist durch seine Haft daran gehindert.

Mein Vermögen besteht im wesentlichen aus dem Hause Wien, XIII. Kupelwiesergasse Nr. 13, und aus der Hälfte des Grundstückes Wien, XIII. Tratzerberggasse Nr. 4. Ich bin gegenwärtig noch nicht in der Lage eine Bewertung anzugeben, doch dürfte dieses Grundstück und die Realität einen Wert von mindestens RM 100.000.- haben.

Ich bitte, mir zur Einbringung des Vermögensverzeichnisses eine Frist bis 31. August 1938 zu gewähren.

Wien, am 28. Juni 1938.

Cäcilie Smetana

Above, Cäcilie's statement, written a few days before Josef's. It reads:

I am 75 years old and suffer from serious heart disease. My husband, Mr Josef Smetana, who manages my business affairs, has been in custody for three weeks. I am unable myself to acquire the documents for the list of assets on time. My husband is unable to do so since he is in custody.

Essentially, my assets consist of the house at Kupelwiesergasse 13, Vienna XIII, and half of the plot at Trazerberggasse 4, Vienna 13. I am at present unable to state a value, but this plot and the real estate might have a value of at least 100,000 Reichsmark.

I request that to allow me to submit the list of assets, I be granted time until 31 August 1938.

Vienna, 28 June 1938. Cäcilie Smetana

There appears to have been a degree of co-ordination, so perhaps they were assisted by their lawyer, or, more likely, the lawyer assigned by the Nazi regime to administer the Smetana company, who was no doubt determined to get all the necessary information as soon as possible.

In dreifacher Ausfertigung!

An die Vermögensverkehrsstelle, Wien 1, Strauchgasse 1.

Ansuchen um Genehmigung der Erwerbung.

Vor- und Zuname: Franz H o t s c h e w a r

Wohnort und Fernruf: Innsbruck 231

Geboren am: 1.Juni 1904 in: Innsbruck

Staatszugehörigkeit (auch die frühere): Österreich

Arier? ja

Verheiratet? ja Rassezugehörigkeit der Ehegattin? Arierin

Kinder (Anzahl, Alter)? 1

Haben Sie einen Verkäufer? ja Fa.Josef Smetana Wien XIII,Linzerstr.104-106

Sind Sie mit diesem verwandt oder bestehen sonstige Abhängigkeitsverhältnisse? nein

Beruf: Färbermeister

Bisherige berufliche Beschäftigung, eventuell Zeugnisabschriften: Tätigkeit als Färbergehilfe und Färbermeister in verschiedenen deutschen Färbereien und Wäsche - reien,Geschäftsführer im väterl.Betriebe in Innsbruck und derzeitiger Inhaber dieses Betriebes.

Welche Art von Betrieb wollen Sie erwerben? Färberei u.chem.Reinigungsanstalt

Haben Sie einen bestimmten Betrieb in Aussicht? ja , Josef Smetana,Wien XIII,Linzerstr.

Wie hoch ist ihr Gesamtvermögen? etwa RM 120.000.--

Wie hoch ist das eigene Barvermögen? Infolge grosszügiger Investitionen nur etwa RM 8.000.--jedoch Kreditgrundlagen

Welchen Betrag wollen Sie investieren?

Wie hoch sind die fremden Geldmittel? zur Zeit RM 30.000.--

Wer ist der Geldgeber? Sparkasse der Stadt Innsbruck,Maria Herbst.

Haben Sie oder Ihr Ehegatte schon ein Geschäft? wie oben angegeben Färberei u.chem. Reinigungsanstalt Franz Hotschewar Innsbruck,Andreas Hoferstr.16

Innsbruck , am 30. Juli 1938.

Franz Hotschewar
Unterschrift:

Unwahre Angaben sind strafbar!

Siehe 2. Seite!

Franz Hotschewar's application for the acquisition of the Smetana company (translation Appendix 9). Note this was written on 30 July 1938, before Josef had signed a form saying he was willing to sell

1

In dreifacher Ausfertigung!

Drw

An die Vermögensverkehrsstelle, Wien 1, Strauchgasse 1.

Ansuchen um Genehmigung der Veräußerung.

Vor- und Zuname: Josef Smetana

Wohnort und Fernruf: Wien

Geboren am: 5/7 1858 in: Hallenkau

Staatszugehörigkeit (auch die frühere): Wien

Rassezugehörigkeit (Jude, ~~Mischling~~ ersten ~~oder zweiten Grades~~):? Jude

Verheiratet: ja

Kinder (Anzahl, Alter)? 4, 50, 45, 35, 49

Beruf: Fabrikant

Haben Sie einen Kaufwerber? ja

Sind Sie mit diesem verwandt oder bestehen sonstige Abhängigkeitsverhältnisse? nein

Betriebsort: Wien XIII Linzerstr. 104/106

Genaue Bezeichnung des Betriebes (Firmenwortlaut, Sitz):

Josef Sm...
... u. Chem. ...
WIEN
XIII. Linzerstrasse 104

Bei gewerblichen Betrieben mit Buchführung ist die Bilanzabschrift 1937 anzuschließen. Außerdem die Anzahl der Beschäftigten im Jahre 1937 und der derzeitige Stand:

1937 210 Beschäftigte davon 8 nicht-arisch derzeit 230 (wieviele davon nicht-arisch?): keiner

Bei allen anderen Betrieben den Umsatz 1937 und die Anzahl der Beschäftigten:

(wieviele davon nicht-arisch?):

Schätzung nach dem Sachwert:

Begehrter Preis: Schätzwert

Wien, am 3. 8. 1938.

Josef Smetana
Unterschrift:

Unwahre Angaben sind strafbar!

Siehe 2. Seite!

Josef Smetana's application to "sell" his company, signed on 3 August 1938 (translation Appendix 10). His declaration of assets (next page) was written 10 days later

/.a. 27064 Sw
1. DEZ. 1939

Vor Ausfüllung des Vermögensverzeichnisses ist die beigefügte Anleitung genau durchzulesen!

Zur Beachtung!

1. **Wer hat das Vermögensverzeichnis einzureichen?** Jeder Anmeldepflichtige, also auch jeder Ehegatte und jedes Kind für sich. Für jedes minderjährige Kind ist das Vermögensverzeichnis vom Inhaber der elterlichen Gewalt oder von dem Vormund einzureichen.

2. **Bis wann ist das Vermögensverzeichnis einzureichen? Bis zum 30. Juni 1938.** Wer anmelde- und bewertungspflichtig ist, aber die Anmelde- und Bewertungspflicht nicht oder nicht rechtzeitig oder nicht vollständig erfüllt, **setzt sich schwerer Strafe (Geldstrafe, Gefängnis, Zuchthaus, Einziehung des Vermögens) aus.**

3. **Wie ist das Vermögensverzeichnis auszufüllen?** Es müssen sämtliche Fragen beantwortet werden. Nichtzutreffendes ist zu durchstreichen. Reicht der in dem Vermögensverzeichnis für die Ausfüllung vorgesehene Raum nicht aus, so sind die geforderten Angaben auf einer Anlage zu machen.

4. Wenn Zweifel bestehen, ob diese oder jene Werte in dem Vermögensverzeichnis aufgeführt werden müssen, sind die Werte aufzuführen.

45738 ~~16546~~

Verzeichnis über das Vermögen von Juden

nach dem Stand vom 27. April 1938

des Josef Smetana, Firmengesellschafter
der (Zu- und Vorname) (Beruf oder Gewerbe)

in Wien, XIII. Kupelwiesergasse ~~Straße, Platz~~ Nr. 13.
(Wohnsitz oder gewöhnlicher Aufenthalt)

Angaben zur Person

Ich bin geboren am 5. Juli 1858

Ich bin Jude (§ 5 der Ersten Verordnung zum Reichsbürgergesetz vom 14. November 1935, Reichsgesetzbl. I S. 1333) und — deutscher¹) — Staatsangehörigkeit¹) — staatenlos¹) —.

Da ich — Jude deutscher Staatsangehörigkeit¹) — staatenloser Jude¹) — bin, habe ich in dem nachstehenden Vermögensverzeichnis **mein gesamtes inländisches** und **ausländisches** Vermögen angegeben und bewertet¹).

Da ich Jude fremder Staatsangehörigkeit bin, habe ich in dem nachstehenden Vermögensverzeichnis mein **inländisches** Vermögen angegeben und bewertet¹).

Ich bin verheiratet mit Cecilie geb. Neumann.
(Mädchenname der Ehefrau)

Mein Ehegatte ist der Rasse nach — jüdisch¹) — nichtjüdisch¹) — und gehört der Religionsgemeinschaft an.

Heftrand

Angaben über das Vermögen

I. Land- und forstwirtschaftliches Vermögen (vgl. Anleitung Ziff. 9):

Wenn Sie am 27. April 1938 land- und forstwirtschaftliches Vermögen besaßen (gepachtete Ländereien u. dgl. sind nur aufzuführen, wenn das der Bewirtschaftung dienende Inventar Ihnen gehörte):

Lage des eigenen oder gepachteten Betriebs und seine Größe in Hektar? (Gemeinde — Gutsbezirk — und Hofnummer, auch grundbuch- und katastermäßige Bezeichnung)	Art des eigenen oder gepachteten Betriebs? (z. B. landwirtschaftlicher, forstwirtschaftlicher, gärtnerischer Betrieb, Weinbaubetrieb, Fischereibetrieb)	Handelte es sich um einen eigenen Betrieb oder um eine Pachtung	Wert des Betriebs RM	Bei eigenen Betrieben: Wenn der Betrieb noch Anderen gehörte: Wie hoch war Ihr Anteil? (z. B. ¼)
1	2	3	4	5

II. Grundvermögen (Grund und Boden, Gebäude) (vgl. Anleitung Ziff. 10):

Wenn Sie am 27. April 1938 Grundvermögen besaßen (Grundstücke, die nicht zu dem vorstehend unter I und nachstehend unter III bezeichneten Vermögen gehörten):

Lage des Grundstücks? (Gemeinde, Straße und Hausnummer, bei Bauland auch grundbuch- und katastermäßige Bezeichnung)	Art des Grundstücks? (z. B. Einfamilienhaus, Mietwohngrundstück, Bauland)	Wert des Grundstücks? RM	Wenn das Grundstück noch Anderen gehörte: Wie hoch war Ihr Anteil? (z. B. ¼)
1	2	3	4
E.Z. 627 Neubau (handwritten)	Mietwohngrundst.	110.800.-	
E.Z. Ober St.Veit	Bauland	30.667	½ - 15.333
E.Z. 1297 K.G.Penzing, Linzerstr. 104-106	Fabriksobjekt	40.000.-	

¹) Nichtzutreffendes ist zu durchstreichen.

Vermögensverzeichnis (VO v. 26. 4. 38)

Kt. 166

Front page of document in which Josef declared his assets, completed on 12 August 1938, following his return to his home in Kupelwiesergasse, after having been held in custody (translation Appendix 11)

Finanzamt Innere Stadt-Ost
Reichsfluchtsteuerstelle
für das Land Österreich

457/38

Rfl. Smetana — Zimmer 516
Bitte, stets angeben!

Wien I, 19. September 1939.
Riemergasse 2
Fernsprecher: R-22-5-95, Hausanschluß
Parteienverkehr Montag, Dienstag, Donnerstag und Freitag von 11 bis 13 Uhr.

Sicherheiten nimmt die Vollstreckungsstelle entgegen, Einzahlungen nur im Wege der Postsparkasse auf Kontonummer A 43.167

Nummer Ihres Kontos:

An Herrn
Josef Israel Smetana
Wien, 13.,
Hietzinger Hauptstr. 53

Abschrift!

Vorläufiger Sicherheitsbescheid

A. Festsetzung der Sicherheit

Meine Feststellungen lassen darauf schließen, daß Sie den Wohnsitz — gewöhnlichen Aufenthalt im Land Österreich oder im übrigen Reichsgebiet — aufgeben werden. Auf Grund des § 7 des Reichsfluchtsteuergesetzes*) ersuche ich Sie daher, sofort

in Höhe von 41.600.— RM

Sicherheit zu leisten. — Dieses Ersuchen ergeht hierdurch auch an Ihre Angehörigen (Ehefrau, Kinder), soweit sie mit Ihnen zur Einkommensteuer oder zur Vermögensteuer zusammen veranlagt worden sind oder zusammen zu veranlagen sind. — Die Sicherheit kann zum Beispiel durch Hinterlegung von Geld, durch Hinterlegung oder Verpfändung von Wertpapieren oder Hypotheken oder durch Bürgschaft geleistet werden (§§ 132 bis 141 der Reichsabgabenordnung).

Dieser Bescheid ist sofort vollstreckbar.

Die Sicherheit ist wie folgt errechnet worden:

Reichsfluchtsteuer, die mit der Auswanderung fällig wird: Nach meinen Ermittlungen betrug das Ihnen und Ihrer Ehefrau ~~sowie Ihren Kindern~~ gehörige Gesamtvermögen am 1. Januar 1938 — einschließlich der Hinzurechnungen gemäß § 3 Absatz 3 des Reichsfluchtsteuergesetzes und § 2 Absatz 1 zu b der Verordnung zur Durchführung der Reichsfluchtsteuer im Land Österreich vom 14. April 1938 —:
166.133.— RM, davon ein Viertel 41.533.— RM

Sonstige Ansprüche: RM

ergibt zusammen 41.533.— RM
Aufgerundet 41.600.00 RM

B. Rechtsmittelbelehrung

Gegen diesen Sicherheitsbescheid steht Ihnen die Beschwerde an den Oberfinanzpräsidenten Wien zu, dessen Entscheidung endgültig ist. Die Beschwerde kann bei mir schriftlich eingereicht oder zu Protokoll erklärt werden. Dies kann nur bis zum Ablauf eines Monats nach der Zustellung des Bescheids, d. h. nach dem Tage, an dem der Bescheid zur Post gegeben ist, geschehen. Die Kosten einer erfolglosen Beschwerde haben Sie zu tragen.

Durch die Einlegung der Beschwerde wird die Wirksamkeit des Sicherheitsbescheids nicht gehemmt, insbesondere die Vollstreckung nicht aufgehalten.

*) Siehe Rückseite.

gez. Unterschrift

Verteiler:

Rfl. 8. (Abschrift des Sicherheitsbescheids.) — 8. 39. — 2000. — Staatsdruckerei Wien. 7776 39

12

Security notice received by Josef and Cäcilie Smetana about the cost and conditions of their leaving the country. The amount was later increased to 48,400 RM. Note that by this time they had moved to Hietzinger Hauptstrasse (translation Appendix 12)

Hietzinger Hauptstrasse 53, Vienna XIII, in October 2006

In September 1938, Josef and Cäcilie moved to Hietzinger Hauptstrasse 53, Vienna XIII. During 1939, they applied to the *Reichsfluchtsteuerstelle für das Land Oesterreich*, (office for tax on flight from the country of Austria) for permission to leave the country, and they were informed in early 1940 that they must first pay 48,400 Reichsmark.

It is unclear whether or not they paid this sum, but given the events leading up to this, it is unlikely that they had any money left. Nevertheless, in order to gain permission to emigrate, there was a requirement for them to leave their abode. Hence, on 23 April 1941, they went to live at Pension Atlanta, Wahringerstasse 33, Vienna IX, where the family thought they were protected. (Chillingly, a document giving details of Josef and Cäcilie's ancestry bears the same date. While its contents have been conveyed to me, this is the only document of which the Austrian State Archives have refused to send me a copy, on the grounds of its "*fragility and poor state of preservation*".)

However, they left the Pension on 29 November 1941, and shortly after were taken to Seegasse 9, Vienna IX, a home for the elderly (and the former Jewish hospital), almost certainly for deportation. According to the *Yad Vashem* database, many other people living at that address were deported to concentration camps from as early as 1938. The elderly couple must have witnessed other people leave from Seegasse 9, taken away on the very trains on which Josef had once worked.

Here Josef and Cäcilie, aged 83 and 78, took their own lives on 2 December 1941, using poison from their factory, obviously fearful of the consequences of deportation. They were buried with my grandfather, their son Fritz, in *Zentralfriedhof* (central cemetery) 4, Group 22, Row 29b, Grave number 19.

No-one was left to attend the funeral.

The final indignity suffered by Josef and Cäcilie was that following their suicide, they were found to be in possession of 8 Reichsmark-worth of jewellery and 680 Reichsmark in cash. A letter was sent on 25 May 1942 by the notary dealing with the estate to the *Oberfinanzpräsident* in Berlin, informing him of these "Jewish assets".

I managed to find their grave when I visited Vienna with my daughter, Bambo, in 2006. There was no headstone for them, nothing to show that Josef and Cäcilie had ever existed. What a sad and lonely ending to such successful and fulfilled lives.

Why did Josef and Cäcilie remain in Vienna? This is a question to which I have not been given an answer, possibly because I dare not ask it. Perhaps they thought they could manage to save the family business which they had spent a lifetime building up. Maybe they thought it would all blow over, only to discover, too late, that the situation was far worse than they could ever have imagined. Or perhaps they simply felt that at their age and in their state of health, relocation to another part of the world was unthinkable. Whatever the reason, their surviving children must have suffered extreme anguish and grief on learning of their fate, and there must also have been a measure of guilt or even of recrimination. No doubt these complex emotions were experienced by numerous other survivors of the Holocaust when contemplating the loved ones they lost.

FITTING MEMORIALS

A memorial to commemorate the 65,000 Austrian Jews killed by the Nazis between 1938 and 1945 was unveiled in Judenplatz, central Vienna, in October 2000. It was conceived by the Nazi hunter Simon Wiesenthal, and designed by British artist

Rachel Whiteread. It depicts a library of books with the spines turned inwards, so that the titles cannot be read, to represent the many lives whose stories would never be told.

A huge portrait of Josef, painted in his later years, is hung in Heinz's home in the USA. A portrait of Cäcilie hangs in Helga's home in Australia. The two portraits originally graced their home in Vienna. Perhaps these paintings, together with their large number of descendants, are their most fitting memorials.

Portrait of Josef Smetana now in USA

During our stay in Vienna, Bambo and I also visited a memorial to the Hietzing Synagogue, erected by Dr Robert Streibel who has conducted research into the Jews of Hietzing. The picture of the original synagogue has been etched in glass, and when one stands in the right place, it becomes imposed on the building which has been erected in its place. The translation of the inscription is:

Only from the correct standpoint can one understand history

Memorial erected by Robert Streibel to commemorate the Hietzing synagogue built in 1928 and destroyed by the Nazis in 1938

Chapter Eight

THE TRAGIC LIFE OF FRITZ SMETANA

PROMISING BEGINNINGS

Throughout my childhood and early adulthood, my mother had said virtually nothing about her parents. Until I was 50, they had remained nameless. But from then on, a picture gradually started to emerge. In particular, I gained the impression that her father, Fritz, had been very special to her.

Below is one of the photos of Fritz which I found in my mother's album in 1995. When I showed this to my daughter, Bambo, she commented that it must have been snapped by a child, because of the low angle at which it had been taken. I asked my mother about this, and she confirmed that the photo was indeed taken by her at about the age of 10, during a family trip to the Schönbrunn Palace, seen in the background, not far from their home in Hietzing.

Photo of Fritz Smetana taken by my mother at the Schönbrunn Palace in the late 1920s

Although my great grandfather, Josef, regularly attended synagogue, it seems the rest of the family, including my grandfather Fritz, was not very religious, though they did attend major festivals, as well as funerals and weddings.

When they reached adulthood, Fritz and his brother, Otto, joined their father's dry cleaning business, each taking a 30% share. No doubt this was something that was expected of them, and they would have been trained for it from an early age. Their younger brother, Karl, did not join the family business, instead entering the paper-manufacturing company of his father-in-law, Richard Bruchsteiner.

My grandparents married in 1918. According to my mother's cousin Ully, Fritz visited Berta's home and heard her singing a "beautiful chanson", with someone accompanying her on the piano. This was apparently when he fell in love with her. The newly married couple moved to Hietzinger Hauptstrasse 69, Vienna XIII, and my mother was born the following year.

Fritz also carved out a diplomatic career for himself. In 1926, he was appointed the Austrian Consul General for San Marino, a post he held until his death in 1938. I have in my possession a card, giving his title and address, contained in an embossed envelope bearing the San Marino coat of arms. The card had been lovingly preserved by my mother, one of the few possessions she had to remind her of her beloved father. The family moved to this residence in 1927.

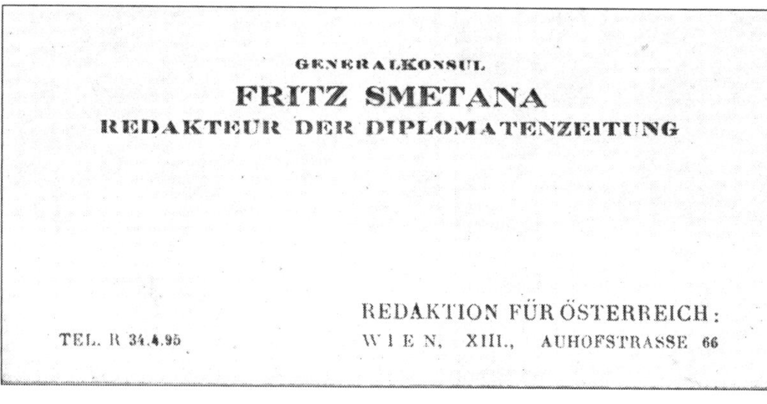

GENERALKONSUL
FRITZ SMETANA
REDAKTEUR DER DIPLOMATENZEITUNG

REDAKTION FÜR ÖSTERREICH:
TEL. R 34.4.95 WIEN, XIII., AUHOFSTRASSE 66

CONSOLATO GENERALE
DELLA REPUBBLICA DI SAN MARINO
VIENNA
XIII.AUHOFSTRASSE 66

A photo of the foyer of Auhofstrasse 66, taken in the late 1920s, is shown below, together with a photo I took when I visited Vienna in 2006. The current owners of the property were interested to see the early photo, and recognised it as their home, even showing us the original architectural plans. They were happy for us to look around the house until they realised that we were Jewish, at which point they asked us to leave in a somewhat aggressive manner, declaring that it was not the same house: *"Das ist nicht das Haus! Das ist nicht das Haus!"*

The foyer of Auhofstrasse 66, left taken in the late 1920s, and right in 2006

Below is a photo we managed to take of the exterior of the house as we left.

Auhofstrasse 66, Hietzing, the San Marino Consulate, and my mother's childhood home

On 1 December 1927, my aunt Sonja was born. My mother remembers how happy her father initially was. However, it transpired that she was not Fritz's daughter, but the daughter of Berta's lover, Norbert Sachs, though Sonja retained the Smetana name. As a consequence, Fritz and Berta divorced on 26 April 1932, and Berta moved, with my mother and Sonja, to Schubertring 12, one of the boulevards in central Vienna. One can only imagine how devastated Fritz must have been.

During the period following the divorce, Fritz remained in Hietzing, and continued to pay regular visits to his parents, sister and brothers and their families. My mother's cousins in Australia have strong and fond recollections of him. By all accounts, including those of my mother, he was a kind, gentle and cultured man.

Following the *Anschluss* in March 1938, all Jews were required to declare their assets, and the Nazis started making arrests. As we have already learned, Fritz's brother-in-law Jacques Steininger was arrested by the Nazis on 27 May 1938, and interned for some months. Fearing arrest himself, Fritz, my grandfather, committed suicide on 31 May 1938, using poison from the factory. At the time of his death, he was living at Auhofstrasse 11b, Vienna XIII, a short distance from the Consulate at Auhofstrasse 66.

Auhofstrasse 11b, where my grandfather, Fritz, was living prior to his suicide

Just a few yards beyond this house, at Auhofstrasse 2, is the famous *Kaffeehaus Dommayer*, where concerts are held, and where many famous musicians have played. Here, my daughter and I met Robert Streibel, who later conducted us around Hietzing. There is no doubt in my mind that my mother must have visited this coffee house on many occasions with her father and other family members.

COMMEMORATION IN SAN MARINO

In January 2008, my brother Stephen and I were invited by the government of San Marino to attend a ceremony to commemorate the work of our grandfather in that country. This ceremony was organised in the context of a programme to celebrate, for the first time in San Marino, the International Day dedicated to the victims of the Holocaust on 27 January. The invitation was made following my correspondence with Christoph Petsch, the present Austrian Consul General for San Marino.

The Republic of San Marino is a tiny hilly country, stunningly beautiful, whose capital, San Marino, is perched on a mountain top. Only 61 square kilometres (24 square miles) in size and with a population of just 30,000, it is situated within the heart of and entirely surrounded by Italy.

Although landlocked, San Marino is only 10 kilometres from the seaside resort of Rimini, on Italy's east coast. It was first founded in 301 by Marino, a Christian stonecutter coming from the Dalmatian island of Rab to flee religious persecution. He founded a community on Mount Titano, from which the Republic of San Marino took its origin.

San Marino is the oldest and smallest sovereign state in the world, fiercely defending its freedom and independence, and has developed a unique political system. It has a democratic parliament (the Great and General Council) of 60 members elected every five years, which then appoints the government (Congress of State), composed of 10 members, and the Council of the Twelve, another ancient institution composed of 12 members.

Every six months, the parliament elects two Heads of State, called the Captains Regent, and during our visit, we met the currently serving Captains Regent. Given the small size of the country, a large percentage of the population has the opportunity to become actively involved in government.

I was surprised, even shocked to learn that San Marino had a fascist government from 1923 to 1943, during the time that my grandfather was the Austrian Consul General. This was largely due to the fact that the upper middle classes tried to maintain their social and economic privileges over the rest of the population, by modeling themselves on the National Fascist Party of surrounding Italy. The San Marino fascists managed to retain power for two decades by banning other political parties, in effect making San Marino a single-party state, quite contrary to its constitution. Anti-Semitic laws were, however, never enacted and the fascists were ousted by the socialists in 1943.

Photo of San Marino taken during our visit in 2008

We were most warmly welcomed in this unique country. The ceremony was a formal event which took place in the historic Government Building and was broadcast on San Marino television. During one of the speeches, we learned that our grandfather had "*regularly offered contributions to the San Marino State aimed at social interventions in favour of the poorest groups of the population ... Some of these donations were made (towards) seaside holiday camps and the San Marino Mutual Aid Society.*"

After my brother and I each delivered a speech to thank our hosts, we were presented with a silver plaque in Fritz's honour, inscribed with the words:

REPUBLIC OF SAN MARINO

In memory of
Friedrich Smetana
Consul General of the Republic of San Marino
in Austria from 1926 to 1938
renewing the sentiments of the highest esteem
and gratitude for his service and commitment.
On the occasion of the
"Annual International Day of Commemoration
in Memory of the Victims of the Holocaust"

Fiorenzo Stolfi
Secretary of State for Foreign Affairs
San Marino, 27 January 2008

Ceremony in San Marino where we were presented a plaque, which I am holding, to commemorate our grandfather. Christoph Petsch and my brother, Steve, are 2nd and 3rd from the left. The two Heads of State, Mirko Tomassoni and Alberto Selva, are centre, together holding the gift we presented to them. The Secretary of State for Foreign Affairs, Fiorenzo Stolfi, is on the right

There has been a small Jewish population in San Marino for at least 600 years and during our visit, a plaque was erected at the site of the former Jewish quarters. Because of its own history, San Marino has had a long-standing reputation for giving refuge to the victims of persecution. During World War Two, the country provided harbour for more than 100,000 Italians (approximately 10 times the Sammarinese population at the time) and Jews fleeing Nazi persecution.

Plaque erected on 27 January 2008, Holocaust Memorial Day, at the site of the old Jewish quarter in San Marino. My brother Steve and I are accompanied by two ceremonial guards

One of the dignitaries invited to the ceremony was the Counsellor for Political Affairs and Foreign Relations of the Israeli Embassy to San Marino, who was there to represent his Ambassador. During our conversation, I told him some of our family history, in particular the possible connection to the composer Smetana. He remarked, to my astonishment, that the Israeli national anthem, the *Hatikvah*, is based on Smetana's composition, *The Moldau*, one of the six symphonic poems which form his great work *Ma Vlast* "my homeland". I found confirmation of this on the State of Israel website, while other sources explained that Smetana's work was itself based on Romanian folk music. Of all the strange coincidences in this story, I found this one to be the most startling.

I later visited the San Marino Archives and discovered correspondence between my grandfather and the San Marino government between 1925 and 1938, 75 pages in all, much of it hand-written by Fritz in fluent Italian. There were six letters written between April and May 1938, from the time of the *Anschluss* to the time of his death, in which he explained to the San Marino government the difficulties he was experiencing as Consul since Hitler's arrival in Vienna on 13 March of that year.

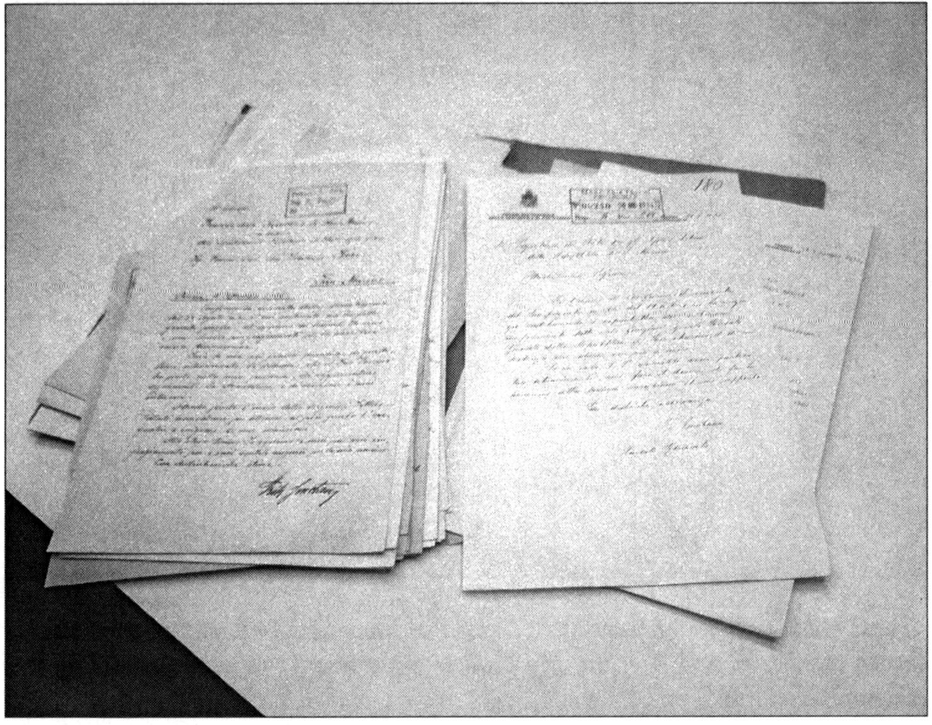

My visit to the San Marino archives in 2008

The response of the San Marino government was to express confidence in him by reaffirming his appointment. In his last letter, dated 25 May 1938 he thanks the San Marino government for this honour bestowed on him. There was no indication of his impending suicide just six days later.

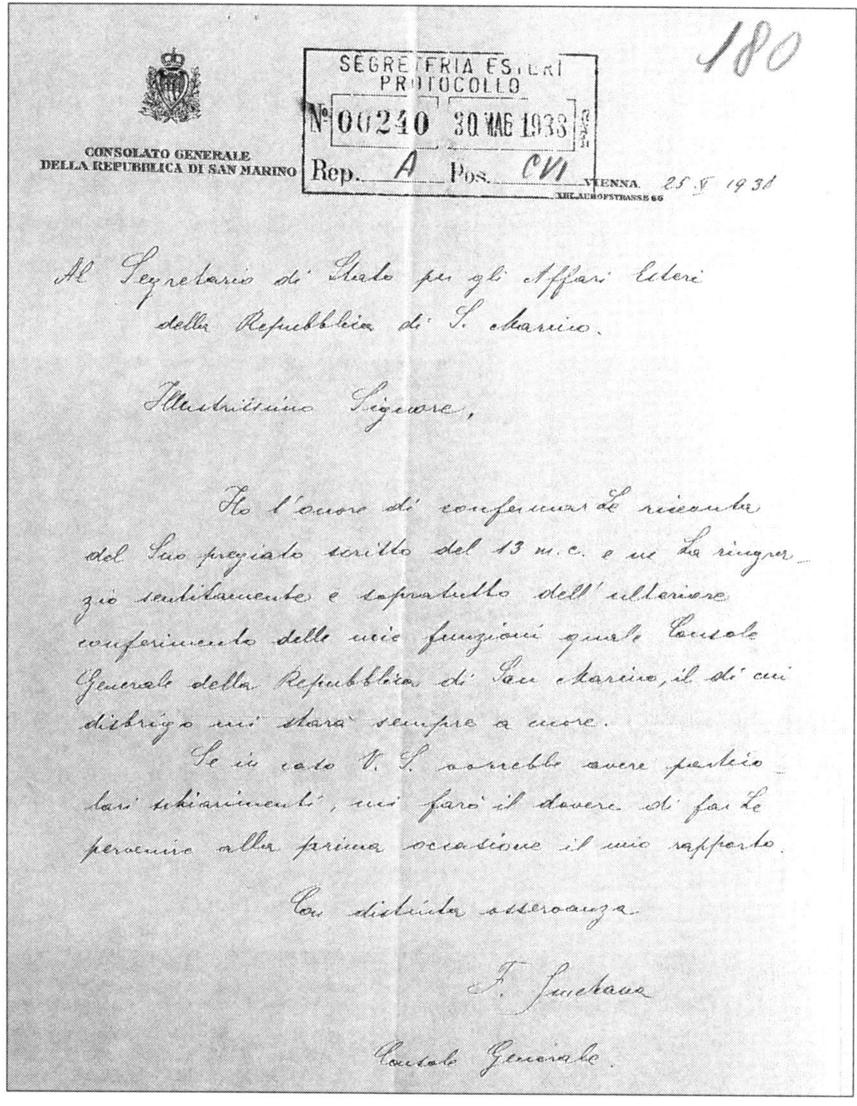

180

SEGRETERIA ESTERI
PROTOCOLLO
Nº 00240 30 MAG 1938
Rep. A Pos. CVI

CONSOLATO GENERALE
DELLA REPUBBLICA DI SAN MARINO

VIENNA, 25.V.1938
XIII. AUHOFSTRASSE 66

Al Segretario di Stato per gli Affari Esteri
della Repubblica di S. Marino.

Illustrissimo Signore,

Ho l'onore di confermarLe ricevuta del Suo pregiato scritto del 13 m.c. e mi La ringrazio sentitamente e soprattutto dell'ulteriore conferimento delle mie funzioni quale Console Generale della Repubblica di San Marino, il di cui disbrigo mi starà sempre a cuore.

Se in caso V. S. vorrebbe avere particolari schiarimenti, mi farò il dovere di farLe pervenire alla prima occasione il mio rapporto.

Con distinta osservanza.

F. Smetana

Console Generale.

Fritz's last letter, dated 25 May 1938 (translation Appendix 13)

On 2 June 1938, a letter was sent from Fritz's colleague, Fritz Reichsfeld, using headed paper from Auhofstrasse 66, and informing the San Marino government of Fritz's death. Herr Reichsfeld referred to my grandfather as *"il mio amico"*, my friend.

A LONELY END

Fritz was buried at *Zentralfriedhof* (central cemetery) 4, Group 22, Row 29b, Grave number 19. My mother remembered being driven there with her mother in the family car. Given the political circumstances, this must have been a difficult and dangerous time for a Jewish funeral. I visited the cemetery on 1 October 2006 when I went to Vienna for the first time with my daughter, Bambo. We managed, with great difficulty, to find my grandfather's grave.

There was a very small headstone for Fritz, and nothing at all for Josef and Cäcilie, who were buried, three years after their son, in the same plot.

We also visited my mother's former homes, which were beautiful, and the *Israelitische Kultusgemeinde*, where the Jewish archives are kept. The records are stored in huge books and I was able to see the original entries of several family members. I learned that my mother had lost eight members of her immediate family: her father, mother, sister, grandfather, two grandmothers, an uncle and a cousin. This number does not, of course, include the many distant relatives and friends who also perished.

My visit, in 2006, to the Israelitische Kultusgemeinde in Vienna, where Wolf-Erich Eckstein, shown here, was particularly helpful

Fritz's siblings survived and there are numerous descendants in Australia and the United States. However, Fritz himself had only one survivor: my mother, Lucy Fowler, née Smetana.

Chapter Nine

IN SEARCH OF BERTA SMETANA

BERTA AND THE WEINBERGERS

While it became clear to me that my grandfather, Fritz, was a kind and gentle man, I started to gain an altogether different picture of my grandmother, Berta. My mother deeply resented her, though she was fond of other members of the Weinberger family.

Berta was born on 9 January 1896, daughter of Heinrich Weinberger and Cäcilie Weinberger née Klausner. The family lived at Herminengasse 10, Vienna II. She had three younger siblings, the one immediately following her being Josefine, who died at the age of 21 due to a weak heart and lungs. She had been cared for at a special climatic health resort. The next sister was Emma, who had been close to Josefine and, when she died, cared for her grave. The youngest member of the family was Josef.

Emma (known as Emmy) was born on 26 April 1899. She married Ludwig Perlberger and lived close to her parents at Herminengasse 6, Vienna II. They had one daughter, Lydia, born on 11 July 1925. Emmy escaped to England with her husband Ludwig, and when the couple arrived, Emmy begged her husband to send for Lydia, but he insisted that she was safe where she was. Tragically, Lydia was shot by the Nazis in Yugoslavia, together with a family of seven relatives, to whom she had been sent for safety. Understandably, this remained a permanent source of tension between her parents. They lived fairly separate lives, each spending several months a year in Switzerland.

In July 2012, I discovered a picture of Lydia on the *Yad Vashem* database, posted by her relative Jacqueline Neuman née Perlberger, whose family had escaped to Australia. I had never before seen an image of my mother's young cousin.

Left: Aunty Emmy, die schöne Tante. *Right: Lydia Perlberger in the late 1930s, shortly before she was murdered by the Nazis*

Aunty Emmy was my mother's only surviving relative on the Weinberger side of the family and was my only contact with my mother's former life in Vienna. Although she and her husband had lost everything, and in spite of the tension between them, they quickly re-established a textile business and became our "rich" relatives, often sending us clothes and gifts.

My father, in particular, received numerous expensive suits worn only once or not at all by Uncle Ludwig, so was permanently well-dressed. These suits were my father's pride and joy, especially so as he had come from an impoverished background. However, he became acutely embarrassed by Aunty Emmy's behaviour towards him on the few occasions they met. Even in his middle age, she would pinch his cheek as if he were a small boy.

Aunty Emmy was very much of another era with its own clearly defined social mores. I remember a comment she made when she first heard I was going to Africa: *"Sie weiss nicht doch dass sie alle dort schwartz sind."* (Doesn't she know that they are all black there!) At the time, I thought this comment was amusing rather than shocking. On reflection, I realise the sad irony of this thoughtless racism expressed by someone who was herself the victim of racism on a massive scale.

My mother called her *"die schöne Tante"*, the beautiful aunt, and I recall weekly phone conversations in German, which my mother always conducted in a highly animated fashion. I remember also visiting Aunty Emmy at her home in Maida Vale, London, and being taught how to hold a cup of tea! I was in awe of her as, I think, was my mother. Emmy died on 20 December 1969 in Zurich, Switzerland. Following Emmy's death, my mother was the sole survivor of the entire Weinberger family.

It has occurred to me only as I write her story that Emmy, having lost her sister and father before the war, then lost her daughter, her mother, her brother and her sister in the Holocaust. She must have carried the most tremendous burden of grief, something of which I was never aware as a child.

Berta's brother, Josef, known to my mother as Uncle Joshi (pronounced Yoshi), was born on 29 May 1902. He remained single and lived with his mother. He owned a business called JAWO (pronounced Yawo), a men's clothing store, together with his brother-in-law Ludwig Perlberger and partner Emil Schmitt.

The business was based at Weihburggasse 5, Vienna I. My brother and I each have a coat hanger bearing the JAWO logo and address. I wonder what clothes were once stored on these hangers, to whom those clothes were sold and what kind of life they lived. If objects could talk, I imagine that these hangers would have many tales to tell about the rich clientele of this elegant store in central Vienna, which I believe still existed until recently.

I was initially unable to trace Joshi's details at the IKG, due to the fact that he apparently renounced his religion on 14 March 1931. This did not prevent him from being interned, at one point, in Dachau, and ultimately being deported from Drancy to Auschwitz on 2 September 1942, together with his sister, Berta and niece, Sonja. The difficulty in locating his records may partly explain why my mother always said that she did not know what had become of her Uncle Joshi, as her Aunt Emmy, his sister, was unable to trace him. I did not ultimately learn of his fate until I came across his name on the *Yad Vashem* database, where it was misspelt as Winberger, but with his correct date of birth.

BERTA: WHO WAS SHE?

Following her marriage to Fritz in 1918 and the birth of my mother in 1919, my grandmother Berta moved with the family to Auhofstrasse 66. Here, on 1 December 1927, she gave birth to my mother's sister Sonja, whose full name was Sonja Renate Renée Erika Smetana. After the initial excitement, arguments began and Berta moved with Sonja to another part of the large house. For Sonja was not Fritz's child, but the daughter of Norbert Sachs, Berta's lover. Divorce was inevitable, and Berta moved, with both daughters, to Schubertring in central Vienna. Such stories are not uncommon in the modern world, but in early 20th century Vienna, this must have caused a shocking scandal.

Left: Sonja on the steps of Auhofstrasse 66, c. 1930. Right: Lucy, Berta and Sonja Smetana, c. 1937

I understood from my mother that the wife of Herr Sachs was in an institution, and it was therefore impossible for him to obtain a divorce, according to Jewish law. He had three daughters, Ilse, Hilde and Lia, who were evidently well known to my grandmother, as I have a postcard written to them, and one from Hilde to Berta, addressing her as *Tante Berta* and signed *Viele Grusse* (many greetings). Some of my mother's cousins also referred to my grandmother as *Tante Berta.*

Clearly, the marriage between Fritz and Berta appears to have been a disastrous one. My mother has very fond recollections of her father, who, she felt, did his very best for her, and also of her maternal grandmother, Cäcilie Weinberger, who she remembers took care of her when she was ill, and visited her when she was in hospital.

However, she experienced only coldness and distance from her mother who, she felt, never had any time for her. As a result, my mother was largely brought up by nannies and had an unhappy, almost loveless childhood, in spite of her parents' wealth. Following the divorce, it seems Berta tried to prevent my mother from having any contact with the Smetana family and my mother led a somewhat lonely existence, seeing her father only occasionally.

My mother remembers that at 11 or 12, she was obliged by her mother to testify in court against her father in order to gain more alimony. Berta also dressed my mother in dowdy clothes to try to get even more money. Given the fact that Berta herself had six fur coats, the bitter resentment experienced by my mother remained with her throughout her life. On almost all the photos I have seen of Berta, Sonja and my mother, Berta's arm is placed lovingly around Sonja, never around my mother.

FLIGHT FROM VIENNA

My grandmother Berta and aunt Sonja left Vienna on 8 October 1938, followed by Berta's mother Cäcilie and brother Josef on 20 January 1939. Before leaving Vienna, Cäcilie, my great grandmother, was obliged, like other Jews, to sign a declaration that she was Jewish, and to declare her assets.

On 15 July 1938, Cäcilie signed a document, commencing *Ich bin Jude* ... (I am a Jew ...). On this occasion she wrote in firm clear handwriting. Less than five months later, on 9 December 1938, Cäcilie signed another document, where her handwriting is wobbly like that of a very old woman (she was 66 at the time, my own age at the time of writing). I imagine a Nazi officer in uniform standing over her as she signed, and she fearful for her life.

The second document was headed *Gildemeester. Aktion Gildemeester* was set up in Vienna in the spring of 1938 and enabled wealthy Jews to emigrate, provided that they agreed to hand over their entire fortune. The action was open mainly to *nichtgläubige Juden*, that is, non-believing Jews.

It has been suggested to me by Dr Kristen Rundle that when Jews first started signing the forms as demanded of them from April 1938, they may not always have been fully aware of the implications, and were willing to comply with the law. However, following the events of *Kristallnacht* on 9 November 1938, when synagogues and Jewish shops were smashed and burned, it became abundantly clear just how dangerous the situation was becoming. Cäcilie's fear is palpable in the second signature.

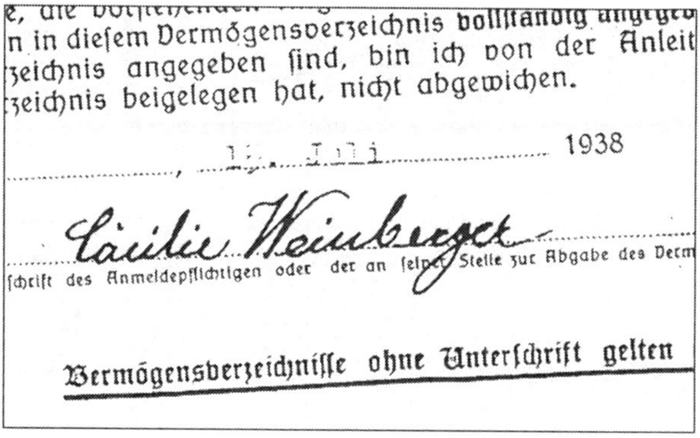
n in diesem Vermögensverzeichnis vollständig angege
zeichnis angegeben sind, bin ich von der Anleit
zeichnis beigelegen hat, nicht abgewichen.
Juli 1938
Cäcilie Weinberger
schrift des Anmeldepflichtigen oder der an seiner Stelle zur Abgabe des Verm
Vermögensverzeichnisse ohne Unterschrift gelten

Cäcilie's signature above, on 15 July 1938 and below, on 9 December 1938

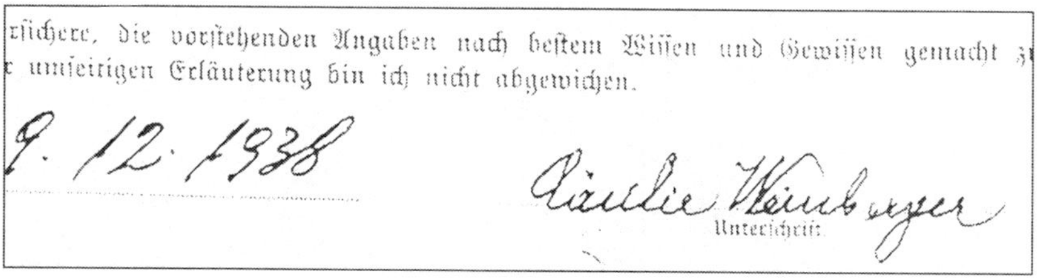
rsichere, die vorstehenden Angaben nach bestem Wissen und Gewissen gemacht z
umseitigen Erläuterung bin ich nicht abgewichen.
9. 12. 1938
Cäcilie Weinberger
Unterschrift

The family escaped to France, initially Paris, from where Berta sent postcards to my mother, at that time working at Peel Street Hospital for Women in Nottingham. Berta visited the Consul General for San Marino in Paris, probably to seek refuge. A letter was sent from the consulate in Paris to the government of San Marino, dated 17 December 1938, informing them of her visit and of the fact that documents from the consulate had been seized by the Nazis. The letter also indicates that Berta may have been planning, at one point, to escape via Brussels, to where she had sent a trunk.

TÉL. : OPÉRA 16-20

274
8.6.938

LÉGATION
DE LA
RÉPUBLIQUE DE SAINT-MARIN
EN FRANCE

PARIS, LE 17 Dicembre 1938.
195, RUE DE RIVOLI

1943/SM/D.

Egregio Commendatore,

Immaginando che la cosa potrebbe avere un interesse per Loro costi, ritengo opportuno di segnalarLe che in questi giorni ho avuto l'occasione di incontrare qui a Parigi la Signora Berta SMETANA, vedova del nostro ex Console Generale in Vienna. La Signora Smetana avendomi intrattenuto del suicidio di suo marito (Fritz Smetana, Auhofstrasse 11.B) a seguito agli avvenimenti politici Germano-Austriaci (Anschluss), mi permisi di domandarle cosa ne addivenne dell'archivio di quel Consolato Generale. Mi disse infatti che l'archivio era stato sequestrato, messo sotto sigilli dalle Autorità con quanto altro che si trovava in casa sua. Le domandai se conosceva il nome dell'usciere che appose i sigilli ma non si è ricordata , aggiunse poi che l'indirizzo dell'usciere l'aveva in un suo baule a Brusselle.

Non so se cotesto Eccellentissimo Governo è al corrente di quanto sopra, comunque Gliene avro' dato a Lei conoscenza a titolo privato.

La saluto ben distintamente.

P.Mally.

Egregio Commendatore Federico GOZI
Cancelliere di S.E. Il Segretario di Stato
per gli Affari Esteri
SAN MARINO

Letter to the government of San Marino from the consulate in Paris where Berta had gone, probably seeking refuge (translation Appendix 14)

Following the German invasion of France in the summer of 1940, an armistice was signed between the two countries. It was agreed that France would be divided into the occupied zone of the north and west, controlled by the German *Wehrmacht*, and the unoccupied zone of the south, where the "free" French government, known as the Vichy government, had authority. In the occupied zone, the Germans immediately established anti-Jewish measures, including arrests and deportations. However, some racial laws were also initiated by the Vichy government, and implemented in the south, but directed mainly against foreign Jews, as officials were more reluctant to take action against French Jews.

Fearing the Germans more than the French, thousands of Jews fled south to avoid the Nazi occupation, including French Jews as well as those of foreign origin. It was probably around this time that my own family travelled to the south of France, where Berta's mother, Cäcilie, died a natural death, I believe of cancer, no doubt induced by fear and terror, but nevertheless a merciful escape from Auschwitz. At some point, the family moved on to Nice, situated on the south-east coast.

I have obtained an identity card from the *Archives Départementales des Alpes-Maritimes*, in Nice, dated 3 January 1942. It was issued to Berta when she renewed a visa originally obtained in Paris three years earlier, and was stamped with a large **J** for Jew. Her address in Nice was given as 34 Rue de la Buffa, and she was described as *ex-autrichienne*, ex-Austrian, having been deprived of her nationality. The document contains a photo of Berta looking fearful and distraught. She was wearing a fur coat which she must have brought with her from Vienna, the last remnant of her dignity to which she was desperately clinging.

The round-up of Jews in France accelerated in 1942. One of the worst events occurred in July of that year, when about 13,000 Jews were arrested in Paris and its suburbs, and incarcerated in the *Vélodrome d'Hiver* for several days, in unspeakable conditions, before being deported. This atrocity was ordered by the Germans but in fact carried out by the French police. On a further notorious occasion which took place on 26 August 1942, over 7,000 foreign Jews in the unoccupied zone were arrested and handed over to the Germans, an action carried out entirely by the Vichy police, actively supported by the authorities of the SNCF, the French state railway company.

It was during the August round-up that Berta and Sonja were arrested in Nice, Alpes Maritimes, and taken to the Caserne Auvare, the local police barracks, where they were detained for five days until the 31 August, in a bedroom with 22 other women and children.

My mother had told me that Sonja's natural father Norbert Sachs, with whom Berta had had a long-standing relationship, may have been arrested with them. I did not find his name on the lists, but did discover the name of a Luba Sachs, possibly a woman, about whom there were few personal details, but who was arrested in Nice at the same time as Berta and detained in the same location.

Josef was picked up at the Quartier des Bouleaux, in Le Périer, Isère, some distance north-west of Nice, just south of Grenoble, and initially held in a French internment camp at Fort-Barraux.

All four, Berta, Sonja, Luba and Josef were transferred by rail from the south of France to Drancy, a transit camp on the outskirts of Paris. I have received evidence from Nice that Berta and Sonja made this 580-mile journey in a *wagon couvert*, a closed wooden boxcar normally used for transporting goods. They were all then deported from Drancy to Auschwitz in Poland, a further 760 miles, no doubt in similar trucks. The date was 2 September 1942, and they travelled on *convoi 27*, transport 27, along with a total of 1,000 Jews on that day alone. 877 of these men women and children were gassed on arrival.

Berta and Sonja's fates are recorded in the two documents below. The first is a letter to me from the International Red Cross (which, significantly, uses the French spelling of Berta's name), while the second is Sonja's entry on the *Yad Vashem* database.

SERVICE INTERNATIONAL DE RECHERCHES
INTERNATIONAL TRACING SERVICE
INTERNATIONALER SUCHDIENST

Bad Arolsen, 20th September 2000
gei/Hy

Re: Your inquiry concerning your family members
Mr Yoschi WEINBERGER, born around 1900, Ms Sonya SMETANA, born in 1927 and Mrs Bertha SMETANA nee WEINBERGER, born in Vienna on 9.1.1896

Dear Ms Soyinka,

referring to your previous letters we advise you that based on the particulars given by you a check was made of the documentary material available here.

The following particulars could be taken from the records available here:

SMETANA, Sonia, Nationality: Austrian
(no further personal data)

and

SMETANA, Berthe, Nationality: Austrian
(no further personal data)

were confined to Camp Drancy by the "Befehlshaber der Sicherheitspolizei und des Sicherheitsdienstes Frankreich" (date not indicated) and transferred to Concentration Camp Auschwitz on September 2, 1942.
Category: "Jüdinnen"

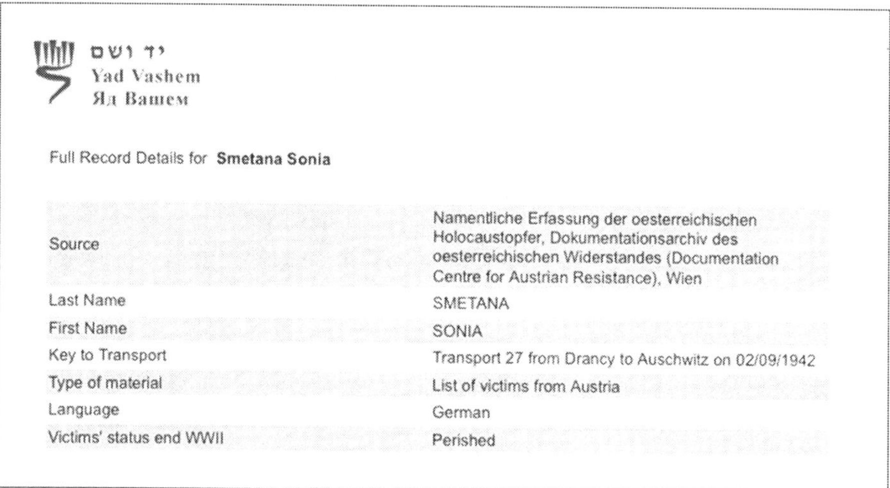
יד ושם
Yad Vashem
Яд Вашем

Full Record Details for **Smetana Sonia**

Source	Namentliche Erfassung der oesterreichischen Holocaustopfer, Dokumentationsarchiv des oesterreichischen Widerstandes (Documentation Centre for Austrian Resistance), Wien
Last Name	SMETANA
First Name	SONIA
Key to Transport	Transport 27 from Drancy to Auschwitz on 02/09/1942
Type of material	List of victims from Austria
Language	German
Victims' status end WWII	Perished

When I first received notification from the International Red Cross about the fate of my aunt Sonja, it was accompanied by a covering letter from the British Red Cross, which read:

> Dear Mrs Soyinka.
>
> Re: Fate of Susan Soyinka in the Holocaust.

They had confused my name, Susan Soyinka, with that of my aunt, Sonja Smetana. It was a typographical error, but one which sent shivers down my spine. It made me realise that, yes, it could have been my fate, too.

I visited Drancy, once, in the suburbs of Paris, and remember standing on the station platform thinking that this must have been the very spot from which Berta, Sonja and Josef were deported. It was a bleak and tearful moment.

"TANTE BERTHE WAS A GOOD WOMAN"

Once I became aware of my mother's poor relationship with her mother, I wondered how this had made her feel when she had learnt what happened to her. She even told me in 1995 that, 20 years after she had left Vienna, she had had nightmares that her mother would one day come knocking on her door.

I realised that these nightmares had continued to occur, even after my mother had learnt of her mother's arrest and deportation. I could not understand this. For all that she resented Berta, my mother was definitely not a person to wish such a fate on anyone. Indeed, she hated and deplored violence of any kind and could not bear to see it on the television.

I wondered if she felt guilty at having almost wished her mother dead. So one day I asked her, *"At what point did you tell yourself that your mother must be dead?"* The reply was swift: *"Oh, I never told myself that she was dead. The letter didn't say that she was."*

So my mother never came to terms with her mother's death, because if she had done, she would have had to come to terms with her own sense of guilt at never wishing to see her again. 50 years on, I realised the extraordinarily powerful and overwhelming emotions that my mother had had to cope with.

Learning of my grandmother Berta's behaviour was a difficult issue for me, particularly in view of the fact that I looked so much like her. She clearly did not treat my mother well, and almost everything I had heard about her was negative. All the stories conveyed a shallow, selfish, unthinking woman.

One tiny snippet suggested that this may not have been a true, or at least a complete picture. One day, my mother said to me in a childish, petulant voice, *"My mother wouldn't let me wear a* dirndl (the Austrian national costume). *She said that was what the Nazis wore." "But Mum,"* I urged, *"your mother was right. Why should you wear such a potent symbol of the Nazis?"* Slowly, a look of surprise came over my mother's face, for until that point she had been trapped inside her childhood perception of her mother, and had carried that perception for all these years. *"Of course,"* she said quietly.

Much later, I came across postcards written by my grandmother in 1939, shortly

Liesel, ich wünsche Dir zu Deinem Geburtstag alles, alles Gute und vor allem Gesundheit, Gesundheit und wieder Gesundheit. Ein [illegible] Dir von Paris aus senden. Schreibe sofort Paris 24, Bld. Malesherbes. Es kann noch ein – zwei Tage dauern bis ich dort ankomme. Es küsst Dich herzlichst u. innigst Deine Mutti

after she had escaped to Paris in which she clearly addressed my mother in loving terms. (One is shown on the previous page and its reverse side at the bottom of this page.) It was comforting and reassuring to know that this woman, whom I resembled so much, had some saving graces. The card, translated by Margret Vince, reads in English:

3 IX 39

My dear, precious little Lucie,

I am desperate as I have had no mail from you for two weeks now. I have been travelling for 24 hours and have just ended up here. If I don't find little Sonja (Sonjali) soon, I may not find her perhaps for months, because the evaluation is kept secret. I don't know where Omi (granny) is either.

Lucie, for your birthday I wish you every good thing, and above all health, health, and once again health. I shall send you a present from Paris.
Write straight away Paris, 24 Bld. Malesherbes
It may take another day or two until I arrive there.

Warm and loving kisses from your Mummy.

VUES DE L'AIN
153 AMBÉRIEU-EN-BUGEY
Vallée de l'Albarine

BRAUN & Cie, Imp.-Edit., Mulhouse-Dornach

Miss
Lucy Smetana
Hospital for Women
Nottingham
Peel Street England

These are hardly the words of a cold-hearted mother. They are the words of a woman desperate to find her own mother and daughter, Sonja, but equally anxious about the safety of her other daughter in England. It would seem that Cäcilie and Sonja, 12 at the time, had been taken in for interrogation and that Berta did not know their whereabouts. Her state of anxiety is palpable. She again attempted to contact my mother just a few days later on 14 September 1939, by which time she had reached Paris:

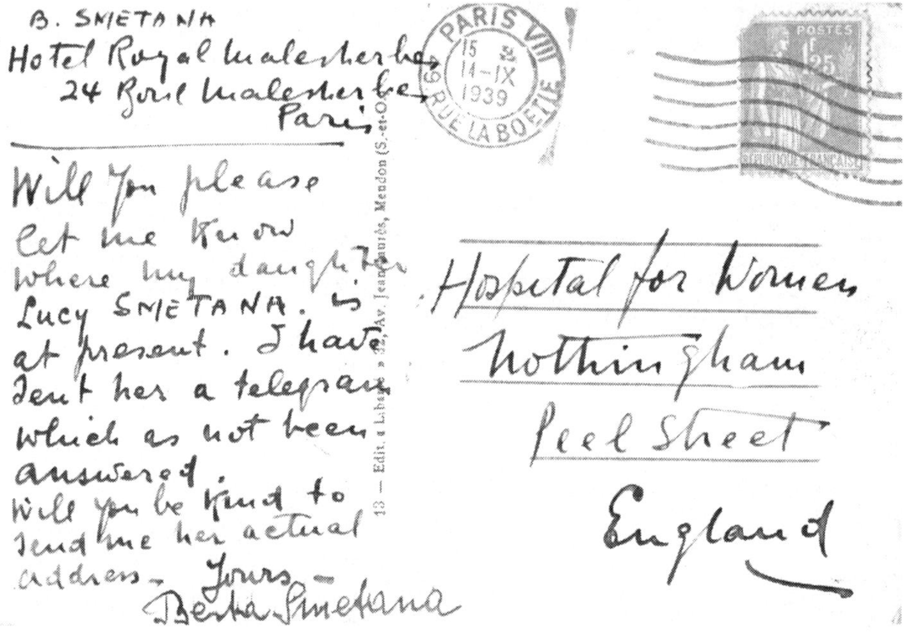

B. SMETANA
Hotel Royal Malesherbes
24 Boul Malesherbes
Paris

Will you please
let me know
where my daughter
Lucy SMETANA is
at present. I have
sent her a telegram
which as not been
answered.
Will you be kind to
send me her actual
address. Yours –
Berta Smetana

PARIS VIII
15
14-IX
1939
RUE LA BOETIE

POSTES
25

Hospital for Women
Nottingham
Peel Street
England

I am not in any way suggesting that my mother was wrong in her recollections of her mother, for it is clear that Berta's behaviour was at times less than motherly. But her memory may well have been partial or selective, clouded by the dark years which followed, which made it difficult for her to recall better times, or to see her childhood experiences through adult eyes.

In December 1995, I visited the newly established Beth Shalom Holocaust Memorial Centre in Nottinghamshire (now the Holocaust Centre), along with a group of people from the Nottingham Jewish community. There I met a wonderful lady called Victoria Ancona-Vincent, an Auschwitz survivor who had been living in Nottingham since the war, with her English husband Alfred.

Left: Victoria Ancona-Vincent at Beth Shalom Holocaust Memorial Centre in Nottinghamshire, 1995

Below: Alfred Vincent, Victoria's husband, my son Alex, my daughter Bambo, and myself at Beth Shalom in 1997

Victoria had written a testimony of her experience at Auschwitz, and this eventually got published in September 1995, to mark the opening of Beth Shalom. She then worked on an educational programme for local schools with Stephen Smith, the remarkable director and co-founder of the Centre (now Executive Director of Steven Spielberg's Shoah Foundation Institute).

As it happened, my son Alex had heard about Victoria and was excited about meeting her. We all had a long chat and warmed very much to this exceptional lady. She signed a copy of her book, *Beyond Imagination*, for Alex, and over the next few days, I started reading it. In the book, Victoria described a group of women in Auschwitz, who over a period of about a year offered one another support. One of them was called, in French, *Tante Berthe.* As I read on, a picture of *Tante Berthe* emerged, and I started to feel a tingle of excitement, mixed with total disbelief.

Tante Berthe was older than the other women, possibly in her mid-forties. She came from a wealthy background and spoke French. Too much of a coincidence, I thought. Anyway, she wasn't French, although maybe by that time she spoke it well, as she had been in France for several years. Then I remembered that one of my mother's cousins had recently referred to my grandmother as *Tante Berta*, the German equivalent.

I eventually plucked up my courage and rang Victoria. *"Look, this is highly unlikely,"* I said, *"but it is just possible that the Tante Berthe you knew was my grandmother."* Victoria asked if I had any photos, and when I said yes, she asked me to bring them along.

When I arrived at Victoria's house, she suggested that I did not show her the photos until we had talked it over, which we did for several hours. As we talked, more facts emerged which made the incredible seem possible. The group avoided talking about the past, as it would have made coping difficult, but on one occasion when she was feeling stressed, *Tante Berthe* spoke longingly of her former life, of visits to the opera and of the fur coats she had once owned.

Victoria remembered that *Tante Berthe* in fact spoke French with an accent and yes, she did speak German. She spoke on her arrival with a young German guard. *"Forget for a moment that I am Jewish and you are German, and tell me how I can help myself."* He asked her her age and, when she told him, suggested that she take off 10 years. So this is how she escaped the gas chambers.

I had always had an image in my head that my grandmother stepped off the train in a fur coat. In fact, whenever I have watched archive footage of the unloading of the cattle trucks, I have looked for a woman in a fur coat, thinking this could be my grandmother. Victoria confirmed that *Tante Berthe* arrived at Auschwitz in a fur coat.

And what about Sonja? Now, Victoria remembered that there was a young woman in her mid-teens with *Tante Berthe*, which would have been roughly Sonja's age. Victoria had thought she was *Tante Berthe*'s niece, but yes, they were very close. The young girl was called Violette or possibly Huguette. Is it possible that Sonja could have taken on a French name in order to go to school in France or to hide her identity? She must have first gone there when she was 12 or 13. Unlike *Tante Berthe*, Violette spoke fluent French. And why niece? Then I realised that by taking 10 years off her age, Berta would have made herself too young to be Sonja's mother, if indeed it was them. Perhaps she said to her, *"Pretend you are my niece, call me Tante Berthe."* Perhaps, even, that is how the name arose.

And then the photos. I now brought them out and showed them to Victoria. She studied them carefully for a long time, and then said slowly, *"Well, it is difficult to say for sure, because you know, our heads were shaven, and we were naked for much of the time. But yes, I think that is her. I would say between 60% and 80% certain."*

By this time I was shaking. We talked over their fate. The whole group left Auschwitz with many others, including the author Elie Wiesel, on 17 January 1945, and embarked on the first Death March. It seems Violette (Sonja?) died during this march, but the older *Tante Berthe* survived. Several more months of excruciating misery, and then the second Death March in April 1945. Just a few days before the end of the war, and after all she had endured, *Tante Berthe* stumbled, fell, and was shot.

A long pause.

And then, one more question. What was she like, this *Tante Berthe*? *"Oh, she was wonderful,"* enthused Victoria. *"She kept up the morale of the younger girls, telling stories, and even jokes. She was like a mother and sister at the same time. We always looked up to her because of her age, but at the same time, she was always one of us. We were devastated when she died. The Tante Berthe I knew was a good woman."*

Thus, finally, I had been given the answer to my questions. Even if, in the final analysis, *Tante Berthe* was not my grandmother (though somehow I believe she was), still, I had been given the answer to my questions. Not just about my grandmother, but also the questions implicit in my search. For if it was not my grandmother, then it could have been.

No doubt all of us are capable of committing evil acts, as the Nazi period demonstrated most clearly. But equally, and more hopefully, we are also capable of rising from the depths of despair, and reaching out a helping hand to others.

I was extremely moved to learn later from Victoria that at a *Yom Hashoah* ceremony (Holocaust Remembrance Day) held at Beth Shalom in April 1996, she had planted a rose tree, in remembrance of *Tante Berthe* and Violette. This became part of a rose memorial garden to Victoria herself.

Victoria died on 5 August 1996. I had known her only for a few short months, but in that time, she had become hugely significant in my life. I shall be for ever grateful to her. The poem on the following page was written by Stephen Smith.

Immortal

I thought you were immortal
When I saw you smile
And watched you cry.
I thought you were immortal
When you laughed in the face of death
And told me how you went to hell
And returned to the land of the living.
I thought you were immortal
When I saw the number on your arm.
That death wish
Indelibly printed on your soul and on your mind.
I thought you were immortal
As you chastened and you warned,
Of bitter things to come,
Lest we think its all over and gone.
But you were no prophet of doom
You were a sign of life
And all that can grow out of pain.

I know how you admired the brave.
Rosa, Regina, Ella, Tusia,
Hanging on the gallows.
They were your martyrs and heroes.
You never failed them,
And so now you join them,
Warrior among the brave.

You know,
I really thought you would be here forever.
But the passage of time takes its toll.
And even the strong have their moment to go.

I thought,
I foolishly thought you were immortal
My true, true friend.

You are not.
But you will always be with me.

S.D.S.

שלום

Written on the passing of
Victoria Ancona-Vincent, 5th August 1996

LE DEVOIR DE MÉMOIRE

In June 2012 just as I was completing this book, I joined the social network site Twitter, on the advice of friends. I did this somewhat reluctantly as I thought that Twitter was a rather superficial means of communication. Within a week, a lady in France, Maryse Banet, picked up on the brief details I had given of my

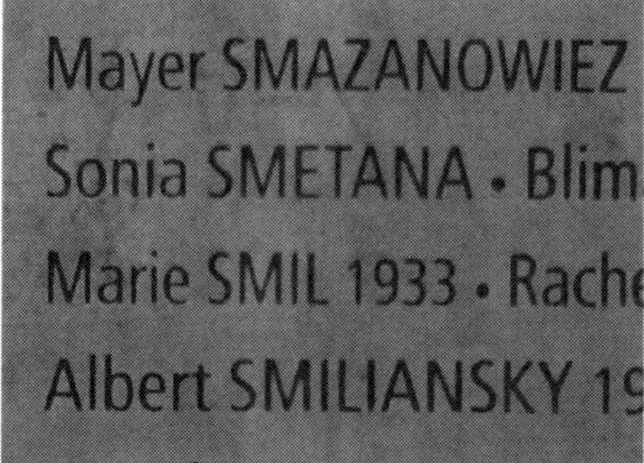

story, and discovered that the names of Berta, Sonja and Josef are inscribed on *Le Mur des Noms* (the Wall of Names) at the *Mémorial de la Shoah* in Paris. Not only that, Maryse visited the Memorial, took photos of my family's names, and lit a candle for them, adding in her tweet the words "*que leur âme repose en paix*", may their souls rest in peace. Her own grandmother had also been deported, and she described this incredibly kind act as "*le devoir de mémoire*", the duty to remember. What a wonderful example, and from such an unexpected source, of what I had already written on the previous page about the human ability to reach out a helping hand to others.

I visited Paris only a month later in July 2012 to participate in the International Association of Jewish Genealogical Societies, and it was there that I made some of the significant discoveries about those members of my family who had gone to France which I have recounted above. I briefly met Serge Klarsfeld, the celebrated Holocaust historian, who showed me the names of Berta, Sonja and Josef in the 2012 edition of his book, *Mémorial de la Déportation des Juifs de France.* This exceptional work records the names and personal details of over 75,000 Jews deported from France, mainly Drancy, on 79 transports between March 1942 and August 1944.

I was also able to visit the *Mémorial de la Shoah* and see the names of my family engraved on the Wall of Names. This was an incredibly moving experience.

Chapter Ten

MY MOTHER'S LIFE IN VIENNA (1919–1938)

Lucy Smetana in Vienna c. 1937

Hietzinger Hauptstrasse 69, Vienna XIII, my mother's first home

~~Tax~~frei

Geburts-Zeugnis.

Unterzeichneten wird hiemit bestätigt, daß laut Geburts-Protokoll der israelitischen Kultusgemeinde in Wien 1919 Reihezahl 1584

Lucie Edith Smetana

am 6. IX. 1919 sechsten September

Eintausend neun hundert neunzehn

als eheliche Tochter des Friedrich Smetana

und der Bertha geb. Weinberger

in Wien II, Pelikang. 15 geboren wurde.

Wien, am 3. Mai 1938

MATRIKELAMT DER
ISRAELITISCHEN KULTUSGEMEINDE
IN WIEN

MATRIKELAMT DER ISRAELITISCHEN KULTUSGEMEINDE IN WIEN

beeideter Matrikelführer.

Taxe S [illegible]
Stem. S 1.50
S 6.50

My mother's birth certificate, issued in May 1938 by the Israelitische Kultusgemeinde, when she was trying to obtain authorisation to leave Austria

CHILDHOOD IN HIETZING

My mother was born Lucie Edith Smetana in Vienna on 6 September 1919. Records show that she was originally called Ilse, but this was changed after only two days. I wonder whether this was a straightforward change of mind, or whether it had been consequent to an argument between Fritz and Berta. The change was made by Fritz.

At the time of my mother's birth, Fritz and Berta lived at Hietzinger Hauptstrasse 69, Vienna XIII, which I visited in 2006. My mother would have been delighted to know that her childhood home now houses an ice cream parlour on the ground floor. She often used to say how much she loved Viennese water ices. The family then moved to Auhofstrasse 66, also in Hietzing, and I discovered several photos of this home in my mother's album. There were no photos of her home in Schubertring, on the boulevards in central Vienna, where she lived during her teenage years.

During our visit to Hietzing in 2006, my daughter Bambo and I walked first down Hietzinger Hauptstrasse, passing number 53 where Josef and Cäcilie had lived at one time, and then number 69 where my mother was born. Just past number 69, we cut through a short road called Feldmühlgasse which runs between the Hietzinger Hauptstrasse and Auhofstrasse, which are parallel roads, and discovered Auhofstrasse 66 as we emerged from Feldmühlgasse.

To our surprise, we passed the home and last studio of Gustav Klimt on Feldmühlgasse, so my grandparents had lived just round the corner from the artist. My mother was born shortly after his death in 1918, but I later learned that her primary school, which she attended for six years, was also situated in Feldmühlgasse. Some of Klimt's most famous paintings are of wealthy Jewish women living in Hietzing. Clearly, my family had lived in a time and place of enormous cultural, social and artistic significance.

My mother had several pictures of the interior of Auhofstrasse 66, including one of her sitting at a desk in her bedroom doing her schoolwork. While she remained living in her own home, in her old age, her photo album of Vienna, which I did not discover until 1995, lay on the small table beside her chair, and I imagine she looked at it on a daily basis. This kept alive the memories of her childhood, even though she remained largely silent about them. In 1997, she moved into a residential home, Miriam Kaplowitch House, and this disruption to her routine meant that she stopped looking at her album. The memories started to fade away rapidly.

Gustav Klimt's studio in Feldmühlgasse which we passed during our visit to Hietzing

Memory is a strange and unpredictable phenomenon. Memories that appear to have been lost forever can sometimes be triggered inexplicably by some visual or other kind of stimulus. In 2001, my son Alex visited Vienna and brought back photos of my mother's former home, but she did not recognise anything, so I wondered if Alex had perhaps photographed the wrong house. I nevertheless placed a framed copy of the photos in her room at the home. Just a few weeks before she died in 2003, I persuaded her to go out with me into the garden at M.K. House. She had always loved the garden of her own home, spending a great deal of time lovingly cultivating it, but had now become apathetic and unwilling to exert herself.

As we sat in the spring sunshine, I noticed a large tree with a circular bench around it. My mother suddenly commented that she had had a bench like that at her home in Vienna. I instinctively knew that she meant Auhofstrasse 66, and rushed upstairs to her room to fetch down the photos. She brightened up and said, yes, that room was her bedroom, and that one was the room where her grandmother stayed when she came to visit. How I would love to have seen, during our visit, if that tree still existed, and the bedroom where she had sat at her desk. Sadly, we were ejected from the house before that was possible.

It was evident from my mother's belated comments that she had spent at least some happy times in her early years. And yet, her recollection, insofar as she communicated it, was that she had had an unhappy childhood, and felt that no one really cared for her. She actually remembers lying on her bed in Vienna when she was 16 or 17 thinking to herself, *"If only someone would love me."*

As we have seen, the marriage between Fritz and Berta was not a good one. Though she never said as much, for she was never one to judge or criticise, it is clear that she blamed her mother for this, and remained bitter towards her throughout her life. However, my grandmother's postcards to my mother are addressed in affectionate terms. Certainly, my mother was largely brought up by nannies, but that was probably the norm for wealthy families at that time.

In fact, up until 1932, while she was still living in Hietzing where the rest of the Smetana family lived, my mother had had lots of contact with her grandparents, aunts, uncles and cousins, and frequently went on holiday, as the photos below show. An early school photo also shows her looking happy.

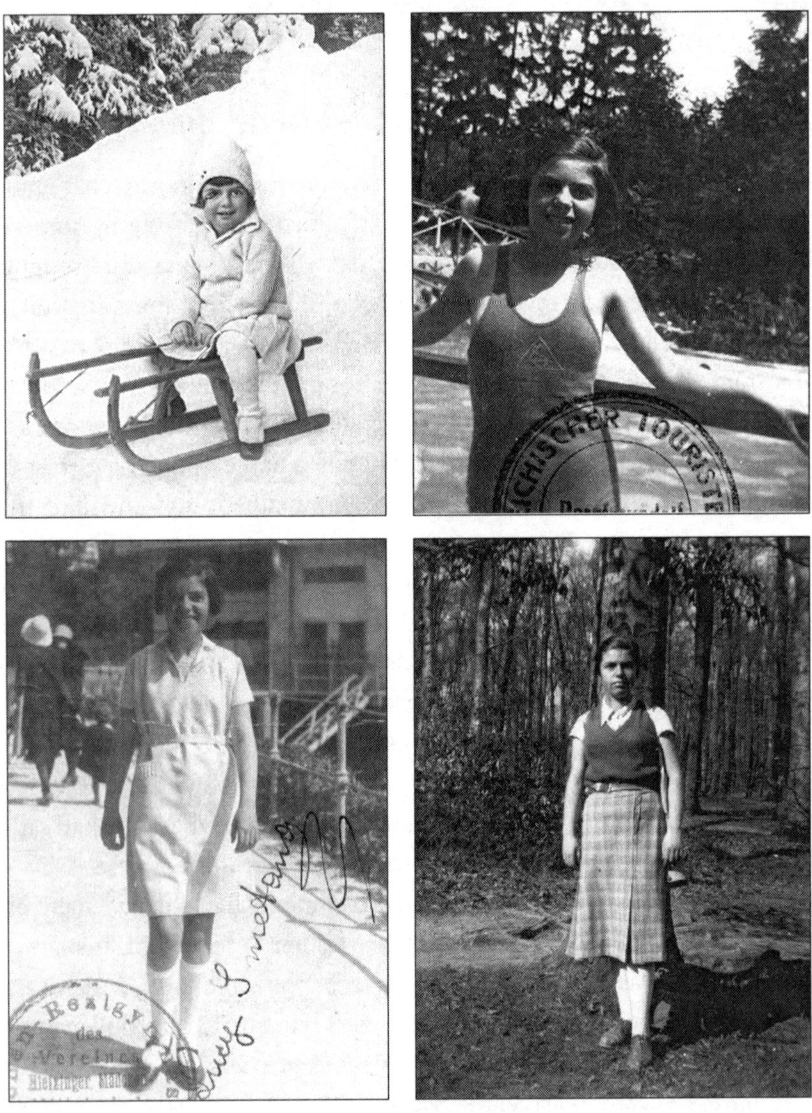

Top: Lucy Smetana as a young child on holiday. Bottom: as a schoolgirl and teenager

I now have in my possession many more family photos, some showing her with her cousins. In one of them, shown in Chapter One, she is seen playing happily with her cousin Helga. She simply could not recollect this; in fact, when I first established contact with her cousins in 1995, the only one she could remember at all was Ully. She had no recollection of her cousins Helga, Heinz, Peter, Lori and Gerda, all on the Smetana side of the family. It seems that in cutting out the painful times, she also succeeded in cutting out the happy ones. But some of her memories did come back. I remember, in 1995, her speaking with Ully on the telephone for the first time in almost 60 years, using a mixture of English and German. My mother asked Ully, *"Do you still have your long blonde plaits?"*

It would seem, therefore, that her sense of sadness and isolation probably began with the move away from the Smetana family in 1932. Although she was now closer to the Weinberger family in central Vienna, and had a good relationship with her maternal grandmother, my mother had only one cousin on this side of the family, Lydia, daughter of her Aunty Emmy, *die schöne Tante.* However, Lydia was born in 1925, and was much younger than her.

My mother's only really happy memories as a teenager are of the times she spent with her school-friend Annie Altschul, who also came to England, and Annie's mother, with whom she spent every Sunday, and with whom, therefore, she was able to gain a much greater sense of family, something she had lost due to her parents' divorce.

Left: Fritz, on holiday with my mother, and his sister, Gusti, in the 1920s. Right: Lucy, Helga and Ully in the 1920s

When Helga visited us in April 1995, bringing with her the exquisite cut glass bowl described in Chapter One, she also brought photos and stories of the family, most especially of "*Uncle Fritz*", my grandfather, of whom she had been very fond.

From 1924 to 1930, whilst still living in Hietzing, my mother attended the *Volkschule, Mädchenschule*, Feldmühlgasse, Vienna XIII, shown in the photograph below, where she is sitting in the middle of the second row.

My mother's primary school class in Feldmühlgasse, Hietzing

I have a poem written in German in 1928 by my mother's primary school teacher, in which a verse is devoted to each child in the class, and where my mother is criticised for her untidy writing. (Her handwriting never did improve!) She often used to tell us also how her teacher called her a snail because she worked so slowly. There is even a verse about Ully and her brother Heinz. Ully was rather indignant about the teacher's description of her as in need of a padlock to close her mouth, but thought the teacher's name was Frau Klier. Perhaps the teacher in the photograph is the one who wrote the poem. Below are two verses beautifully translated by Margret Vince, with some poetic licence.

Nun bitte: SMETANA LUCIE!
Machst schon die Punkte auf dem "i";
auch "u" - Häckchen ich nicht vermisse.
Was aber soll'n die Krähenfüsse?
Du schmierst im Heft ja wie ein Hahn! -
Mein gutes Kind, denk doch daran:
die Schrift muss schöner stets gelingen;
drum will ich Dir hier Federn bringen.

I ask you: LUCIE SMETANA!
You dot the "i"s
and cross the "t"s
But just what kind of scrawls are these?
You smudge your book with hen's footprints! -
My dear child, just stop and think:
your handwriting needs to get better;
a fountain pen will help your letters.

STEININGER OLLY macht's nicht besser ...
Euch beiden send' ich Vorhangschlösser!!
Ja, Olly, - Heinz, Dein Brüderlein,
für das Du sorgst, so treu und fein,
darf diese Unart nie erlernen;
drum - Plaudertaschen kurz entfernen!!
Dann hör'ich weiter, - ganz erschreckt-,
dass Emmy beim Erzählen steckt
das Zungenspitzl keck heraus
und vorlaut ist im Klassenhaus!

OLLY STEININGER is no better ...
The pair of you fidget and chatter!
Must I chain you to the desk?
Separation may be best.
We don't want little brother Heinz
Copying such classroom crimes.
But moving on, I am aghast
At Emmy's forwardness in class
Gossiping to all and anyone
And even sticking out her tongue!

It is likely that many of the 25 children named in this poem were Jewish and did not survive the Holocaust.

GROWING UP IN CENTRAL VIENNA

My mother also attended the *Hauptschule* (high school) in Hietzing, from 1930 to 1931, and the *Realgymnasium* (grammar school), Wenzgasse, also in Hietzing, from 1931 to 1932. It seems, therefore, that she had two years of secondary schooling before leaving Hietzing.

Following the move to central Vienna, she transferred to a new secondary school, where she met her life-long friend, Annie Altschul. This school was the *Realgymnasium des Wiener Frauen Erwerb Verein*, Wiedner Gürtel 68, Vienna IV. She remained in this school from 1932 to 1937, and even brought with her to England some of her school reports.

My mother's class at the Realgymnasium in central Vienna. She is at the right on the back row, while Annie, with glasses, is first left on the front row

I remember a story Annie told me long ago that she was extremely short-sighted, but that this was not discovered until she was five years old. When she started wearing spectacles, she was amazed to discover that trees had leaves, and houses had roofs! Annie was an extremely intelligent child who had hoped to become a Professor of Maths, and went on to study Maths and Physics at Vienna University. However, like other Jews, she was obliged to leave, and in 1938 came to England with her mother and sister. She took up nursing, the only avenue open to her, eventually rising to the position of Professor of Nursing Studies at Edinburgh University. Annie became internationally renowned in the field of psychiatric nursing. In her retirement she fulfilled in part her childhood ambition by taking a degree in Mathematics. Annie died in 2001.

Annie and Lucy, several years after their escape to England, with me and my brother, Peter, 1949

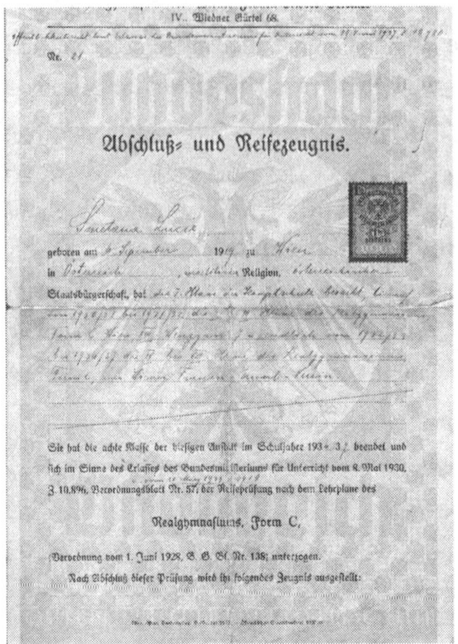

IV., Wiedner Gürtel 68.

Nr. 21

Abschluß- und Reifezeugnis.

geboren am ... 1919 zu Wien

in Österreich ..., Religion, ...

Staatsbürgerschaft, hat ...

Sie hat die achte Klasse der hiesigen Anstalt im Schuljahre 1936/37 beendet und sich im Sinne des Erlasses des Bundesministeriums für Unterricht vom 8. Mai 1930, Z. 10.896, Verordnungsblatt Nr. 57, der Reifeprüfung nach dem Lehrplane des

Realgymnasiums, Form C,

(Verordnung vom 1. Juni 1928, B. G. Bl. Nr. 138) unterzogen.

Nach Abschluß dieser Prüfung wird ihr folgendes Zeugnis ausgestellt:

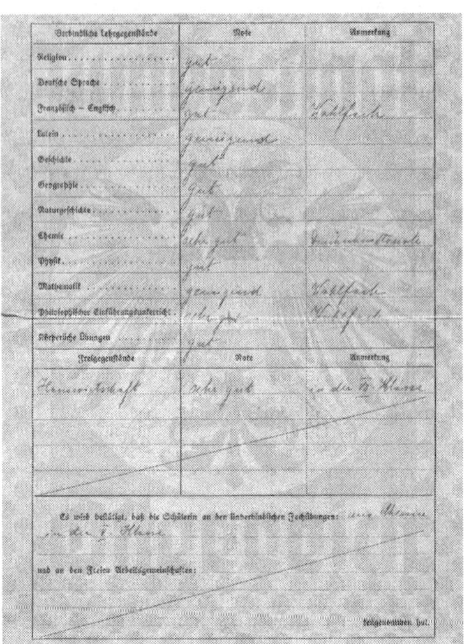

Verbindliche Lehrgegenstände	Note	Anmerkung
Religion	gut	
Deutsche Sprache	genügend	
Französisch – Englisch	gut	Wahlfach
Latein	genügend	
Geschichte	gut	
Geographie	gut	
Naturgeschichte	gut	
Chemie	sehr gut	[illegible]
Physik	gut	
Mathematik	genügend	Wahlfach
Philosophischer Einführungsunterricht	sehr gut	[illegible]
Körperliche Übungen	gut	
Freigegenstände	**Note**	**Anmerkung**
[illegible]	sehr gut	in der ... Klasse

Es wird bestätigt, daß die Schülerin an den unverbindlichen Fachübungen: ... in der ... Klasse

und an den Freien Arbeitsgemeinschaften:

teilgenommen hat.

My mother's school leaving certificate, issued on 17 June 1937. She had to get this document authenticated when she was trying to obtain permission to continue her university studies in France

In 1937, when she was 18, my mother started studying medicine at the *Universität Medizinische Fakultät,* University of Vienna Medical Faculty, where she remained for almost a year until her precipitous departure in 1938.

Vienna University has recently published an online Memorial Book for the Victims of National Socialism in 1938. I came across this site quite accidentally and discovered that it contained documentation about my mother, as well as her friend, Annie. The memorial book confirms that my mother was a *Vertriebene Studierende*, an expelled student.

My mother had told me that she was enrolled in the Jewish Faculty of Medicine attended by socialists and non-conformists as well as Jews. However, the site indicates that while she was indeed enrolled in the Faculty of Medicine, there was no Jewish Faculty of Medicine at Vienna University. My mother may have got her facts confused, but I do wonder if perhaps there was some separate registration system for Jews which accounts for her recollection. Certainly, there was a space on the registration form where she was required to declare her religion, which, given the political circumstances, was not a benign piece of information.

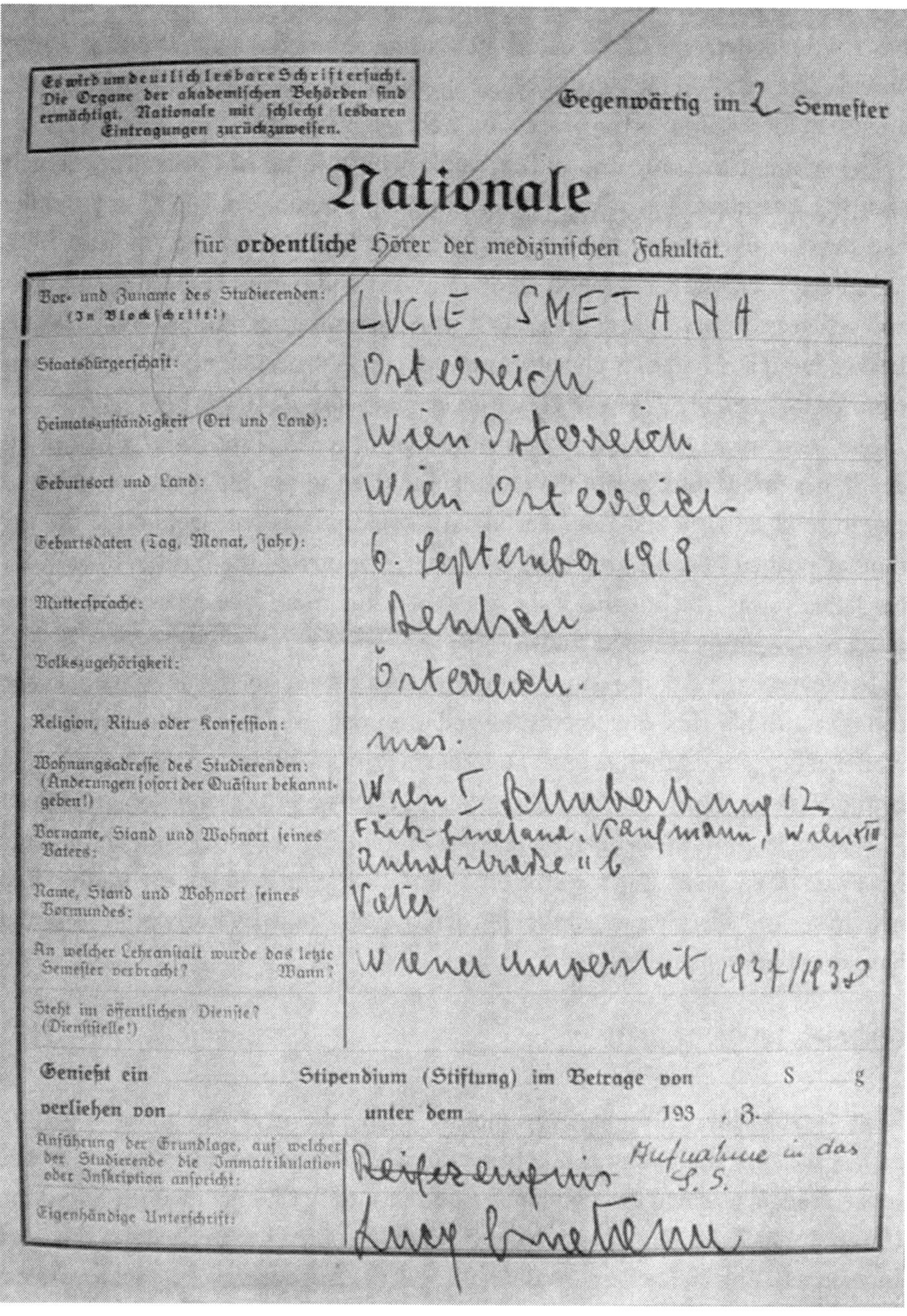

Es wird um deutlich lesbare Schrift ersucht. Die Organe der akademischen Behörden sind ermächtigt, Nationale mit schlecht lesbaren Eintragungen zurückzuweisen.

Gegenwärtig im 2 Semester

Nationale

für **ordentliche** Hörer der medizinischen Fakultät.

Vor- und Zuname des Studierenden: (In Blockschrift!)	LUCIE SMETANA
Staatsbürgerschaft:	Österreich
Heimatszuständigkeit (Ort und Land):	Wien Österreich
Geburtsort und Land:	Wien Österreich
Geburtsdaten (Tag, Monat, Jahr):	6. September 1919
Muttersprache:	deutsch
Volkszugehörigkeit:	Österreich.
Religion, Ritus oder Konfession:	mos.
Wohnungsadresse des Studierenden: (Änderungen sofort der Quästur bekanntgeben!)	Wien I [illegible] 12
Vorname, Stand und Wohnort seines Vaters:	Fritz Smetana, Kaufmann, Wien VIII [illegible] 6
Name, Stand und Wohnort seines Vormundes:	Vater
An welcher Lehranstalt wurde das letzte Semester verbracht? Wann?	Wiener Universität 1937/1938
Steht im öffentlichen Dienste? (Dienststelle!)	

Genießt ein Stipendium (Stiftung) im Betrage von S g

verliehen von unter dem 193 . 3.

Anführung der Grundlage, auf welcher der Studierende die Immatrikulation oder Inskription anspricht:	Reifezeugnis — Aufnahme in das S. S.
Eigenhändige Unterschrift:	Lucie Smetana

My mother's registration for her second semester at the Universität Medizinische Fakultät, *the Faculty of Medicine at Vienna University, shown in an online Memorial Book for the Victims of National Socialism in 1938*

Her studies were disrupted when Hitler annexed Austria in March 1938. She has vivid recollections of the occasion: a bright sunny day with cheering, happy crowds. She stood on the balcony of her apartment in Schubertring watching, with a sense of foreboding, as the procession went by.

She was not the only one in her family with a sense of foreboding. Shortly after the *Anschluss*, her father, Fritz, committed suicide. Until 1995, my mother had never spoken about this episode or how it had affected her. In June 1995, I attended a Second Generation Conference for children of Holocaust survivors and refugees, where I participated in a workshop on grief. On my return home, I asked her if she had ever gone through a grieving process for her parents. I was stunned by her reply: *"I grieve for my father every day of my life."*

She went on to tell me a story she had never told before. Shortly before his death, her father took her to the cinema and tried to put his arm around her as a gesture of fatherly affection. Feeling self-conscious as teenagers often do, my mother pushed his arm away. For ever after, she carried the burden of guilt for her father's death, feeling that if she had shown him more love, he would have had more reason, more courage, to live.

In November 1996, the daughter of my mother's cousin Helga visited me. She brought with her Nazi documents she had just uncovered in Vienna. Together we read that her grandfather, Jacques Steininger (Fritz's brother-in-law), was arrested by the Nazis on 27 May 1938 and interned in Dachau. Fritz committed suicide on 31 May 1938, most probably fearing arrest himself. His fears were not unfounded: his own father, Josef, was arrested on 3 June 1938. For decades, my mother had needlessly and silently carried that burden of guilt, though clearly nothing could have eased her sense of loss.

ESCAPE TO ENGLAND

After leaving the university, my mother spent the next five months getting papers to leave the country. She had originally planned to go to France as she spoke French, and had even obtained a place to study Chemistry at the Sorbonne University in Paris. She does not know what prompted her to abandon this idea and come to England, where she did not speak the language, except that her friend Annie was already here. Of course, had she gone to France, she would probably not have survived.

Throughout the months of running from office to office getting the necessary stamps, complete with swastikas, on her birth certificate, she recalls a man in a

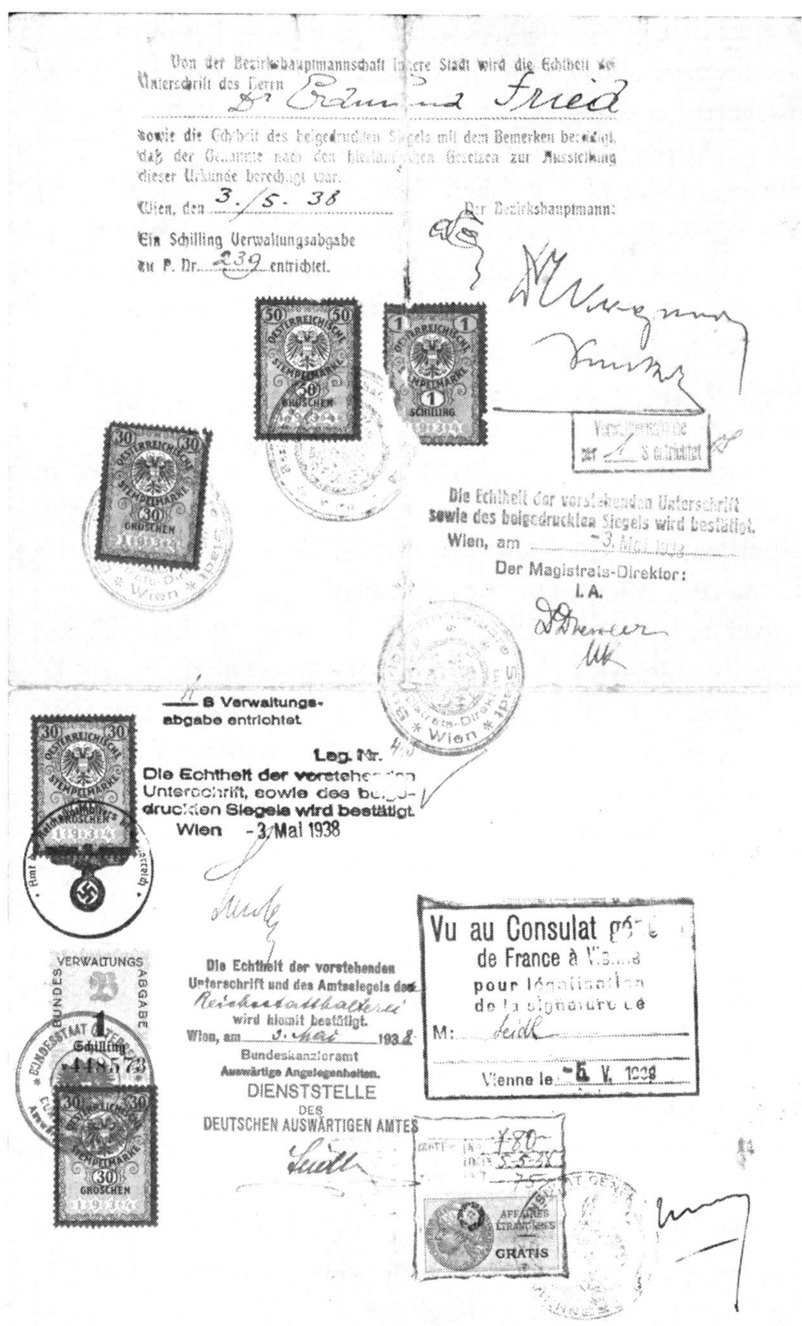

Von der Bezirkshauptmannschaft innere Stadt wird die Echtheit der Unterschrift des Herrn Dr Edmund Fried sowie die Echtheit des beigedruckten Siegels mit dem Bemerken bestätigt, daß der Genannte nach den hierländigen Gesetzen zur Ausstellung dieser Urkunde berechtigt war.

Wien, den 3./5. 38

Der Bezirkshauptmann:

Ein Schilling Verwaltungsabgabe zu P. Nr. 239 entrichtet.

Verwaltungsabgabe 1 S entrichtet

Die Echtheit der vorstehenden Unterschrift sowie des beigedruckten Siegels wird bestätigt.

Wien, am 3. Mai 1938

Der Magistrats-Direktor:

I.A.

1 S Verwaltungsabgabe entrichtet.

Leg. Nr.

Die Echtheit der vorstehenden Unterschrift, sowie des beigedruckten Siegels wird bestätigt.

Wien - 3 Mai 1938

Die Echtheit der vorstehenden Unterschrift und des Amtssiegels der Reichsstatthalterei wird hiemit bestätigt.

Wien, am 3. Mai 1938

Bundeskanzleramt

Auswärtige Angelegenheiten.

DIENSTSTELLE DES DEUTSCHEN AUSWÄRTIGEN AMTES

Vu au Consulat général de France à Vienne pour légalisation de la signature de M: Seidl

Vienne le 5 V. 1938

Reverse side of my mother's birth certificate, showing the authorisation she had to obtain from various offices before being allowed to leave the country

green hat standing, day after day, outside her apartment. It is chilling to think how close she may have been to arrest. When she finally left Vienna on 27 August 1938, she remembers her mother and grandmother waving goodbye on the platform, the last time she was to see them.

She managed to take a number of family mementoes with her, including photographs and documents, and also two crystal bowls and a set of leather-bound books by Goethe. She sold the books on her arrival, in order to obtain cash for her survival, but I still have the bowls, which I treasure, together with the third bowl given to my mother by Helga.

During her journey of escape, she wore a wedding ring, also as a means of carrying money with her. As the train passed through Germany, a woman on the train noticed the ring and started to ask her questions about her "husband". My mother had to invent a story on the spot, clearly a very scary moment. In subsequent years, she sometimes said that she thought, throughout this period, that she had been protected by a guardian angel.

I learned in the late 1990s that after her arrival in England, my mother corresponded at length with her sister Sonja, but sadly never kept the letters. She was also convinced that, after the war, she had received a letter from the Red Cross, stating that her mother and sister had been transported to Theresienstadt, but that their fate was unknown. Again, she did not keep the letter.

Theresienstadt, or Terezín, was a concentration camp in the present Czech Republic, which was used as a Nazi propaganda tool to promote the myth that Jews were treated well. In reality, it was a transit camp from which Jews were deported to death camps, often Auschwitz. In June 1944 the Germans permitted the International Red Cross to visit, but this was an elaborate deception. Deportations from the camp took place shortly before the visit, and the ghetto itself was made to look beautiful. Social and cultural events were staged for the visiting dignitaries, but once they left, the Germans resumed deportations.

My mother divulged the information about the letter she had received, after agreeing to watch a television programme with me about Theresienstadt, some time after her first revelations to me. She sat through it in silence and without any apparent emotion, for she must have been holding on very tightly to her feelings, for fear of them spilling over uncontrollably.

When the programme had finished, she said in a small quiet voice: "*My mother and sister went to Theresienstadt.*" She had never told me this before.

Later I received documentation from the International Red Cross, shown in Chapter Nine, informing me that Sonja, Berta and Josef had been taken to Drancy on the outskirts of Paris, and from there directly to Auschwitz. Given my mother's very clear recollection, I wonder if it is possible that they went to Theresienstadt first before their final journey to the extermination camp.

I also learned in 2011 that throughout the war years, my mother (referred to in the correspondence as "*die Jüdin*", the Jewess) was being hunted down by the Gestapo in Vienna and Berlin, as they wished to deprive her of her inheritance from her father, following his death. Finally, it was declared in 1944 that my mother's inheritance had become the sole property of the German Reich (" ... *das Vermögen obgenannten Person dem Reich verfallen ist*").

This document was one of the 3,000 pages of Nazi documents, discussed earlier, which I received at the same time, giving details of how various family members had fared under the Nazi regime. They were chilling in the extreme. At last, I understood the shadow of the Holocaust which had hung over my mother as she arrived in England in early September 1938, and for the rest of her life.

Chapter Eleven

MY MOTHER'S LIFE IN ENGLAND: LIVES ENTWINED

The shadow cast by my mother's horrendous experiences was but one part of her story. I came also to recognise and admire her enormous courage in dealing with her many difficulties and, despite them, in making a meaningful life for herself in the country in which she had sought refuge.

EARLY DAYS

My mother initially worked as an *au pair* with a family just outside Nottingham. An Englishman had helped her, and other young women in her situation, to find a post in this country. At one point he tried to abuse my mother's vulnerability by pressing his attentions on her, but fortunately she was strong enough to resist. How sad that a man who performed such brave and commendable actions in rescuing the victims of persecution was to sully these by some of his subsequent behaviour.

She was initially regarded as an "Enemy Alien" and had to report to a police station every fortnight, and appear before a tribunal. On 30 October 1939, she was declared "exempted from internment" as she was a:

> Genuine refugee from Nazi oppression. Father dead. Mother and sister in Paris. No relatives in Germany. Has no sympathy with Nazis and no desire to return to Germany. No danger to this Country.

Jewish women refugees at that time had only two alternatives for employment: domestic work or nursing. In 1939, after a brief stint in domestic work, my mother started to train as a nurse at Peel Street Hospital for Women in Nottingham and within a short time was top of her class, despite not speaking English at the beginning of her course, assisted by the knowledge she had gained on her medical studies in Vienna.

Nottingham Hospital for Women

This is to Certify
that
LUCY EDITH SMETANA
has completed a Two years' course of training in
the nursing of Surgical Conditions peculiar to Women
During this period she has received instruction
in Elementary Anatomy, Physiology, Hygiene, Nursing
and has passed the requisite Examinations in these subjects
Her work has been Good and her Conduct Good
Signed this 12th day of September 1941

Chairman of Committee
Senior Surgeon
Matron

My mother's first nursing certificate

She threw herself whole-heartedly into her new life. During the war years, she worked first at Harlow Wood Orthopaedic Hospital near Mansfield, then as a district midwife in a poverty-stricken area, delivering babies in homes without running water. This gave her insights into an aspect of life she had never before encountered. Following a house move, she transferred in 1952 to the Children's Hospital in Nottingham, where she remained for many years, and became a well-known and respected figure.

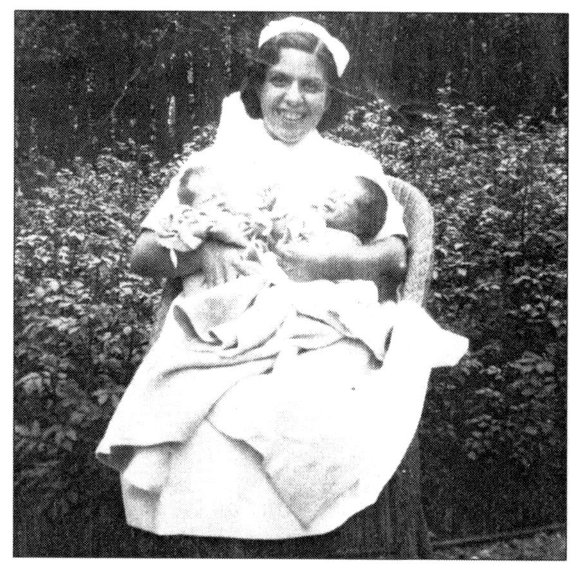

My mother as a midwife, mid–1940s

In 2003, I contacted my godmother, Liesel Tilles née Holzapfel, a German Jewish refugee who trained as a nurse with my mother during the war years, and subsequently emigrated to America. She sent me a copy of her own life story, which contained this fitting, and for me very poignant, description of my mother:

Matron had mentioned that there was another refugee student nurse, and before long she barged into my room. Lucy was always a barger, always lively, with a brilliant mind full of ideas. When she was happy, she was ecstatic, when she was sad, she was very, very sad. Lucy was short and a little on the chubby side with short black hair and pretty dark brown eyes. She came from Vienna and had been at the hospital for several months already. She spoke German with a musical, lilting accent. Our friendship was instantaneous: we became each other's family.

My mother's ability, so aptly described here, to experience not only extreme sadness, for evident reasons, but also extreme joy, was something we all learned to appreciate in her.

Throughout this period, she maintained contact with other young women of her background. There was an older woman who organised regular Sabbath evening meals for the group, and my mother derived great enjoyment from these meetings.

She also attended the International Friendship League (IFL), along with other Jewish refugees, and this was where she met my father. He was six years her junior, a very sensitive, artistic, intelligent and handsome young man, but from a working-class background and with little formal education. He had passed his school entrance exams, but his parents had insisted that he leave school at 14, as they wanted him to earn a living.

At the age of 16, he had taught himself to speak German fluently and went to the IFL to practise it. Only recently, I learned from his diaries that the reason he wanted to learn German was so that he could read the works of German philosophers in their original language. He also spent his early teens in London visiting museums and art galleries and sketching paintings and statues. He was clearly a talented young man.

My father, John Fowler, in RAF uniform, 1946, shortly after my birth

My mother was not concerned by the fact that he was not Jewish, nor that he was from a different social background. Indeed, she told herself that a Jewish man would want to control her and demand too much of her. This very vulnerable young woman was emotionally attracted by the excessive devotion that this young Englishman displayed towards her. She yearned for the love she had never had during her childhood. On one occasion he lay in the snow outside her nurse hostel, refusing to leave until she came out, an action which must have seemed romantic at the time.

Tragically, it did not take her long after her marriage in 1944 to realise that his behaviour towards her was pathological and that, in fact, he was seriously mentally ill, and quite incapable of sustaining a stable emotional relationship. At one stage, he became self-conscious of the fact that she was six years older than him and refused to be seen in public with her. She was once more thrust back into loneliness and isolation. In spite of this, she remained loyal to him for many years.

My father, born in 1925, was only 14 years old at the beginning of the war, and married with a child on the way by the end. He was, therefore, too young to fight during the war, and instead worked down the mines as a pit boy. Shortly after their marriage, my parents moved into a two-bedroom terraced mining house in Mansfield, with coal fires, an outside toilet, and a tin bath which we used in the kitchen. Now my mother was never a snob, and certainly did not feel any entitlement to wealth, but this must have been something of a culture shock to someone whose childhood had been spent in large houses with chandeliers and central heating, not to mention paintings by well-known artists.

I learned recently, while looking at his diaries, that my father attempted suicide just after my birth in October 1945. It was rather galling to know that my birth had not been sufficient reason for him to want to live.

This was a double rejection. While my mother was still alive, we were looking together, one day, at some old Fowler family photos, which included my father's parents and sisters, as well as me as a baby. My mother told me that while the photos were being taken, my grandfather commented, *"There is someone here who is not welcome."* I assumed he was referring to her, but learned, to my horror, that it was in fact me he was speaking of. I had known something of my grandfather's anti-Semitism but was shocked to hear that, because of his prejudice, he had even rejected his own grandchild.

In early 1946, my father was sent on national service to Egypt for two years and also visited Cyprus while on leave. I discovered, again very recently while sorting out his photos, that he also visited Palestine, and while there, made a trip to Jerusalem. This period of his life was to leave a profound impression upon him, though he never ventured abroad again.

My father, John Fowler, on the left with two friends at their post in Egypt, 1946

My mother told me that after my birth, and during my father's absence, she experienced the most peaceful period of her life. She felt that, for the first time, she was able to establish an intimate relationship with another human being. I have often wondered what secrets this tortured young woman whispered to her little companion as she cradled her in her arms. What language did she speak to me? And what did she tell me of her innermost soul?

I am convinced that, whatever words she used or even without words at all, she must have communicated to me the depths of her emotions. This could explain why I feel so much more compelled to delve into these matters than my two younger brothers, Peter and Stephen, born in 1948 and 1950, though they both, also, had a very close relationship with our mother.

My mother and I, shortly after my birth in 1945

When he returned from his national service, she arranged for my father to enrol on a teacher training course, a one-year emergency training scheme introduced by the post-war government. Like her grandmother before her, she encouraged her husband to better himself. And so he went into the teaching profession. Now a professional, he remained fiercely loyal to his working-class roots and continued to regard himself as working-class throughout his life, a belief he drummed into me, though clearly, my situation is rather more complex than that.

AN UNUSUAL FAMILY LIFE

There were many disruptions to our family life, so my childhood years were mixed. My school experience was positive: I was bright, sociable and academically successful, and this somehow shielded me from the tensions I experienced at home. My lives at home and at school were totally separate, almost as if I were two different people. My mother always did her very best for the three of us, particularly in the way she encouraged our education, but she had inevitably been affected by her experiences and seemed almost always on the point of explosion.

Now, she had a new problem to deal with: her sick husband. My father suffered from a condition which at that time was called obsessive compulsive disorder. He was highly obsessive, emotionally incapable of relating to others, and as a result had no understanding of what it was to be a husband and father. These things were entirely beyond his control, and at his best he could be a very pleasant person, a point I need to emphasise. Although I have tried to present my father in an honest way, I have no wish to humiliate him, or to stain his memory. He was, in my view, a gifted person, who was unable, tragically, to fulfil his considerable potential.

In 1952, he underwent a pre-frontal leucotomy, a brain operation (now called lobotomy), in an attempt to change his obsessive behaviour. I clearly remember visiting him in hospital. It was a shock for a seven-year old to see her father with a shaven, scarred and bandaged head.

I continued to live my dual life, and now have only the vaguest memory of that early period. Perhaps I have learnt, like my mother, to blot out what is painful.

I remember my father saying in his quiet English voice, *"Lucy, will you stop shouting,"* and my mother shrieking back at him, in a very loud voice, *"I am not shouting."*

I remember my father forcing me to stand naked for an entire day, when I was six years old, while he sketched me, totally oblivious to my humiliation and shame.

I remember the long nights when my mother's repressed fears and anxieties would come to the surface and she would lie on the stairs, moaning over and over again that she was dying. I lay frozen in my bed, listening to her conversation with my father. This was the only time he ever genuinely attempted to care for her. She would say, *"I need a cup of tea,"* and he would dutifully go and get her one, only to be greeted with, *"no, no. Get me some water."* The poor man was totally bewildered, but clearly my mother was beside herself and had ceased, temporarily, to function normally.

The next day, she would carry on as usual as if nothing had happened, with the entire burden of running home and family, as well as working in the busy casualty department of the Children's Hospital in Nottingham.

I remember having recurrent nightmares of my own, when I would dream I was being pursued by some unspeakable horror. Just as it was about to engulf me, I would force myself, with every ounce of physical and mental energy, to rise above it and fly away. Was I being pursued by the spectre of the Holocaust, which I had somehow come to know in my infancy? Like my mother, I have spent a lifetime deploying such efforts to force myself over any obstacle that has come my way, but at what emotional cost?

My mother went to enormous lengths, against the odds, to create a warm and caring home. I remember her repeated attempts to establish a normal family life and routine. She insisted on a Sunday family lunch but could never get my father to clear the table of the work with which he was currently obsessed. She tried to establish a pattern of family holidays, but my father always opted out, saying he preferred his maths books, which he always took away on holiday with him.

Despite this, I have some wonderful memories of summer holidays organised by Erna Lowe in Cornwall. Erna Lowe, also a Viennese Jew, was an innovative tour operator who invented the concept of "house party". She rented St Clare's School in Penzance, a private boarding school, to use as a base for one of her famous house parties which we attended. Later, we also went on holidays organised by the Humanist Association, with which my mother was actively involved at the time. For many years, she was Secretary of the Nottingham Humanist Association.

Fowler family album1940s/1950s

My parents, Lucy and John Fowler, myself, and my two brothers Peter and Stephen in the early 1960s at our home in Redhill, Nottingham, where we lived from 1952

There were moments when my mother experienced intense gloom. At such times, she would sometimes make the most unfathomable comments. I remember that, at the beginning of spring, when the clocks had just been put forward, she would say, *"Oh dear, it's soon going to be dark, the days will start drawing in."* I would laughingly respond: *"But Mum, it's the beginning of spring, not the beginning of winter!"* I was amused by her eccentricity, by what seemed to be an unreasonable pessimism, until one day I suddenly realised that the coming of spring, the advent of hope and joy, had forever been marred for her on that day in March 1938 when Hitler had entered Vienna triumphant. I do not think she ever consciously made that connection, that association, but I am convinced that it existed in the deepest recesses of her mind.

When I visited Vienna in 2006, I decided to go to Heldenplatz, the plaza where Hitler had been ecstatically received by over 200,000 people. I climbed onto the plinth of a statue in front of the balcony of the Hofburg Palace, from where Hitler had addressed them, and turned to face in the direction he had faced. There was a vast open space, which on that day had been packed with the adoring, cheering crowds. I gained a very strong sensation of the power and invincibility he must have felt, of the belief in his destiny to rule over these people, and to do with them what he wished.

On that day when Hitler seized power and control in Austria, he took away power and control from those, like my mother, who became his victims. There were many times in my mother's life when I believe she became quite overwhelmed by that sense of powerlessness, of worthlessness, and she spent her whole life striving to overcome this.

She expressed this sense of worthlessness in a letter she sent to my brother, Peter, in 1968, and which I saw for the first time when I was putting the finishing touches to this book. Earlier that year, she had returned to Vienna with her friend, Annie, for the first time since her departure in 1938. She found the trip hugely distressing because of the memories it triggered.

On her return to England, she developed a painful skin condition for which her doctor was unable to find a cause, so could not offer treatment. I was away at university at the time and Peter spent many hours taking wonderful care of her. She felt the need, therefore, to share her thoughts with him.

This letter shows that, even in her darkest moments, she managed to find the strength to struggle through towards the light. She never allowed what had happened to her to strip life of meaning and purpose. And perhaps because of this, my brothers and I were brought up by a woman who had a highly developed sense

To my son, Peter.

THE RETURN

L. E. Fowler

I am ill. I am in bed. Getting up, going to work, visiting friends, - all these activities are in the past. Life has become restricted, expectations narrow and more limited. The past has become shadowy; there is no future; only the present. Life is this minute, may be the next, but there the horizon falls.

How to sit up, on which side to lie, how to tolerate the pain, how not to be submerged by a flight of terrifying ideas and emotions - these are the problems which press upon me.

There are the friends who endeavour to help, there are the ones who stay away.

In the end one is alone, - in isolation. There is the pain, there is the fear, there is the struggle, the despair and the resignation. The clouds gather round, ever denser, ever bleaker and blaker. But still the rays of hope are flickering, they persist in shining through, though more and more rarely.

There is fear of the night, fear of death, fear of the unkown and fear of fear.

There are moments of regret, of anguish over past deeds, that one would like to forget.

The struggle goes on. Then as my strength leaves me there is a moment of terror - a realisation that the fight cannot go on. An endless weariness invades me, - I am tired, Iam resigned; - I am at peace. The unavoidable has to be faced.

I try to review my life in a flash. Were there even a few isolated instances that have made my life worth while to others? Have I made any kind of imprint for the good? May be one only kidds oneself in thinking there were, after all a few of these instances.

And just as one has resigned oneself, given up, - rays of hope attempt to stir up this uneasy peace. No, one is not going to let go of the threads of life.

I am going to live. I can take up the struggle again. I want to return. But from where do I want to return? And whereto do I want to go?

Part of a letter written by my mother to my brother, Peter, in 1968

of values, no doubt shaped by her experiences. She taught us to value education, travel, freedom and tolerance, and encouraged us to recognise and respect other cultures and ways of life. Internationalism was a dominant theme in our lives and my brothers and I all travelled abroad alone from our mid-teens.

And despite the obvious traumas and difficulties, there were many moments of joy and even of sheer hilarity. My mother was a larger than life character, who when not weighed down by her past, was full of energy and exuberance, and incredibly dynamic.

My younger brother, Steve, had a more relaxed upbringing than I did, as by then she had managed to suppress some of her anxieties. During the 1960s Steve became something of a hippie and, like many others of his generation, dabbled in drugs. There were frequent animated discussions about the merits of drug-taking, when my mother would argue heatedly that the drugs Steve was taking were addictive. His reply was always that his drugs were no different from hers. She took Sodium Amytal at the time, a now discontinued medication, which she took to calm her down and help her sleep. On one occasion, she yelled back at him, "*I've been taking Sodium Amytal for 20 years, and I'm not addicted!*" We all fell about laughing, but she could not see the funny side.

On one memorable occasion, Steve persuaded our mother to take a small amount of hash in her tea, as smoking it would have been out of the question. She then had a wonderful day, so asked Steve to leave her a little before going back to university. He left some hash in a piece of silver paper, which became misplaced, and I remember my mother wandering around asking, "*Where's my hash?*" I hasten to add that she did not make this kind of drug-taking a habit, though it is true to say that she depended on medication for the remainder of her life.

Throughout this entire period, my mother continued to demonstrate an extraordinary capacity for rising above her difficulties, and for gaining the most from life. Towards the end of my childhood, when we started to leave home, she decided to recapture the education of which she had been deprived. From the age of 40, she spent 10 years diligently studying sociology part-time. At one point, when she was enrolling on yet another course, the lecturer said to her, "*Mrs Fowler, I don't think there is any more we can teach you!*"

Eventually, at the age of 50, she became a social worker and spent the last 15 years of her working life putting tremendous energy into helping others. She worked with total commitment and dedication and was dearly loved by her patients and clients. She always regretted having to retire at 65, as for her, her life only had meaning when she was busy, and giving to others. Furthermore, staying active helped to keep at bay unwelcome thoughts of the past, and she dreaded having too much time on her hands when those thoughts might once again resurface.

When she became a social worker, my mother needed to learn to drive. She spent two and a half years, starting at the age of 50, having lessons twice weekly and went through 17 driving instructors. She became legendary at the driving school. As it happened, her 17th instructor was my first and only instructor. He told me that everyone called her "*Vi*". When I asked why, he said, *"Because she is always asking 'Vi? Vi must I do zis? Vi must I do zat?'"*

She eventually passed her driving test on her third attempt, to everyone's relief. She had already bought her first car, a little Morris Minor, but had great difficulty adjusting the seating, because of her short legs. We tried putting a piece of wood under the back of the seat, but this caused the seat to tip forward in such a way that her large bosom was then pressed against the steering wheel. This caused great hilarity. Steve remembers having a deal with her to take her out before she passed her test, in return for using the Morris Minor, but threatened to wear a crash helmet if she was driving!

Her driving remained erratic. A friend remembered being driven through Sherwood by her, and a woman on the pavement leaping out of the way. My mother and her friend Vera both took a Valium before they went out for a drive together to calm them down. On one occasion, my mother, by then in her late 60s (Vera was nine years older as she always liked to tell her), drove into a wall which turned out to be a police station. Happily, they were not badly injured, but the police station was in uproar for the next few hours, as was the hospital they were taken to. The two elderly ladies insisted on comparing and showing off the injuries to their chests to everyone in sight, each declaring, *"My bruises are bigger than yours!"*

A similar incident occurred in France, which my mother decided to hitch-hike around at the age of 60. She arrived at a hotel in a small town in the mountains, only to discover that some of her clothes were missing. Again, she caused havoc at the local police station for several days. On her way back, she arrived late at night in Paris, exhausted and with no money. She went into an expensive hotel and asked if she could sleep in the foyer. She was ejected from the hotel, accused of being "*une femme de la rue*", a street woman! On her return home, she discovered that she had never, in fact, packed the missing clothes.

Another incident which illustrates the character we knew and loved was when, shortly after her retirement, she realised there were very few seats at the Victoria Shopping Centre in Nottingham. She demanded to see the manager, dragged him out of a meeting, and took him around the centre to show him where seating was needed for the elderly. Within a short while, the Victoria Centre became equipped with more benches.

Her doctor, a much younger man than her, asked her one day whether he could call her by her first name, Lucy. Always one to speak her mind, she asked him if she could also call him by his first name. When he said that this would not be possible, she declared: *"In that case, Dr Sparrow, you will call me Mrs Fowler."*

My mother had always had a cyclical personality, which developed into manic depression (now called bipolar disorder) when she was 60. In her high or manic phases, she was, well, manic. She would race around excitedly, throwing huge energy and enthusiasm into everything she did, and in the process, sometimes brushing people up the wrong way. She was ejected from numerous banks and restaurants because of her wild behaviour, though the people she crossed always spoke of her with great affection.

She was an enormously energetic grandmother, and her grandchildren adored her. My daughter, Lara, described her Nana as full of colour and character, though there were moments when, as a teenager trying to look "cool and trendy", she became somewhat embarrassed by her grandmother's eccentric ways. Lara remembers one occasion when her Nana took her to see a concert. At the theatre, Lara saw one of her old primary school teachers, and mentioned this to her Nana, who immediately demanded to know where the teacher was. Lara replied that she was not telling her! Nana then proceeded to jump up and down, waving her arms and shouting excitedly, *"Mrs Kennedy! Mrs Kennedy!"*

My daughters Bambo and Lara with their grandmother on Lara's 18th birthday

Friends and colleagues, too, thought very highly of her. My oldest school friend, Shirley, recalled with amusement her first meeting with my mother:

> *"The first time I met your Mum, I was about 11 and didn't know she was*

your Mum. It was at the Children's Hospital. The doctor was foreign and spoke with a heavy accent and your Mum was making sure I understood what he said. I didn't dare admit that I didn't understand what she said either!"

After my mother died, Shirley wrote to me:

"Your mum couldn't be ignored, but people loved her, partly because she made them feel special. I don't know why, but she did. She was the sort of person who made quite an impression on people. She was and always will be someone rather special."

A younger colleague of my mother's wrote to me:

"I will always remember Lucy, with great fondness. She was a tremendous support to me. I recall having lengthy in-depth discussions with her in a way which simply was not possible with many of my contemporaries. Susan, I salute your mother for her character and fortitude, her intellect, her joy in life despite periods of bleak depression."

A RETURN TO ROOTS

I remember that one day, when I was about 10, my father asked me to go to the library to fetch a book by Bertrand Russell, a particular hero of his, called *Why I am not a Christian*. My father's family were Catholic, but he had become an atheist and enjoyed examining religious subjects from an intellectual perspective. On the two-mile walk home from the library, the book weighed heavily in my hand. Everyone I met asked what book I was carrying and I sensed their horror when I told them. In those days in provincial England, not being a Christian was unthinkable and if you were not, you did not advertise it.

I did not in fact have any religious upbringing, though inevitably, I encountered Christian teaching at school. I believe I was a naturally spiritual child, and these spiritual leanings led me to join the local chapel of my own volition at about the age of eight, and I remember singing solo at a public event.

I have always been vaguely aware of my Jewish background, or at least I thought I had until my mother told me that she never mentioned it to me for several years. One day, when I was about 10, a Jewish family friend (one of the very few Jews I knew as a child) said to me in front of a family gathering, *"Well, of course, Susan, you are Jewish, because your mother is Jewish."* Apparently, I ran out of the room shouting, *"I am not Jewish,"* but I have no recollection of this.

I must have come to terms with it very quickly, as I do remember at the age of 11, a student teacher talking to the class about the New Testament and explaining the difference between Jews and Gentiles. *"Of course, all of us here are Gentiles,"* she declared. I proudly put up my hand and said, *"Please Miss, I am not a Gentile."* I was puzzled by her cold, almost hostile reaction. My first taste, perhaps, of anti-Semitism.

My mother's own experience of Judaism had been fairly loose. As a child, she had attended synagogue for the major festivals and received Jewish instruction, along with the other Jewish children at school. She remembered the children in the class behaving badly during these sessions, as the teacher was unable to control them.

In marrying our father, she appeared to turn her back on her religion of origin, though in her later years, Jewish artefacts appeared in her home and she started corresponding with Jewish friends and acquaintances to try to re-educate herself. There is no question in my mind that she set out on a spiritual search, and she told me at one stage that she always knew that in her old age she would return to Judaism. In fact, I believe that she had never quite forgotten her Jewish roots.

One day, in 1977, she went to a London venue to watch a performance of *The Diary of Anne Frank*. She was so moved by this experience that at the end of the

28.11.77

Moved to thank cast of play

A JEWISH REFUGEE from Hitler's Europe surprised everyone when she stepped on to the stage at All Saints' Church, Queensbury, on Saturday evening, after seeing an amateur production of "The Diary of Anne Frank," to thank the cast and producer.

The anonymous woman had come to London from Nottingham especially to see the play, which she had heard about from the daughter of a member of the cast, Mr. Len Webber.

The Minister, the Rev. L. D. Mackenzie, said: "At first the audience responded with stunned silence, not critical silence. People did not know whether they should clap, but they did.

"She was a social worker, I think, and she spoke about her family who had perished in concentration camps. She had gone around to the back of the stage and asked the producer if she could say a word to the audience."

The minister said that after thanking the cast individually off stage the woman "Seemed to vanish" but she had expressed everyone's appreciation.

performance, she climbed on to the stage and, to everyone's astonishment, spoke of her family who had perished, and said how much the play had meant to her as a Jewish woman. She thanked the cast and left the stage. Reporters tried to pursue her, but by then she had gone.

The next day, the national press printed the story of this "unknown Jewish woman". When I learned of this in later years, what surprised me most was that she had been able to say to strangers what she was never able to say to her own family.

My mother had a favourite poem, written by Leonard Nimoy, which she shared with many people. The poem encapsulates much about her:

What mark will I leave behind?
How will anyone ever know that I have been here?
What sign will tell the future traveller that I existed?
Shall I carve it on a door?
"I am here! Today ... I exist."

I believe the deepest impression is made
In those moments when I can say

I care

I love

Lucy Fowler was an extraordinary and very special woman. I could use many adjectives to describe her, none of which do her justice, but here are a few: she was strong, intelligent, dynamic, passionate, enthusiastic, energetic, often over-energetic. She was also deeply caring, abhorred violence and deplored social injustice. She was never afraid to make her views known, or to take action to rectify a wrong. In her later years, she sadly declined and lost much of her physical and mental energy, much to her frustration, yet those who knew her only in those years saw her as a dear sweet lovely person. The years seemed to have mellowed her and her true inner beauty shone through.

Chapter Twelve

A LIFE OF MY OWN?

"The past is a presence between us. In all my mother does and says, the past continually discloses itself in the smallest ways. She sees it directly; I see its shadow. Still, it pulses in my fingertips, feeds on my consciousness. It is a backdrop for each act, each drama of our lives. I have absorbed a sense of what she has suffered, what she has lost, even what her mother endured and handed down. It is my emotional gene map." *Fern Schumer Chapman, Motherland: Beyond the Holocaust: A Mother-Daughter Journey to Reclaim the Past*

What was the impact on three children of growing up in such an apparently dysfunctional family, where psychiatrists and mental hospitals loomed large? There was clearly an assumption on the part of professionals working with my parents that we would inevitably be affected. I remember a psychiatrist saying to me at some point in my life that it had always been considered a miracle that three such normal children should emerge from such an abnormal background.

Perhaps the reason for that was that we had such an extraordinary mother, who in her own unique way, and despite her horrendous experiences, had managed to create a loving, albeit unusual family, and set us a wonderful example.

Certainly on the surface, I appeared to emerge unscathed, and my brothers have both built rewarding lives for themselves. I was successful at school, becoming head girl (though the headmaster said this was a calculated risk!), and gaining five GCE A levels. I went on to study Psychology and French at Keele University in 1964. Given my experiences, I had always been fascinated by the study of the mind and languages came easily to me. I found French a convenient form of escape: slipping into another language was rather like taking on a new identity.

I felt less at ease with German, which I had studied to GCE O level, because I had already understood as a teenager the connotations of this language for a person of my background. Perhaps, also, I was aware from my childhood that one way of coping with emotional and family difficulties is to focus on those areas of your life where success comes more easily, and where there is more control. I therefore concentrated on my education and the relationships that arose out of that, and left unresolved my family traumas. Besides, beyond my home a very different world beckoned. I was swept along by the optimism of the sixties, a carefree, cheerful, joyous decade, when looking back or looking inwards seemed irrelevant.

Throughout my secondary school and university period, I had no difficulty with social relationships, and yet always had a sense of being different, apart. I knew I was not like my English peers, that I did not share the same experiences, partly because of my unorthodox family relationships, but also for more simple reasons.

I remember, for example, queuing with my mother at the delicatessen in Nottingham to buy camembert, yoghurt, pickled herrings and salami, even brains, foods which were largely unheard of in the area where I lived at that time. No doubt, this would have been a different matter for people living in London or other cities, where refugees had gathered to re-establish their lives. I cannot say that I disliked being different, in fact, I rather enjoyed it. I never experienced the desire, so prevalent among teenagers, of wanting to be like my friends.

While at university, I spent a year at Bordeaux in France, and there I got involved with a circle of French-speaking African students. I was drawn by their warmth and vivacity, which struck a chord in me, and by the way they seemed at ease with themselves. I almost married a Togolese student of medicine. When I graduated in 1969, I decided to go to Africa, partly because of my experience in France, but also I feel, because of the need to escape the tensions at home. To feel free to be myself. Perhaps within me was a certain Jewish restlessness, for I have never truly felt my roots to be in this country. At that stage, I was young and adventurous, and also to some extent impulsive and irresponsible.

I taught initially at a teacher training college in Akrokeri, Ghana. My students were mainly older than myself and I gained from them some fascinating insights into African life, especially when supervising teaching practice in small and remote village schools. During the holidays, I visited Togo and there met my husband, Kayode, who came from a highly distinguished and educated Nigerian family. Many of his relatives, including some of his siblings, had achieved prominence, in particular his brother Wole, who later won the Nobel Prize for Literature, the first black African to do so. He was awarded this honour in 1986, the same year that Elie Wiesel, author and Auschwitz survivor, received the Nobel Peace Prize.

Kayode, however, was also very talented, but rebelled against his parents, opted out of formal education and pursued instead a variety of interests in the world of the arts, which took him to many parts of the world. He was an enormously attractive young man, with huge charisma and a unique capacity to draw people to him. Wherever I went with him, he was loudly and cheerfully greeted by friends and acquaintances.

Kayode and myself in Nigeria in 1970, about six months after we first met

During 1973, we worked together on the *Changing African Family Project*, conducted by Professor Jack Caldwell of the Australian National University. As part of the project, Kayode travelled with Jack and his team around Nigeria, visiting hundreds of towns and villages. I remember Jack telling me that wherever they went, in whatever part of that large country, someone knew Kayode. And it seemed many people knew him even beyond Nigerian borders. The first time he came to England with me, he was hailed on the street in both London and Nottingham.

Kayode made me feel very special. But sadly, and in spite of his many gifts and qualities, he was also, at that time, irresponsible, and spent little time with me. In later years, I came to recognise some similarities between my mother's marriage and my own. We had both been drawn to talented men from very different backgrounds and cultures to our own, who ultimately, in their different ways, absented themselves from the marriage.

By the time I had my first child, Lara, in 1971, I realised that I was going to have to fend for myself. Kayode came and went as he pleased, and I learnt to cope with this, even learnt to value the independence it afforded me. Perhaps in retrospect, I can see that my childhood had not prepared me for a close and intimate emotional relationship, and the rather unconventional arrangement I had with Kayode gave me the emotional space I needed. In any event, there were many aspects of my life in Nigeria that I enjoyed, and I was beginning to feel at home, even to feel "African".

My brother Peter and husband Kayode, shortly after Lara's birth in 1971

I took on my step-daughter Egbin, had a second daughter, Bambo, in 1975, and went to teach French in the University of Ilorin, Nigeria, where I was also student warden. One of my students fell pregnant, and I invited her to come and live in my house on the university campus, as she was no longer allowed to live in student accommodation. She was joined not just by her newborn baby, but also by her mother. Other students wandered in and out of my house, and I developed a definite sense of belonging. This may have been in part due to Kayode's family connections, but I always felt accepted for myself. In Africa, so it seemed to me, there was a much greater tolerance of difference than in my part of England, where to be different in any way, at that period, was not acceptable.

However, there were problems also. Kayode's easy come, easy go attitude became increasingly difficult to accept as the economic, social and political circumstances in Nigeria started to deteriorate. His prolonged absences left me feeling insecure and unsupported. In 1977, Lara contracted tuberculosis, and the following year, Bambo developed trachoma, an illness which almost made her blind.

Although they recovered, I was no longer able to tolerate these conditions, especially following student riots, when tear gas was deployed. Since I lived very close to the university gates, I could not prevent the gas from entering my house and affecting my children. I decided to come "home" in 1979. However, I returned to the country of my birth only to discover that both the country and I had changed to such a degree that I felt like a foreigner.

Perhaps I had always been a foreigner. I remember distinctly feeling as though I were outside a goldfish bowl, looking in. I also felt trapped inside my little house, where doors and windows were kept firmly shut, and where, for a long period, visitors were few and far between, in stark contrast to my experience in Nigeria. I suffered from huge culture shock and remained traumatised for many years, as I tried to re-establish myself at a personal, social and professional level.

To add to my difficulties, I was once again confronted directly with the problems of my parents, which had reached a critical point just a short time prior to my return. My father had become so sick mentally and physically (he suffered a stroke in the mid-seventies) that the situation had become intolerable for my mother. He would make demands of her, and if she would not comply, he threatened to commit suicide, saying that she would then carry the guilt for the rest of her life.

This was the most horrendous emotional blackmail, most especially in the light of the guilt she already felt, quite unjustifiably, for her own father's suicide. The emotional burden now became too great for her.

During one of my visits from Nigeria in 1975, he was threatening towards me when I was pregnant with Bambo. For my mother, this was the last straw. She finally walked out on him after 31 years of marriage. But she did not escape the feeling of guilt. For ever afterwards, she felt responsible for abandoning a sick man. Not long after this, she developed manic depression at the age of almost 60. Having coped magnificently for years, her spirit had eventually broken.

I have always seen this illness as a reaction to her traumatic life. Both the mania and the depression were a form of escape, a way of refusing to confront the reality of the pain of her existence. Remarkably, the doctors made no such connection and managed to convince her that this was a genetic condition which required medical treatment. She remained on lithium for the rest of her life. Never was there any attempt to help her work through her traumas. Even then, she used her experiences to help others, becoming for many years secretary of the Nottingham Manic Depressive Society, so that she could assist fellow sufferers.

For my own part, I eventually met an Englishman, Andy Trembath, by whom I had a son, Alex, in 1983. At the time Alex was born, I was still married to Kayode, whom I had not seen for several years, and who refused to allow a divorce. I therefore had to wait five years to obtain one. I am not proud of this, but at the time, it seemed the only way of making a new life for myself.

But even as I married Andy, my mother's words from years previously echoed in my ears. *"Susan, never marry an Englishman."* The marriage was doomed from the outset. I could not rid myself of my love for Kayode and yearned for him daily. Andy was everything a "proper" husband and father should be, and his family were most welcoming. But somehow, I could never feel a part of this solid English family. I knew that I had had so many experiences that placed me outside their world. Again there was that sense of being a foreigner. I must have married Andy for security, and when I got it, I could not cope with it. Why? Because I had spent a lifetime coping with crises, and I did not know how to relate to normality.

During my marriage to Andy, I was also having difficulty adjusting to my professional situation. I had returned to secondary school teaching, but had found that my lengthy experience in Africa was not considered to be relevant or worthwhile. If I had gone to Africa, married a black man, and taught Africans, it must have been because I could do no better for myself!

I remember one head teacher ignoring my experience as a university lecturer and researcher, and telling me that I was *"just a little girl"* (I was 35 at the time!). I desperately wanted to do something which drew more fully on my experiences. Eventually in 1986, I retrained as an educational psychologist, an occupation I found immensely satisfying. Once again, I followed in my mother's footsteps, retraining and changing professional direction in my forties.

Shortly after I started this course, my father died. A few days later, I heard a lecture on Able Autism, more commonly called Asperger's Syndrome. It described my father exactly. Finally, I came to understand him, but too late to offer help. This caused me huge and unexpected grief.

Also during the mid-eighties, I returned to the spiritual quest of my childhood. I had, in fact, dabbled a little during the seventies in Nigeria when I became acquainted with a number of American missionaries. I was drawn by a need to believe in God and in some sense of purpose and process in life, but was appalled by some of the missionary activities. I remember a conversation with a 19-year-old Canadian missionary. I asked her what she hoped to achieve, and she said she was going into the bush to teach African women to bake bread. *"But do you really think that Nigerian women don't know how to cook?"* I asked, astounded by the assumption of superiority.

Anyway, back in England, I started to attend a black Pentecostal church. The music and enthusiasm were infectious, and it took a while to recognise that while I was attracted by the outward form, I very much disliked the content. I found it difficult to relate to the constant talk of hell and was puzzled by the idolisation of Jesus, which seemed to put him above God. I could not understand the need for an intermediary between God and man.

In late 1990, Kayode suddenly reappeared in my life, ostensibly to see his children whom he had not seen for more than 10 years. We immediately fell in love again, and I felt that this time our relationship could be more successful, as he had in the meantime become a devout Christian and seemed in every way more responsible than in his youth. We remarried in early 1992, and for a couple of years, things went extremely well.

However, as time passed, our religious differences became more apparent. Kayode became increasingly fanatical and evangelical, or so it seemed to me, and I realised this was something to which I could not relate. My own venture into Christianity was largely centred on a search for God, and I felt strongly that this was something everyone had to do in their own way. I was very worried by Kayode's apparent intolerance of other faiths. For me, there could be no prescriptive path to God. I stopped attending church, but carried on thinking about spiritual issues, wondering which path I could follow that would be meaningful to me.

After my visit to the synagogue in January 1995, it suddenly dawned on me with great clarity that the reason I had lost my way spiritually was because I had started halfway down the path. I needed to go back to the beginning of the path, to my own Jewish roots.

In the months that followed, when I uncovered my mother's family, this reinforced my sense of Jewishness. Why did I have a family scattered around the world that I had never known? The answer was because of our common Jewish heritage. I realised that the effect of the Holocaust had been to cut me off from this heritage, and that were I to remain cut off, Hitler would have succeeded, in my case at least. It therefore became of vital importance to me to re-embrace my heritage, my true self.

For some months I took instruction from Rabbi Amanda Golby who was most helpful and sympathetic. It was not all plain sailing. I recognised many conflicts and tensions within the Jewish world. Perhaps that is inevitable, given its history, but it was a world to which I belonged, and at least I now felt more comfortable with myself.

Finally, I recognised that I am not English, French or African. I am Jewish. And from that vantage point, I can reach out to others.

My mother started attending synagogue with me and said that she always knew that in her old age she would return to Judaism. Her knowledge of the Hebrew language and of Jewish customs, buried for more than 60 years, began to re-emerge in bits and pieces. She started attending a Jewish old people's home, Miriam Kaplowitch House, for three days a week, where she very much enjoyed being with people of her own background. In December 1997, following a fall in her home, she was admitted full-time to M.K. House. At last, I started to see some of her old spirit resurfacing, and she seemed to be more at peace with herself.

As for my husband, he has been bewildered, to say the least, by where events have taken me over the past few years. We remain married but lead largely separate lives, as, sadly, we have followed different paths. Nevertheless, we care deeply for one another, and I have come to recognise and appreciate that what I once saw as his fanaticism is in fact a deep compassion for humanity.

Kayode is a man of enormous integrity, who spends his entire life caring for others, most especially those who have been rejected by the rest of society. For me, the only difficulty in that is the over-zealous religious language with which his actions are accompanied. There is no question that Kayode has become a recognised and respected community leader. A mutual friend, Dr Fírinne Ní Chréacháin, once wrote of him:

> *"Pastor Soyinka is a remarkable person by any standard. He has a genuine love for humanity. Should the majority of Christians practise what they preach as he does, the world would be a better place. He has a refreshing ability to communicate across boundaries of class and culture. I have watched him in encounters with groups of 'challenging' white teenagers on the London Council estate where I work, and marvelled at his immediate rapport with kids that others have failed to connect with. His empathy with the disadvantaged is inspiring: his work with the homeless has even led him on occasion to offer a bed in his own home to those in need."*

Kayode is equally at home with the elderly. I shall never forget the devotion he showed to my mother in her last few years. He visited her on a regular basis when she was a resident at M.K. House and took her out on trips which she enjoyed immensely, especially given that her world at that time was closing in on her. The two of them became very close and loved one another dearly.

Myself and Kayode with our grand-daughter, Faith, in 2003

It is my sincere hope that Kayode and I shall one day be able to reconcile our religious differences, be able to accept and tolerate one another, each for what we are, and take together our place at the heart of our beautiful rainbow family.

My children, Alex, at the back, Lara, Bambo and Egbin, my step-daughter, on my 65th birthday

Shortly after writing my original story, *A Journey in Time*, I was offered a post as educational psychologist at Binoh, the Jewish Special Educational Needs Service of Norwood, a major Jewish charity in London, where I started working in January 1997. Two years earlier, I had never even heard of Yom Kippur, the Jewish Day of Atonement. Now I was working full-time in the Jewish community.

This was a truly amazing learning curve.

I had already had almost 10 years' experience as an educational psychologist in the Midlands, and was confident in my professional skills. However, I was now required to go into Jewish schools, including those in the ultra-orthodox community, speak with head teachers and rabbis, and offer educational advice, with virtually no knowledge of Judaism or of the Jewish way of life. Who was I to offer such advice? I found speaking with rabbis particularly intimidating at first, as I felt almost like an imposter.

A defining moment came for me, early on, when I was asked to assess an eight-year-old boy from the Chasidic community. He recognised that I was in some way different from him and wanted to know if I was Jewish. I replied that I was, and he cannily tested this out by asking me to read from a poster on the wall written in Hebrew. I was not, of course, able to comply, so he commented "*You say you are a Jew, but you do not read Hebrew. What are you then?*" A devastating question from one so young (and supposedly with learning difficulties), to which, at that time, I had no satisfactory reply.

Some of the schools I visited were positively Dickensian. I remember on one occasion visiting a nursery school in Hackney, and watching about 20 little boys seated in a straight row in front of a rabbi in full orthodox dress, walking up and down in front of them with a large cane.

While working in the Jewish community, I had decided to remain living in my home in Nottinghamshire and commuted to London on a weekly basis. I remember thinking during some of my drives home that it was as though I were shuttling between two different planets. But I adjusted to my new working environment, came to love dearly my colleagues and clients, and learned a good deal about the Jewish world. This was a world to which, I gradually realised, I most emphatically belonged. I had finally come home.

My only visit to Israel in 1999 when I attended a conference in Jerusalem sponsored by my employers at Binoh

What a journey. It has been both exhilarating and exhausting. I seem to have spent my entire life crossing boundaries and barriers, boundaries between countries, between continents, crossing the barriers of language and culture, climbing the walls between class, race and religion.

I have relatives in four continents, two mixed-race daughters, a white son, a black step-daughter, an Austrian Jewish mother, a lapsed Catholic English father and a Nigerian Evangelical Christian husband. I now also have grandchildren of every hue.

Someone remarked to me that my family is like the United Nations. I once told some of my story to a Nigerian niece. "*Aunty,*" she commented, "*you are a real human being.*" I very much took that as a compliment.

Having criss-crossed my way through such a range, variety and complexity of human experiences, I hope I am now ready to learn from these experiences. To move on from my new home base as a "*real human being*" and to face the world and the future with hope.

Chapter Thirteen

END OF AN ERA

WORDS FOR MY GRANDMOTHER by ALEX TREMBATH

Inspiring. Courageous. Beguiling. Outrageous.
Tragic.
But you rose from the depths of tragedy
To light a fire for all of the world to enjoy.

So I see the end
Of the most beautiful summer I have ever known
Taking with it
The most beautiful woman I have ever known.

So if the frail autumn trees
Protect me not from the chilling breeze,
Where shadows thrown by evening gloom
Disband the light which filled my room,
I illuminate my mind
With a picture of your smile
And the menace of any storm
Is reduced to whispers.

Oh what injustice
For a soul blessed with peace and equity
To be cast into a world
Where war and hierarchy dominate the appetite of mankind.

This world did not deserve you.
You conquered the injustice
And now sleep
With the peace you deserve.

Thank you for enriching my life with your influence.
So ends the summer of bewildering beauty,
I light a candle to rejoice
The light of Lucy.

My mother died on 23 August 2003, a huge loss to us all. As one of my brothers said, her passing was the end of an era. Although she had married out and appeared to have turned her back on her religion, she requested a Jewish funeral and was buried at the Orthodox Jewish cemetery in Nottingham.

We received tributes from family and friends around the world:

> *"What an exceptional lady, and shining example of triumph over adversity, her kindness, generosity and delightful eccentricity are held affectionately in my memories."*

> *"Her life had been lived with so much courage in the face of such impossible difficulties."*

> *"She was an unforgettable character, and we all admired her for battling on, after all she had been through."*

> *"How much she achieved in her lifetime and against such odds. I shall always remember Lucy for her spirit and laughter. She was a wonderful woman."*

> *"Aunty Lucy was such a vibrant, unique and totally energised woman, that it is hard to imagine her as an elderly frail lady. I am sure that her single-minded spirit was with her always."*

> *"Being an individual myself, I appreciated that in your Mum. She faced the challenge of being herself when all the world tried to make her like everyone else."*

> *"Her life and the way she lived it provides both a sanctuary and challenge. May you stay in touch with her wisdom and passion."*

At the funeral, my son Alex read the poem above which he had written for the occasion, while my daughter, Lara, gave this eulogy to her Nana:

> *"I remember her with arms open wide, a smile on her face and a sparkle in her eye. Full of life, joyous, generous with her treasure case full of outings and trips for her various grandchildren – Goose Fair, bonfire night, of course, with*

toffee apples, scenic train trips, leisurely cream teas by the sea, restaurants and pub treats galore. Looking back, I was a truly spoilt grandchild.

"Nana believed in living life to the full. Yes, there were hard times but she always said life was like a wibble wobble: you knock one of those dolls down and it bounces straight back up, a lesson I have always tried to remember."

Lucy Fowler at her retirement party in 1984, with arms open wide, a smile on her face and a sparkle in her eye

Attended by Nigerian members of the family, some in national costume, it was a most unusual Jewish funeral as hardly anyone present was Jewish.

At the ceremony, Rabbi Perez, the wonderful man who permitted this event, asked me for my mother's Hebrew name. I said I did not know, and he replied that he could not bury her without one. I therefore asked him what the Hebrew word for *light* was, since Lucy means light. He told me that it was ***Ora***, and I thought this was a perfect name for my mother. Thus she was given a Hebrew name at her funeral.

The inscription on her headstone reads:

LUCY FOWLER née SMETANA
BORN VIENNA 6 SEPTEMBER 1919
DIED NOTTINGHAM 23 AUGUST 2003

WHAT MARK DO I LEAVE BEHIND?

A SHINING EXAMPLE OF TRIUMPH OVER ADVERSITY
YOUR CHARACTER, COURAGE, WISDOM AND SPARKLE
WILL FOREVER BE OUR INSPIRATION
AND OUR GUIDING LIGHT

YOUR LOVING CHILDREN
GRANDCHILDREN, GREAT GRANDCHILDREN
FAMILY AND FRIENDS

My mother's headstone was made by a stone mason called Smeeton, the anglicised form of Smetana. The name Smeeton is also carved on her grave.

Post-Script

BUTTERFLIES AND OTHER COINCIDENCES

There is a leitmotif flitting through this story which has been difficult to include because it is not based on fact or evidence, but rather on the feeling that it is somehow significant. In the course of my search, there have been many strange coincidences, some of which I have alluded to in the text above.

Once I discovered the existence of my mother's relatives, and began my search in October 1994, events started to unfold before me with surprisingly little effort on my part, giving me the strong impression that the time had come for me to know this story. It was just waiting there for me to find it. Accompanying my search was the frequent appearance of butterflies in rather unusual circumstances.

The first appearance was at a family gathering which included my mother, on 25 December 2002. A butterfly appeared suddenly and unexpectedly and swooped down on my grandson, Joshua, then one year old, who was in the centre of the room playing a drum. Joshua ducked to avoid it, startled, as were we all to see a butterfly indoors in the middle of winter. The butterfly continued to fly around the room for a while before disappearing.

Throughout the following winter, spring and summer, the butterfly (or more probably butterflies) appeared frequently in my home, almost becoming a member of the household. I was never able to determine where it had bred or fed, but I did discover that it was a small tortoiseshell butterfly, which is bright orange and black with a row of blue crescents around the wing edges. It is normally seen in gardens between March and September.

My mother died on 23 August 2003, and from that point on, the appearance of butterflies in my house was much less frequent, but when they occurred, usually in the winter. Once, when I was staying in Cornwall with my brother, Steve, I discovered a small tortoiseshell on the floor in the narrow space between my bed and the wall. I only saw it because I happened to glance down.

At the end of September 2006, I visited Vienna for the first time with one of my daughters, Bambo. My other daughter, Lara, had also hoped to come but was unable to due to her pregnancy. The trip was a 60th birthday present from my children. We stayed in a wonderful hotel, the *Aldstadt*, in the 7th district, fairly close to the city centre. I wanted, before doing anything else, to visit the grave of my grandfather, Fritz Smetana, where his parents, Josef and Cäcilie, were also buried. I had obtained the location from the *Israelitische Kultusgemeinde*: *Zentralfriedhof* 4, Group 22, Row 29b, Grave number 19. As we left the hotel on 1 October, we noticed that two wasps had become trapped between the window panes of our bedroom, and we were unable to release them.

Zentralfriedhof, first opened in 1874, consists of four large cemeteries, situated one after the other in the south-east outskirts of the city, on Simmering Hauptstrasse. The old Jewish cemetery, much of it destroyed by the Nazis, is in *Zentralfriedhof* 1, but a new one was opened in 1917 in *Zentralfriedhof* 4, the furthest from the city centre.

We took a tram from a central location and alighted at *Zentralfriedhof* 4, where we learned that the plot in which my grandfather was buried was right at the back left-hand corner. This location, the furthest plot in the furthest cemetery, is probably the reason it was left untouched by the Nazis. It contained the tombs of Jews buried in the 1930s and was consequently largely neglected and overgrown, since no-one had been left to care for them, though there were a few which had clearly been restored and lovingly tended.

We found Row 29b, but most of the graves were thickly covered with ivy, and it was impossible to say to whom they belonged. We searched, unsuccessfully, for two hours in the place where we felt Grave 19 was likely to be. Eventually, Bambo decided to move further up the row to a point where I could not see her because of the thick undergrowth. She soon called out that she thought she had found it, because there was a wasps' nest on one of the graves, and that the wasps we had seen in our hotel room that morning were trying to tell us that this was the spot.

I called out to her that that was ridiculous, and anyway, that location did not seem to concur with the numbering we had been given. Nevertheless, I circled the undergrowth to join her. There were two large gravestones, both completely covered with ivy, with a space between them. The one with the wasps' nest was to the right as we faced them. In spite of my fear of wasps, I carefully pulled at the ivy, and was fairly sure that the name on the grave was not Smetana. Neither was that the name on the other gravestone, as far as I could ascertain.

We had now spent three hours searching, and I felt there was nothing further we could do, so we decided, reluctantly, to leave. As we stood there, a butterfly hovered over the space between the two graves. It startled me but somehow seemed to confirm that my grandfather was nearby.

On our way out of the cemetery, we sat down on a bench, and I said to Bambo that even though we had not found the grave, I felt happy that my grandfather was buried in this beautiful peaceful spot, rather than having died in a horrible way at some distant location.

Now this may seem absurd, but I had a strange feeling that my grandfather heard me and that he felt I had forgiven him for killing himself. Because of his shame, he had hidden from us, but he was now prepared to reveal himself. As we got up, I saw a grass-cutter, and said to Bambo that we should give it one last shot, and ask this man if he could find the grave for us.

He was from the former Yugoslavia and spoke no English, but when I showed him the number of the grave written down, he nodded, and marched purposefully back up the cemetery to the very spot that Bambo had found, much to my amazement. He counted down the row from the space between the two graves and back up again, arriving once more at the space. He checked the number with me, nodded, then bent down, removed the ivy on the ground between the two graves, then gently pulled up a small headstone bearing the simple inscription:

Smetana
31. V. 1938.

To say that I was astonished is to put it mildly, but my astonishment became wonderment as a large and very beautiful butterfly hovered immediately above the tiny headstone.

In a dazed state, Bambo and I returned to Vienna on the tram, and at the tram terminus, had a pleasant lunch on the terrace of a café, talking over the events of the morning. After an hour, I decided to check on the map where we were, and found to my delight that the café was at the junction of Kärntner Ring and Schubertring.

My mother had spent her teenage years at Schubertring 12, and this was one of the places I wanted to visit. I crossed the junction, and there was number 12, right in front of us, easily within sight of the spot where we were sitting. I could scarcely believe it. My mother must have alighted many times from the tram at this terminus and no doubt spent many hours in this very café drinking coffee or indulging in a Viennese water ice.

The remainder of our visit to Vienna was full of such wondrous encounters: a journey to Hietzing, where my mother had lived as a child, a meeting with Robert Streibel, who has documented the Jews of Hietzing and erected a memorial, and not least a visit to the *Israelitische Kultusgemeinde*, where the kindly and helpful Wolf-Erich Eckstein showed us the family records.

Not long after my return home to England, a close friend, Shirley, visited me and I told her the whole story. I also showed her a beautiful appliqué cushion I had inherited from my mother, on which were embroidered two butterflies, one large, one small, which to me symbolised the two butterflies I had seen at my grandfather's grave. Shirley stared at the cushion, speechless, then said softly, *"Susan, have you not noticed that there are also two wasps?"* There indeed, in full view, were two wasps which I had never noticed, the signposts to my journey, waiting to be discovered.

For several years there were no further appearances of my resident butterfly. Then, in October 2010, I decided to transfer the original family history document I had written in 1996, *A Journey in Time,* to a Word document on my computer. I used voice-activated software, so that I was literally talking to the computer, telling it my mother's story.

After a while, I started to hear a flapping sound, like that of a butterfly, but which appeared to be coming from inside the computer. Several times, I put my ear down to the computer to see where the sound was coming from, but could not work it out, so carried on talking. Then, after about an hour, I glanced to the side, and there, inside the window, just a few inches away from my right shoulder, was a small tortoiseshell butterfly, flapping away as if it were trying to tell me something. Perhaps indeed it was.

APPENDICES ONE TO FOURTEEN TRANSLATION OF DOCUMENTS

APPENDIX ONE: JOSEF SMETANA'S BIRTH RECORD

As a result of the order by the imperial governor's office of 18th June 1902, line 28145, the following is noted:
According to the communication from the imperial governor's office of Lower Austria of 2nd June 1902, line 58120, Josef Smetany, resident of Vienna, is permitted to alter his surname to "Smetana".

Ung. Brod,

8th July 1902

Registrar of births

Official Extract from the Register of Births

Folio	Line	Date, number of notification	Day Month Year Place of birth	Day Month Year Place of circumcision	The names					
					of the child	of the father	of the mother	of the godparent	of the circumcisor	of the midwife
105	26	17th July 1858 No. 5522	5th July 1858, Hallenkau	12th July 1858, Hallenkau	Josef	Baruch Smetany, bar keeper in Hallenkau	Betti nee Hirsch of Karlovitz	Leopold Böck, Karlovitz	Leopold Kukol	Eva Blaha of Hanjesy
21	-	-	23rd February 1836		Aron Smetany[1)]	Abraham Hirsch	Marie			

1) The last letter of this word is written unclearly in the old register, and can also be read as "a".

Ung. Brod, 29th November 1899.

~~Note: The surname of the father and thus also of the child should read, correctly: "Smetany"~~
~~Order of the imperial Moravian governor's office, 11th March 1901, no. 9339~~
~~Ung. Brod, 27th March 1901, registrar of births~~

As a result of the decree issued by the imperial ministry of the interior of 11th March 1902, line 7896, this note concerning the order by the imperial Moravian governor's office of 27th March 1902, line 12906, is cancelled. Ung. Brod, 21st April 1902, registrar of births.

Note: the two entries at the bottom of the page appear to confuse the dates 1901 and 1902, a further puzzling feature to this document (see Chapter Four).

Appendices 1–12 were translated from German by Margret Vince

APPENDIX TWO

DOCUMENT SHOWING ATTEMPT BY GESTAPO TO TRACK DOWN MY MOTHER

(Carbon copy)

Secret State Police [Gestapo]
State police headquarters, Vienna
Log book no.: 5243 IV B 4 a

Vienna, 18th September 1942

To the

Reich security head office
Department IV B 4 b-4
in Berlin.

Re: Forfeiture of property of Jews on the basis of the 11th decree relating to the Reich citizenship law of 25th November 1941 (Reich law gazette I p. 722 ff).
Reference: None
Enclosures: 1 carbon copy

I request that it be determined that the assets of the Jew listed below, who last had German citizenship, have been forfeited to the Reich on the basis of the 11th decree relating to the Reich citizenship law of 25th November 1941 (Reich law gazette I p. 722 ff).

---

1. Name: Smetana — Given names: Lucie Sara
   For women, maiden name also) — (underline name by which known)
2. Date of birth: 6.9.1919
3. Place of birth, and district: Vienna
4. Last residence in this country: Vienna 1, Schubertring 12
   (Exact address)
5. Date of emigration: De-registered 27.8.1938, to England
6. Assets in this country:
   a) Nature and value of assets: She is a joint heir to the estate of Friedrich Smetana. The estate settlement is being handled by the Hietzing local court, no.: 7 A 843/38/36. The trust account hi 203/8 is held at the Creditanstalt Bankverein, Hietzing branch.

   b) Seizure effected? No.
7. Information as to whether pensions, maintenance etc. were drawn and cancellation of payment has been initiated: No.

p.p.:

Form 33 sent: 16.10.44

APPENDIX THREE

LETTER IN WHICH JOSEF SMETANA PURPORTEDLY REQUESTED THE SALE OF HIS COMPANY

Josef Smetana

Dyeing, dry cleaning, fabric repairs, carpet cleaning and storage
Factory and head office: Linzerstrasse 104-106, Vienna XIII. Tel. U-38-0-59 – U-35-0-81
Bankers: Austrian post office savings account no: A 2323; Zentral-Europ. Länderbank, Penzing branch

Vienna, 28 April 1938

[stamp:] The state commissioner for private industry
4 May 1938

Dr. K/H
To the

Reich governor,

Vienna I,
Austrian regional government

Re: Request for approval of sale.

With respectful reference to section 1, paragraph 4 of the law for the protection of the Austrian economy, we hereby submit the appropriate request to be permitted to enter into negotiations with Imperial German Aryan companies that are interested in purchasing our business.

The grounds for this request are that a handover of the company into Aryan hands is in the interests of the numerous workers and employees employed in the business, but that have been unable to find an interested party in Austria who is in a position to take over our business and run it.

In anticipation of your swift agreement, we remain

faithfully,

[signatures]

[stamp:] Ministry for Trade and Commerce
Office for the Transfer of Assets
Received on 30th May 1938
Number: 201437 Encs.: *2*

APPENDIX FOUR
BERTA SMETANA'S DECLARATION OF ASSETS

Before completing the list of assets, the enclosed instructions must be read carefully!

Please note!

1. Who must complete the list of assets?
Each person obliged to make a notification, thus each spouse and child individually. For each minor, the list of assets must be submitted by the holder of parental authority or by the guardian.

2. By when must the list of assets be submitted?
By 30th June 1938. Anyone who is obliged to make a declaration and valuation, but who does not complete this, or does not do so on time or in full, **is liable to a severe penalty (fine, imprisonment, custodial sentence, confiscation of assets).**

3. How should the list of assets be completed?
All the questions must be answered. Items that do not apply must be deleted by drawing a line through them. If the space available on the list of assets is not sufficient for completion, then the details required must be provided on an attached sheet.

4. In cases of doubt as to whether particular values are to be included in the list of assets, the values should be listed.

07027

List of the Assets of Jews
as at 27th April 1938

of *Berta Smetana* (occupation or trade): *Private*
in *Vienna I, Schubertring* house number: *12*
(residence or usual domicile)

Personal details

I was born on *9. I. 1896.*
I am a Jew (§ 5 of the First decree on the Reich citizenship law of 14th November 1938, Reich law gazette I, p. 1333), and have German[1] – ………….. – nationality[1] – ~~am stateless~~ –.
Since I am a Jew of German nationality[1] – ~~stateless Jew~~[1] – I have listed and valued **my entire** assets **in this country** and **abroad** in the list of assets below[1].
~~Since I am a Jew of foreign nationality, I have listed and valued my assets **in this country** in the list of assets below[1].~~
I am ~~married to~~ *legally separated,* maiden name *Weinberger*
My spouse ~~is~~ *was* racially – Jewish[1] – ~~non-Jewish~~[1] *deceased* – and ~~is~~ *was* a member of the *Jewish* religious community.

Details concerning assets

I. Agricultural and forestry assets (cf. instructions, item 9):
If you owned agricultural and forestry assets on 27th April 1938 (leased land and the like are to be listed only if the livestock and equipment belonged to you):

Location of owned or leased business and size in hectares? (Municipality – district – and holding number, including designation in land registry and valuation roll)	Type of owned or leased business? (e.g. agricultural, forestry, horticultural business, viniculture, fishing)	Was this your own business or leased?	Value of the business in RM	In the case of owned businesses: If the business also belonged to others: how much was your share (e.g. ¼)?
1	2	3	4	5
---------------	---------------------	------------------------	------------------------	------------------------

II. Real estate (land, buildings) (cf. instructions, item 10):
If you owned real estate on 27th April 1938 (land that did **not** belong to the assets listed above under I and below under III):

Location of the property? Municipality, street and house number, in the case of building land also designation in land registry and valuation roll)	Type of property? (e.g. single-family home, rental income property, building land)	Value of property in RM	If the property also belonged to others: how much was your share (e.g. ¼)?
1	2	3	4
------------------------------	------------------------------	------------------------------	------------------------------

1) Delete what does not apply.

List of assets. VO of 26.4.1938

APPENDICES FIVE AND SIX

CERTIFICATE OF RACIAL ORIGINS

Interim — Paid

Valid only until: 22nd June 1939 — Number: 31450

NSDAP – Vienna district
Regional office for genealogical research
Vienna 1, Am Hof 3 & 4

Result of examination

To be completed by the applicant:

Address: Stumpergasse 49, Vienna VI Marital status: married

has presented the documents detailed overleaf for

short proof of descent

Accordingly, the person under review is to be regarded as:

of German blood (Aryan) / ~~mixed race of the 2nd order / mixed race of the 1st order / a Jew~~.

This certification shall cease to be valid on 1.1.1942, unless it has, prior to that, become part of the personal file of an authority or party office, and is no substitute for the full proof of descent by the NSDAP.

Vienna, 22nd Feb. 1939 — Signature, official seal

Valid only with the seal of the Regional Office for Genealogical Research in Vienna

Illegibly completed forms will be rejected!

Price: 5 Rpf.

DECLARATION OF NAZI OWNERSHIP OF SMETANA FIRM

Vienna, 18 July 1938

The German Labour Front
District administration VII

I request that party comrade Karl **Seidl**, shop steward at the **Smetana** company, Linzerstrasse 104, district 13, be supported in the Aryanisation of this business. The Smetana company is 100% in the German Labour Front.

Heil Hitler!

[stamp:] NSDAP – The German Labour Front
District administration VII, Vienna

The district officer of the GLF

APPENDIX SEVEN

DECLARATION THAT FRITZ'S ESTATE HAS BEEN FORFEITED BY HIS HEIRS AND HAS BECOME THE SOLE PROPERTY OF THE GERMAN REICH

For processing.

Payment and amount as overleaf

Enclosure: File 7 A 843/38.

To the

Hietzing local court,

Vienna, district XIII,
Trautmannsdorfgasse 18.

The legal heirs, the spouse Berta Sara Smetana and the two daughters Lucie Sara and the minor Sonja Sara Smetana, left the territory of the Reich on 8th October 1938 and 27th August 1938, in other words only after the death of the deceased on 31st May 1938. They have therefore acquired the right to inherit.

Their assets, of which the right to inherit forms a part, have been forfeited to the Greater German Reich on the basis of the 11th decree relating to the Reich citizenship law of 25th November 1941 (Reich law gazette I, p. 722 ff).

In the name of the Greater German Reich (Reich tax administration), in place of the heirs Berta Sara Smetana, Lucie Sara and the minor Sonja Sara Smetana, on the basis of the law and the eleventh decree relating to the Reich citizenship law, I give the conditional declaration of acceptance of inheritance, and request that this declaration of acceptance be accepted by the court, and that the right to inherit be deemed to be shown.

I request that the court commissioner, the notary Dr. ~~Hermann Suchomel~~ *Anton Zimmermann*, Vienna XIII, Lainzerstrasse 3, be entrusted with continuing the settlement negotiations.

If necessary, this declaration of acceptance of inheritance shall also serve as authorisation for the notary Dr. ~~Suchomel~~ *Zimmermann*, as a person authorised to act for the Greater German Reich (Reich tax administration), to carry out the probate procedure until the certificate of inheritance has been issued, and to transfer the net share in the estate to the chief cashier's office of the president of the regional tax office for Vienna - Lower Danube, Vienna (post office account Vienna no. 51, quoting the file reference given above.

p.p.

Sent
with *1* enclosure
28 March 1944

Dr. Suchomel died

APPENDIX EIGHT

JOSEF SMETANA'S RAILWAY SERVICE RECORD

Imperial ministerial commission for the administration of the imperial Dniester and Tarnow-Leluchower state railway, the Archduke Albrecht railway, and the Moravian border railway.

Record of service

Surname: *Smetana* Given name: *Josef*
Date of birth: *5th July 1857*
Place of birth: *Hallenkau, Moravia*

Education
Studies: *Realschule and commercial school*
Language skills: Spoken: *German, Bohemian*
Written: *German*
Other:

Practical utilisation prior to entering into the service of the imperial ministerial commission:

Official of the Moravian border railways for almost ten years, and in fact for five years with the [illegible] service as cashier and traffic officer, and in the subsequent period in the receipts audit office.

Military service: […] *Exempted*

Marital status:
Date of approval and marriage: *7.8.1888 / M 20.8.1888*
Wife: *Cäcilia Neumann*
Born on: *26.10.1863*

Children:	Name:	Born on:
	Friedrich	*18.9.1889*
	Otto	*17.5.1891*
	~~*Marie*~~ … *Auguste*	*17.12.1894*

Signature of superior:
Certificate from the commercial school, otherwise none supplied.
Birth certificate seen subsequently.

Own signature (mark) of employee:
J. Smetana

APPENDIX NINE

FRANZ HOTSCHEWAR'S APPLICATION FOR THE ACQUISITION OF JOSEF SMETANA'S COMPANY

To be completed in triplicate

To the office for the transfer of assets, Strauchgasse 1, Vienna 1.

Request for approval of acquisition

Given name, surname: Franz **Hotschewar**
Residence and telephone number: Innsbruck 231
Born on: 1st June 1904 in: Innsbruck
Nationality (including any previous): Austria
Aryan? Yes
Married? Yes Racial identity of spouse: Aryan
Children (number, age)? 1

Do you have a vendor? Yes. The firm Josef Smetana, Linzerstrasse 104-106, Vienna XIII.
Are you related to this person, or are there any other relationships of dependency? No.

Occupation: Master dyer

Previous occupation, possibly certificate transcripts: Worked as assistant dyer and master dyer in various German dye works and laundries, manager in father's business in Innsbruck, and currently proprietor of this business.

What type of business do you wish to acquire? Dye works and dry cleaning business.

Do you have a particular business in mind? Yes, Josef Smetana, Linzerstrasse, Vienna XIII.

What are your total assets? Around 120,000 Reichsmarks.
What are your own cash assets? As a result of extensive investment, only round 8,000 Reichsmarks, but good credit ratings.
What amount do you wish to invest?
What external funds do you have? Currently 30,000 Reichsmarks.
Who is your financial backer? Sparkasse (savings bank) of the city of Innsbruck, Maria Herbst.
Do you or your spouse already have a business? As above, Franz Hotschewar dye works and dry cleaners, Hoferstrasse 16, Innsbruck.

Innsbruck, 30th July 1938.

Signature

Providing false information is punishable!

See page 2

APPENDIX TEN

JOSEF SMETANA'S APPLICATION TO "SELL" HIS COMPANY

In triplicate

To the office for the transfer of assets, Strauchgasse 1, Vienna 1

Request for permission to sell

First name and surname: *Josef Smetana*

Place of residence and telephone: *Vienna*

Born on *5.7.1858* in *Hallenkau*

Nationality (including previous): *Vienna*

Racial group (Jew, ~~first or second degree mixed origin~~)? *Jew*

Married: *Yes*

Children (number, age)? *4* *50, 45, 35, 49*

Occupation: *Manufacturer*

Do you have a buyer? *Yes*

Are you related to this person, or are there any other relationships of dependency? *No.*

Place of business: *Linzerstrasse 104/106, Vienna XIII*

Precise description of the business (company name, registered office):
Josef Smetana
Dyeworks and Dry Cleaners
Linzerstrasse 104
Vienna XIII

In the case of commercial business with book-keeping, a transcript of the 1937 balance sheet must be attached, together with the number of employees in 1937 and the current status:
1937 210 employees, of whom 8 are non-Aryan
Currently 230 employees (How many of them non-Aryan?): *none*

In the case of all other businesses, the turnover for 1937 and the number of employees: -
(How many of them non-Aryan?): -

Estimate according to the real value:

Desired price: *Estimated value*

Vienna, 3.8.1938

Signature: *Josef Smetana*

Providing untrue information is punishable!

See 2nd page.

APPENDIX ELEVEN
JOSEF SMETANA'S DECLARATION OF ASSETS

See also 27064 *1st DEC. 1939*

Before completing the list of assets, the enclosed instructions must be read carefully!

Please note!

1. Who must complete the list of assets?
Each person obliged to make a notification, thus each spouse and child individually. For each minor, the list of assets must be submitted by the holder of parental authority or by the guardian.
2. By when must the list of assets be submitted?
By 30th June 1938. Anyone who is obliged to make a declaration and valuation, but who does not complete this, or does not do so on time or in full, **is liable to a severe penalty (fine, imprisonment, custodial sentence, confiscation of assets).**
3. How should the list of assets be completed?
All the questions must be answered. Items that do not apply must be deleted by drawing a line through them. If the space available on the list of assets is not sufficient for completion, then the details required must be provided on an attached sheet.
4. In cases of doubt as to whether particular values are to be included in the list of assets, the values should be listed.

45738 ~~46546~~

List of the Assets of Jews
as at 27th April 1938

of *Josef Smetana, company shareholder* (occupation or trade)
in *Vienna XIII, Kupelwiesergasse* house number: *13*
(residence or usual domicile)

Personal details

I was born on *5th July 1858.*
I am a Jew (§ 5 of the First decree on the Reich citizenship law of 14th November 1938, Reich law gazette I, p. 1333), and have German[1)] – .... – nationality[1)] – am stateless –.
Since I am a Jew of German nationality[1)] – stateless Jew[1)] – I have listed and valued **my entire** assets **in this country** and **abroad** in the list of assets below[1)].
Since I am a Jew of foreign nationality, I have listed and valued my assets **in this country** in the list of assets below[1)].
I am married to *Cäcilie,* maiden name *Neumann.*
My spouse is racially – Jewish[1)] – non-Jewish[1)] – and is a member of the .... religious community.

Details concerning assets

I. Agricultural and forestry assets (cf. instructions, item 9):
If you owned agricultural and forestry assets on 27th April 1938 (leased land and the like are to be listed only if the livestock and equipment belonged to you):

Location of owned or leased business and size in hectares? (Municipality – district – and holding number, including designation in land registry and valuation roll)	Type of owned or leased business? (e.g. agricultural, forestry, horticultural business, viniculture, fishing)	Was this your own business or leased?	Value of the business in RM	In the case of owned businesses: If the business also belonged to others: how much was your share (e.g. ¼)?
1	2	3	4	5

II. Real estate (land, buildings) (cf. instructions, item 10):
If you owned real estate on 27th April 1938 (land that did **not** belong to the assets listed above under I and below under III):

Location of the property? Municipality, street and house number, in the case of building land also designation in land registry and valuation roll)	Type of property? (e.g. single-family home, rental income property, building land)	Value of property in RM	If the property also belonged to others: how much was your share (e.g. ¼)?
1	2	3	4
E.Z. 627 New build E.Z. Ober St. Veit E.Z. 1297 K.G Penzing, Linzerstrasse 104-106	Rental income plot Building land Factory	110,800.00 30,667 40,000.00	 ½ - 15,333

1) Delete what does not apply.

List of assets. VO of 26.4.1938

APPENDIX TWELVE

SECURITY NOTICE RECEIVED BY JOSEF AND CÄCILIE SMETANA ABOUT THE COST AND CONDITIONS OF THEIR LEAVING THE COUNTRY

City centre east tax office
Office for tax on flight from the Reich
for the country of Austria

Emigr. Smetana – room 516
Please quote in all communications.

Vienna I, 19th September 1939
Riemergasse 2
Tel. R-22-5-95, extension: ___
Open to the public Monday, Tuesday, Thursday and Friday from 11 a.m. to 1 p.m.
The enforcement office will take delivery of securities, payments to be made only via the Post Office savings bank, to account number A 43.167
Number of your account: ________

To Mr. Josef Israel Smetana
Hietzinger Hauptstrasse 53
Vienna 13

Transcript!

Provisional **security notice**

A. Determination of the security
The information available to me indicates that you will give up your residence – usual domicile in Austria or the remaining territory of the Reich. On the basis of § 7 of the *Reichsfluchtsteuergesetz* [law on tax on flight from the Reich]*), I therefore request that you provide immediately security to the value of 41,600 Reichsmark.
This request is hereby also being sent to your relatives (wife, children), insofar as they have been, or are to be, assessed together with you for income tax or wealth tax. – The security can be provided for example by depositing money, by depositing or pledging securities or mortgages, or by a bond (§§ 132 to 141 of the Reich tax code).

This notice is enforceable immediately.

The security has been calculated as follows:
Tax on flight from the Reich, which is due on emigration: According to the information available to me, the total assets belonging to you and your wife ~~as well as your children~~ on 1st January 1938 – including the additions in accordance with § 3, paragraph 3 of the law on the tax on flight from the Reich and § 2, paragraph 1 to b of the implementing decree for the tax on flight from the Reich in Austria, dated 14th April 1938 –:
..............166,133.00 Reichsmarks, a quarter of which is ......41,533 Reichsmarks.

Other claims: ....

Total:	41,533 Reichsmarks
Rounded to:	41,600 Reichsmarks.

B. Information on rights of appeal
You are entitled to appeal against this security notice, to the president of the regional finance office at Vienna, whose decision is final. The appeal can be submitted to me in writing, or declared for taking down in writing. This can be done only within one month after service of the notice, i.e. after the date on which the notice was posted. The costs of an unsuccessful appeal must be borne by you.
The submission of an appeal does not impair the validity of the security notice, and in particular it does not delay enforcement.

*) See overleaf.

Signature Copy to:

Rfl 8. (Transcript of the security notice) – 8.39 – 2000. – State printers, Vienna 7776 39

APPENDICES THIRTEEN AND FOURTEEN

FRITZ'S LAST LETTER

CONSUL GENERAL
OF THE REPUBLIC OF SAN MARINO **VIENNA** 25.V.1938
XIII, AUHOFSTRASSE 66

To the Secretary of State for Foreign Affairs of the Republic of San Marino.

Dear Sir,

I have the honour of confirming receipt of your esteemed letter of the13 inst. I sincerely thank you, most especially for the further conferring of my office as Consul General of the Republic of San Marino, the accomplishment of which I shall always cherish. Should your Lordship have specific questions, it will be my duty at the first opportunity to convey you my report.

With regards

F, Smetana

Consul General

LETTER FROM SAN MARINO CONSULATE IN FRANCE

PARIS 17 December 1938
198, Rue de Rivoli

EMBASSY OF THE
REPUBLIC OF SAN MARINO
IN FRANCE

Distinguished Commander,

Should it be of interest to you, I write to inform you that I recently had the opportunity of meeting here in Paris, Mrs Bertha Smetana, widow of our former Consul General in Vienna.

Mrs Smetana informed me of the suicide of her husband (Fritz Smetana, Auhofstrasse 11b) as a result of the German-Austrian political events (the Anschluss)

I ventured to ask her what had happened to the archive of the Consulate. She said that in fact, the archive had been sequestrated; put under seal by the Authority, including what was in her house. Asked if she knew the name of the bailiff who affixed the seals, she did not remember, but added that his address was in a trunk she had in Brussels.

I do not know if your Government is aware of this, however, I bring it to your attention in private.

Yours very truly

P. Mally

Distinguished Commander Frederico GOZI
Chancellor of the S.E. Secretary of State for Foreign Affairs
SAN MARINO

Appendices 13 and 14 were translated from Italian by Giorgio Cacciabue

APPENDIX FIFTEEN

A NOTE ON CZECH JEWISH GENEALOGY

JEWISH VITAL RECORDS IN BOHEMIA AND MORAVIA

The historical information in this section is based partly on articles written by Czech Jewish genealogist Dr Julius Müller, published on his website www.toledot.org, and partly on the website www.CzechFamilyTree.com.

In my attempt to uncover Josef Smetana's history, I obtained further information from the Austrian State Archives over several years and in 2011 employed the services of two Czech genealogists, Julius Müller and Martin Kočařík.

Czech Jewish records have been remarkably well preserved for a number of historical reasons. From 1784, Jewish communities in Bohemia and Moravia were obliged to keep their vital records, and thus a system of record-keeping, based on legal requirements, arose within each Jewish community. In 1794, midwives were required to keep separate birth records, giving rise to a first set of duplicates. A little later, in 1799, Catholic priests were also required to produce "catholic duplicates" of Jewish vital records. In 1874, Jewish communities were, themselves, required to keep their own duplicates.

In 1938–39 the Gestapo attempted to collect all Jewish vital records in parts of Bohemia and Moravia, and in 1941–42, a similar campaign was launched in the rest of the occupied country. In 1943, the various duplicate records, including the catholic duplicates, were collected and reposited outside Prague. Those duplicate collections were reportedly recovered and saved by the Czech employees in the repository and thus were not transfered to Prague during the war years. The original records were, however, destroyed by the Nazis in April 1945. After the war, in 1949, the Jewish vital records were included in civil records kept by the state, and were stored in the National Archive in Prague.

These Jewish records have been supplemented by Czech census records. In 1857, the Austro-Hungarian Empire completed the first comprehensive census of its crown lands and censuses were subsequently carried out in 1869, 1880, 1890, 1900 and 1910. Bohemia, Moravia and Silesia, the states which compose the modern Czech Republic, were subject lands of the Austro-Hungarian Empire till 1918, and as such, were included in these census exercises.

The Czech Republic has a large and impressive network of archives including seven regional archives, the repositories for most pre-1900 parish books and 72 district archives, which are the main repositories for the census records.

Searches were made on my behalf by Julius Müller, who checked the Jewish records in the National Archive in Prague and by Martin Kočařík and his wife Šárka Kočaříková, in the east of the country. Martin and Šárka visited the Uherské Hradiště District, where the census records for Uherský Brod (Ungarisch Brod) are stored, and the Vsetín District Archives, where the records for Hallenkau (Halenkov) are kept. Some Jewish records for Hallenkau were kept in the town of Valašské Meziříčí, whose records are kept in both Prague and Vsetín. Martin also visited the Moravian Regional Archive in Brno to examine documents relating to the Smetana family name change.

It was discovered that some of the census records were missing, or too fragile to be made available to the public. This included the Ungarisch Brod census for 1857 and the Hallenkau census for 1869. The latter census record, in particular, would have been invaluable in uncovering Josef's origins.

The chequered history of many of the towns and villages discussed in this book has meant that their names have often been known in several languages. In particular, place names in the current Czech Republic are now known, of course, by their Czech name, but during the era of the Habsburg Empire, they were referred to in official documents by their German name. This has made it difficult to know which form to use.

In general, I have used the German names when referring to the 19th century (for example, Hallenkau and Ungarisch Brod), as that is what appears in the documentation, but the Czech names of the towns where the archives are now stored. However, I have used the English names for Prague and Vienna, as they are so well-known by those names.

The table below shows the names of towns and cities in the Czech Republic, giving the Czech form now in use, and the German form which was in official use during the period of the Habsburg Empire.

Czech Name	German name	Location
Bohumín	Oderberg	Moravian-Silesian Region
Brno	Brünn	South Moravian Region
Český Těšín	Tschechisch-Teschen	Moravian-Silesian Region
Halenkov	Hallenkau	Vsetín District, Zlín Region
Hanušovice	Hannsdorf	
Karlovice	Karlovitz	Vsetín District, Zlín Region
Litomyšl	Leitomischl	Pardubice Region
Ostrava	Ostrau	Moravian-Silesian Region
Praha	Prag, Prague (English)	Capital City
Šumperk	Schönberg	Olomouk Region
Terezín	Theresienstadt	Ústí nad Labem Region
Uherský Brod	Ungarisch Brod	Zlín Region
Uherské Hradiště	Ungarisch Hradisch	Zlín Region
Valašské Meziříčí	Wallachisch Meseritsch	Vsetín District, Zlín Region
Vsetín	Wsetin	Vsetín District, Zlín Region

Other place names mentioned in the book include:

Current Name(s)	Location
Бачки Петровац (Serbian), Bački Petrovac (Slovak), Petrőc (Hungarian)	Serbia
Београд (Serbian), Belgrade (English), Belgrad (German)	Serbia
Bielsko and Biala, now Bielsko-Biała	Poland
Bratislava, Pozsony (Hungarian), Pressburg (German)	Slovakia
Drancy (in the suburbs of Paris)	France
Dresden	Germany
Göteborg (Swedish), Gothenburg (English)	Sweden
København (Danish), Copenhagen (English)	Denmark
Львів (Ukrainian), Lviv (English), Lwów (Polish), Lemberg (German)	Ukraine
Nice	France
Orsova (Romanian), Oršava (Czech), Orşova (Hungarian), Orschowa (German)	Romania
Oświęcim (Polish), Auschwitz (German)	Poland
Paris	France
Steyr	Austria
Trenčín (Slovakian), Trencsén (Hungarian), Trentschin (German)	Slovakia
Villach	Austria
Wiśnicz (Polish), Wisnitz (German)	Poland
Wygoda	Poland

THE CZECH MEMORIAL SCROLLS

Information in this section is based on the website www.czechmemorialscrollstrust.org with the kind permission of Mrs Evelyn Friedlander.

In addition to the Jewish vital records which were saved from destruction by the Nazis, some 100,000 religious treasures were also rescued during the war from the provinces of Czechoslovakia. Prior to 1938 there were some 350 synagogues in Bohemia and Moravia, of which more than 60 were destroyed by the Nazis between 1938 and 1945 and their contents lost. Most of the remaining synagogues were abandoned and left to decay. During the Communist regime following the war, over 80 further synagogues were demolished.

The Jewish treasures of Bohemia and Moravia were saved in 1942 by a devoted group of individuals from Prague's Jewish community. Working in desperate conditions, they brought to the Central Jewish Museum in Prague the possessions of provincial Jewry, which lay at the mercy of vandals and plunderers. They hoped that these treasures would be protected and might one day be returned to their original homes. All the Museum's curators were eventually transported to Theriesenstadt (Terezín) and Auschwitz. Only two of them survived. Their legacy and their gift to the Jewish world was a vast catalogued collection, which included 1,564 scrolls.

In 1964, these 1,564 Czech scrolls were purchased from the Czechoslovak Communist state by Westminster Synagogue. They were brought to London and restored by David Brand, a professional scribe, over a period of 27 years. There followed a stream of requests for the scrolls, and over 1,400 were distributed to recognised organisations around the world on long-term loan, with the Trust retaining ownership. Each scroll was identified by a small brass plaque, with a number, and accompanied by a certificate from the Trust.

Among these scrolls were three originating from the Jewish community in Ungarisch Brod (Uherský Brod). Number 500 went to Congregation B'nai Emunah in San Francisco, number 687 to Temple Beth El in Utica, New York, and number 1012 to Northwest Suburban Jewish Congregation in Morton Grove, Illinois. Sadly, the last has now closed and the scroll is to be returned to London. I have been in touch with all three synagogues and been sent some fascinating information about Uherský Brod, the town from which their scrolls originated.

The remaining scrolls from Czechoslovakia form a Wall of Scrolls in the Czech Memorial Scroll Museum, which was moved in 2008 to Kent House in London, where Westminster Synagogue is also housed. This display, together with the scrolls distributed world-wide, forms a wonderful memorial to the lost Jewish communities of Bohemia and Moravia.

LIST OF ILLUSTRATIONS

CHAPTER 5: THE JEWISH COMMUNITIES OF BOHEMIA AND MORAVIA

CHAPTER 6: THE NAZI MACHINE IN AUSTRIA

CHAPTER 7: THE LIFE AND FATE OF JOSEF AND CÄCILIE SMETANA

CHAPTER 8: THE TRAGIC LIFE OF FRITZ SMETANA

CHAPTER 9: IN SEARCH OF BERTA SMETANA

CHAPTER 10: MY MOTHER'S LIFE IN VIENNA (1919–1938)

CHAPTER 11: MY MOTHER'S LIFE IN ENGLAND: LIVES ENTWINED

CHAPTER 12: A LIFE OF MY OWN?

CHAPTER 13: END OF AN ERA

POST-SCRIPT: BUTTERFLIES AND OTHER COINCIDENCES

BIBLIOGRAPHY

Götz Aly, *Hitler's beneficiaries: plunder, racial war, and the Nazi welfare state*, 2006, translated by Jefferson Chase, Henry Holt & Company, 2007

Victoria Ancona-Vincent, *Beyond Imagination*, Witness Collection, Beth Shalom Ltd., 1996

Marion Berghahn, *Continental Britons, German-Jewish Refugees from Nazi Germany*, Berghahn Books, Rev. Ed., 2007

John Clapham, *Smetana*, The Master Musician Series, J.M. Dent and Sons Ltd., 1972

Jean-William Dereymez (ed), *Le Refuge et le Piège: Les Juifs dans les Alpes (1938–1945)*, L'Harmattan, 2008

Nicholas J. Fogg, *German Genealogy during the Nazi Period*, in Genealogists' Magazine, March 2012, pp. 347–360

Anthony Grenville, *Jewish Refugees from Germany and Austria in Britain, 1933–1970, Their Image in AJR Information*, Vallentine Mitchell, 2010

Serge Klarsfeld, *Mémorial de la Déportation des Juifs de France*, FFDJF, 2012. This impressive book lists the names and details of over 75,000 Jews deported from France

Jean Kleinmann, *La Vie des Juifs à Nice 1938-1944*, part 3 of *Les Étrangers dans les Alpes-Maritimes à travers les Documents Préfectoraux 1860–1944*, doctoral thesis 2003, available on the internet

Rena Kornreich Gelissen, with Heather Dune Macadam, *Rena's Promise, A Story of Two Sisters in Auschwitz*, Weidenfeld & Nicolson, 1996

Liam Nolan and J Bernard Hutton, *The Pain and the Glory: The Life of Smetana*, Harrap and Co. Ltd., 1968

Kristen Rundle, *Law and daily life – questions for legal philosophy from November 1938*, 2012, *Jurisprudence* xxx, Symposium on Nazi Law, September 2012. In this paper, Dr Rundle makes reference to the two very different signatures of my great grandmother, Cäcilie Weinberger.

Karl Schleunes (ed), *Legislating the Holocaust, The Loesener Memoirs and Other Documents*, Perseus, 2001

Fern Schumer Chapman, *Motherland: Beyond the Holocaust: A Mother-Daughter Journey to Reclaim the Past*, Viking Press Inc., 1999

Thea Skyte et al (eds), *Jewish Ancestors? A Guide to Jewish Genealogy in Germany and Austria*, JGSGB. This booklet has some very useful contact information.

Liesel Tilles, née Holzapfel, *Stories from my Life, memoir pieces and fiction*, private publication

SOURCES, CREDITS AND ACKNOWLEDGEMENTS

SOURCES OF INFORMATION

Archives Départementales des Alpes-Maritimes, Nice, from where I received a copy of Berta's registration document, dated 3 January 1942.

Austrian General Settlement Fund, which provides compensation for victims of National Socialism. Catherine Friedmann provided me with information about the current value of the Reichsmark.

Austrian State Archives (*Österreichisches Staatsarchiv*), Nazi documents on individual family members obtained in 1997 and 2011, and other archive materials, including Josef Smetana's service record with the Imperial Railway. Dr Hubert Steiner, *Archiv der Republik*, was most helpful.

Dr Anders Carlsson, Research Coordinator in the School of Music and Drama, Göteborg (or Gothenburg) University, Sweden, with whom I have corresponded extensively since 2006. Dr Carlsson was very generous in sharing his knowledge of the composer Smetana with me.

Czech District and Regional Archives. Research was carried out for me in the Uherské Hradiště and Vsetín District Archives, and in the Moravian Regional Archives in Brno by Martin Kočařík and his wife Šárka Kočaříková. Martin and Šárka work for a private company whose details are available at www.CzechFamilyTree.com.

Czech State Archives. Research was carried out for me in the National Archives in Prague by Czech Jewish genealogist, Dr Julius Müller. Dr Müller was also most helpful in providing information about various aspects of Czech Jewish genealogy. I met him when attending the IAJGS in Paris in July 2012.

Czech Memorial Scrolls Museum, London. Rabbi Ariel Friedlander was most helpful in providing information about the scrolls originating from Uherský Brod.

Conversations and correspondence with cousins of my mother, known to me for the first time in 1995, when my mother started, reluctantly, to tell her story. I am most grateful, in particular to Ully, Helga, Heinz (Henry), Gerda and Lori, and to Helga's daughter, Annette. They provided me with many stories and family photos.

Documents and photographs brought from Vienna by my mother, including her birth certificate and school reports.

FamilySearch, the family history website of the Church of Latter-day Saints.

Holocaust Centre (formerly Beth Shalom Holocaust Memorial Centre) in Nottinghamshire, which I have visited on many occasions, and where I met Victoria Ancona-Vincent and Stephen Smith. Some of the original documents featured in this book, as well as copies of the Nazi documents sent to me, have now been donated to the Holocaust Centre.

International Association of Jewish Genealogical Societies (IAJGS). In July 2012, I attended the 32nd Conference of the IAJGS held in Paris, where I learned new information about the fate of my family in France, and also made helpful contacts and new friendships.

Israelitische Kultusgemeinde Wien (IKG), the Jewish Archives in Vienna, where Wolf-Erich Eckstein has been particularly kind and helpful over many years. I met him when attending the IAJGS in Paris in July 2012.

The Jewish Genealogical Society of Great Britain. I attended a JGSGB workshop in June 2011, which I found most helpful.

JewishGen.org, where I discovered details of Smetana tombs in Ungarisch Brod, and also of the Smetana family in Trenčín, in present day Slovakia. I subsequently made contact with a number of their descendants.

Mémorial de la Shoah, Paris, which I visited in July 2012 to deposit photos and documentation, and where I learned new information about Berta and Sonja Smetana, and Josef Weinberger, whose names are engraved on the Wall of Names at the Mémorial.

Movinghere.org.uk, website which publishes Public Record Office documents about migrants to Britain, and where I found an entry about my mother dated 1939.

MyHeritage.com, whose excellent website I have used for research and to build the family trees used in this book.

Photographs taken by myself and my daughter Bambo when we visited Vienna for the first time in September and October 2006.

Postcards sent from France in 1939 by my grandmother to my mother, by then in Nottingham.

Red Cross International Tracing Service and the British Red Cross.

Dr Kristen Rundle, Lecturer in Law at the London School of Economics and Political Science, who has a special interest in the law and the Holocaust. I have held several interesting conversations with Dr Rundle on this topic, and she has kindly given me permission to quote from these conversations.

San Marino Archives, documents obtained during my visit in January 2008. Maria Lea Pedini, who was, in 2008, Director General of the Foreign Affairs Department of the Republic of San Marino, helped to organise the event, and arranged for the copying of archive materials. She is presently Director of European Affairs of the same department, and was kind enough to edit my section in this book on San Marino. The information on San Marino in Chapter 8 is drawn mainly from the SanMarinoSite.com, with the kind permission of Maria Lea Pedini.

John Smetana, a distant relative, who first introduced me to the story of the composer's illegitimate sons, and who provided me with information about his side of the family, in the course of our conversations and correspondence.

Dr Robert Streibel, Director of the *Volkshochschule*, a community college in Hietzing, Vienna, who has tirelessly conducted research into the Jews of Hietzing. I met Dr Streibel in October 2006 when I visited Vienna.

Victoria Ancona-Vincent, an Auschwitz survivor whom I met at Beth Shalom Holocaust Memorial Centre in Nottinghamshire in 1995. She recorded her experiences in her book, *Beyond Imagination*. It is possible that Victoria knew my grandmother, Berta, in Auschwitz.

Wiener Library in London, where copies of the Nazi documents sent to me are now stored. Howard Falksohn, Archivist, was helpful in discussing with me the significance of the documents and Katharina Hubschmann, Senior Librarian, provided me with information about the current value of the Reichsmark.

Yad Vashem, Israel's official Holocaust Memorial, whose database contains details of over half the 6 million Jews who perished in the Holocaust, including members of my own family.

CREDITS

I would like to thank the following organisations and institutions for their kind permission to use material from their archives and databases:

Austrian State Archives, for reproduction of Nazi documents on various family members and other family records.

Congregation B'nai Emunah in San Francisco, Temple Beth El in Utica, New York, and Northwest Suburban Jewish Congregation in Morton Grove, Illinois, guardians of three Czech Memorial Scrolls originating from Uherský Brod (Ungarisch Brod). A member from each of these congregations kindly sent me information about Uherský Brod.

Israelitische Kultusgemeinde Wien, most especially Wolf-Erich Eckstein, for use of archive information obtained from them, and for reproduction of a photo taken there in 2006.

Mémorial de la Shoah, Paris, for permission to reproduce photos of the names of Berta and Sonja Smetana on the Wall of Names. My thanks also to Maryse Banet who took the photos.

Moravian Regional Archives in Brno, for reproduction of the extract from the Jewish registry of births in Ungarisch Brod, showing details of Josef Smetana's birth in 1858 (MZA Brno, B 13 – Moravské místodržitelství). Martin Kočařík and his wife Šárka Kočaříková kindly helped me to obtain this permission.

MyHeritage.com, for the reproduction of the two family tree charts.

San Marino Government for the reproduction of archive documents relating to Fritz Smetana, and also photos they sent to me.

The Uherské Hradiště Archives, where the Ungarisch Brod archives are stored, for reproduction of the document giving details of John Smetana's parents and grandparents.

University of Vienna, for the reproduction of Lucy Smetana's registration at the Faculty of Medicine, Vienna University, in 1938.

The following individuals have most kindly and generously permitted me to use their images or quote from their materials:

Jim Asher, Butterfly Conservation, for use of the butterfly image.

Dr Anders Carlsson, for the reproduction of almost his entire correspondence with me in 2006 and 2007, as well as the photos of Fröjda Benecke.

Mrs Evelyn Friedlander, for permission to quote from the website www.czechmemorialscrollstrust.org.

Dr Julius Müller, for use of material from articles on his website www.toledot.org to write Chapter 5: *The Jewish Communities of Bohemia and Moravia*, and part of Appendix 15: *A Note on Czech Jewish Genealogy.*

Paul Ptacek, manager of the company www.CzechFamilyTree.com for use of material from his website in the writing of part of Appendix 15: *A Note on Czech Jewish Genealogy*. Mr Ptacek was also kind enough to advise me regarding the correct spelling of Czech place names.

Fern Schumer Chapman, for permission to quote from her book, *Motherland.*

Stephen Smith, for permission to reproduce his poem about Victoria Ancona-

Vincent and for his kindness and generosity in writing the Foreword for this book.

Alex Trembath, for his poem *Words for my grandmother.*

OTHER ACKNOWLEDGEMENTS

I would like to express my sincere and profound gratitude to the many wonderful people who have contributed to the writing of this book.

In addition to all those mentioned above, I would also like to thank my friends Fírinne Ní Chréacháin, Jane Curtis and Mary Vidal who read the draft and made helpful comments and suggestions. Thanks also to my life-long school friend Shirley Chatfield for her unwavering love and support. Shirley knew my mother well and was extremely fond of her.

I am particularly indebted to Margret Vince, who kindly translated many of the archive documents for me, as well as the poem written by my mother's teacher and the postcards from my grandmother. She sat with me for many days to help me with this task.

I am grateful to Amanda Belcher of Spectrum Printers who printed the original family history documents. I would also like to thank my former publishers DB Publishing, particularly Simon Hartshorne, Designer, for his endless hard work, patience and flexibility, and Miles Bailey of The Choir Press, who supported me through the process of republication.

Of course, I could not have completed this project without the much appreciated encouragement and support of my family throughout these painstaking years of research: my brothers Peter and Stephen, my husband, Kayode, and my children, Lara, Bambo, and Alex, and step-daughter, Egbin. I am particularly grateful to Alex, who proof-read and edited the book for me, and in so doing learned much of his own history.

The most recent heirs to this story are my wonderful grandchildren, Joshua, Leon, Faith and Joel, whose boundless joy and energy have sustained and nourished me. Faith was born in 2003, shortly after my mother died, and in honour of my mother (named *Ora* at her funeral), was also given the name Eliora. It seemed natural, therefore, to republish this book under the name Eliora Books, and to use as the logo a delightful piece of artwork designed by Faith Eliora when she was just eight years old. This book is a legacy to all my grandchildren.

It is, after all, their story too.

Lightning Source UK Ltd.
Milton Keynes UK
UKOW050901230413

209613UK00002B/2/P